VALUING NATURE

VALUING NATURE

The Decline and Preservation of Old-Growth Forests

Douglas E. Booth

ROWMAN & LITTLEFIELD PUBLISHERS, INC.

ROWMAN & LITTLEFIELD PUBLISHERS, INC.

Published in the United States of America
by Rowman & Littlefield Publishers, Inc.
4720 Boston Way, Lanham, Maryland 20706

3 Henrietta Street
London WC2E 8LU, England

British Cataloging in Publication Information Available

Library of Congress Cataloging-in-Publication Data

Booth, Douglas E.
Valuing nature : the decline and preservation of old-growth
forests / Douglas E. Booth.
p. cm.
Includes bibliographical references (p.) and index.
1. Old growth forests—Northwest, Pacific. 2. Forest
conservation—Northwest, Pacific. 3. Forest ecology—Northwest,
Pacific. I. Title.
SD387.043B66 1993   333.75'09795—dc20   92-47001   CIP

ISBN 0-8476-7859-8 (cloth : alk. paper)
ISBN 0-8476-7860-1 (paper : alk. paper)

Printed in the United States of America

To Carol, Edward, and Jeremy;
my world would be empty without them.

Contents

List of Tables

Preface

Some ten years ago, I became seriously interested in the connection between economics and ecology. Because I grew up in the Pacific Northwest and returned there frequently after moving away, the connection that was most concrete for me was between the timber industry and the forests. As time passed, I saw the patchwork quilt of clearcuts so common in the Pacific Northwest extending farther and farther up the mountainsides. No one I knew seemed to like this very much, but most accepted it as a necessary price to pay for regional economic prosperity. Still, what I saw did not sit well with me instinctively. This experience led me to devote a sabbatical from teaching to looking into the connection between economic activity in the Pacific Northwest and the ecology of the forests—the final result is this book.

After gaining a basic understanding of the ecology of old-growth forests, I had trouble continuing to accept the cost-benefit approach taken by economists in analyzing resource allocation decisions. Somehow, it didn't seem right just placing a dollar value on something as interesting and unique as old-growth forests. I knew that the cost-benefit framework could take into account the benefits of preserved old growth for recreation and other purposes, but that didn't seem like enough.

In search of a framework appropriate for analyzing the question of whether old-growth forests should be exploited or preserved, I was led to the relatively new field of environmental ethics. In this literature, I found a methodology that seemed to answer my concerns about the cost-benefit approach. While there isn't universal agreement by any means, many environmental ethicists argue that nature is valuable in its own right and should be an object of moral concern. While this view can be rooted in reasonable philosophical principles and is thus attractive to me and to a number of environmental ethicists, what really matters is whether individuals who hold such views can influence political decisions that affect the uses to which old-growth forests are put. Consequently, a central purpose of this book is to investigate historical attitudes toward old-growth forests, the effect of those attitudes on the human uses of forests, and the evolution of those attitudes over time. Once we understand the actual attitudes that people have toward forests, we can then consider whether the cost-benefit approach to valuing old growth is legitimate, and we can investigate the implications of ethical standards for the question of whether old growth should be exploited or preserved.

This book would not have been possible without the support for research Marquette University has afforded me over the years, including a sabbatical, for which I am very thankful. I would also like to extend my thanks to the University of Washington Forestry Library for its able assistance. The manuscript was significantly improved by a reader who provided me with extensive comments but wishes to remain anonymous. Many others commented on research papers directly connected to the book and thus also played a major role in improving the final product. The book has been immeasurably improved through the diligent efforts of the editorial staff at Rowman and Littlefield. Finally, I would like to give special thanks to my wife, Carol, and my sons, Edward and Jeremy, who put up with my grumpiness when things were not going well and provided plenty of encouragement.

1

Valuing Nature: Introduction

When asked about how the natural world should be valued, economists would generally say that benefits and costs should be calculated for the various human uses of nature, and the use should be chosen that brings the maximum difference between benefits and costs. If the exploitation of nature accomplishes this objective, then that's what should be done. If profits from logging, for example, exceed the economic value of a forest as a recreational resource, then logging should be undertaken. Some environmentalists and environmental ethicists would disagree, arguing that we must go beyond consideration of simple instrumental uses to address our own moral obligation to nature apart from any material benefits human beings receive from the natural world. Moral attitudes, in this view, should place a restraint on exploitative tendencies. Who is right? This depends on how people look at nature in practice.

The purpose of this book is to investigate how nature has in fact been valued in the context of a most interesting specific case: the decline and preservation of old-growth forests in the Pacific Northwest. What attitudes motivated the exploitation of these forests that contain trees ranging in age from 200 to more than 600 years old? Conversely, what attitudes motivated the movement to preserve the remnants of old-growth forests? Why would people's attitudes shift from favoring the exploitation of forests to advocating their preservation? Did declining economic dependency on forests in the Pacific Northwest allow such attitude shifts to take place? Do advocates of forest preservation look at forests in moral terms? If they do, should the cost-benefit approach to valuing forests be used, or should ethical standards be established? These are the kinds of questions that will be addressed in the chapters to come. This first chapter provides a framework for valuing nature that will be used throughout the book.

Valuing Nature

Philosophers have suggested two alternatives for valuing nature. Nature can be valued instrumentally, as a means to achieve some end, or it can be valued for itself, independent of any instrumental value it may deliver. An instrumental valuation of the natural world implies a moral commitment limited to human beings and their goals; a noninstrumental valuation implies a moral commitment to nature for its own sake.[1] The latter form of valuation is purely altruistic, while the former can be oriented to either self-interest or the interest of others.

In many ways, the instrumental evaluation is the easiest to understand. Nature, above all, is instrumental to human survival and well-being. Without the oxygen produced by plant respiration, the appropriate atmospheric balance between oxygen and carbon would be upset and the earth would become uninhabitable for human beings and other oxygen-using species. Without the nutrients and materials provided by nature, human beings could not survive, much less achieve material prosperity. Human beings thus find nature to be of value for its capacity to provide for instrumental needs and wants.

The human species can fulfill its material wants and needs through the utilization of naturally evolved ecosystems or, alternatively, through the development and exploitation of human-created "anthropogenic" ecosystems. In an anthropogenic system, human beings substantially modify and shape nature and its evolutionary process, creating new "symbiont" species, which are dependent on human cultivation or care and provide for human needs and wants. The list of these species is lengthy, including a large number of agricultural crops, a variety of domesticated animals, urban garden plants, fast-growing tree species for industrial forestry, and even genetically altered organisms for breaking down spilled oil or preventing the formation of frost on crops. The human species has thus created anthropogenic plant and animal species and ecosystems that would largely disappear without human effort to preserve them.

Naturally evolved ecosystems, on the other hand, persist in the absence of human intervention, although human intervention may bring changes to the relative mix of different types. For example, the large amount of land in tall-grass prairie prior to European settlement of the American continent was partly the result of fires set by Indians. In the absence of fire, some of these prairies probably would have been replaced through succession by forests. Indians rarely introduced new species to a locality, but they did reset natural successional processes through burning to favor species desired for consumption.[2]

Like their anthropogenic counterparts, naturally evolved ecosystems can be utilized for commodity production that satisfies human needs. Wood fiber can be extracted from old-growth forests for human use, although if clearcutting is employed in harvesting, and if the land is converted to tree farms where trees are harvested at relatively frequent intervals, then in the process the natural ecosystem is replaced by an anthropogenic one.[3] If, alternatively, timber harvesting is selective and modest in extent, retention of the naturally evolved, old-growth ecosystem is consistent with human material use.

While anthropogenic ecosystems exist solely for the material resources they deliver, naturally evolved ecosystems can be valued instrumentally for nonmaterial reasons. (1) Natural ecosystems can be valued instrumentally as places to be enjoyed for aesthetic observation and spiritual reflection, the opportunities they provide for solitude and escape from the bustle of modern urban life, the challenges of outdoor recreation, and the experiences of observing wildlife or hunting and fishing. (2) Natural ecosystems can also be valued instrumentally as storehouses of chemicals, species, and genetic material that are currently of value or may be of value to humans at some point in the future. These storehouses also provide abundant research opportunities for scientists. (3) Species, ecosystems, and their landscape can also be of symbolic value for a society. The American eagle, for example, is a symbol of national strength for the United States, and wilderness remnants represent and symbolize conditions faced by pioneering settlers. Without the actual existence of wilderness remnants or eagles in the wild, their power as symbols would inevitably be diminished. In such cases, there may be a public demand to preserve species and ecosystems simply to maintain the potency of what they represent culturally.[4] Finally, (4) ecosystems and species can have transformative value. Some individuals may want to see species or ecosystems preserved so that others will have the opportunity to observe and experience them and as a result have their values transformed. One who observes, say, an eagle may experience enhanced national pride as well as the desire to see eagles preserved. The experience of nature has the potential to transform the way individuals look at the world.[5] Thus, instrumental evaluations of nature need not be material. They can be founded on preservation rather than exploitation of nature.

The way nature has been valued instrumentally as well as noninstrumentally in the United States historically has been addressed by several authors. Their findings provide an interesting frame of reference for analysis of the decline and preservation of old-growth forests. Before considering this, however, we need to take a closer look at the philo-

sophical underpinnings of the notion of valuing nature noninstrumentally for itself.

While many environmental ethicists agree on extending the realm of
direct moral concern beyond human beings to the rest of nature, there is
extensive disagreement over the philosophical foundation for doing so.[6]
There are also some environmental ethicists who are skeptical that reasonable philosophical foundations can be worked out for this view.[7] The
position taken here is that the most reasonable basis for viewing nature
as morally considerable is a subjectivist holistic environmental ethic.

In contrast to a subjectivist approach, an objectivist environmental
ethic claims that something should be morally considerable if it has a
certain characteristic, such as the capacity to reason, the ability to feel
pain, the ability to self-replicate, or the capacity to pursue some end.[8]
The existence of value, in this view, is the result of an objective feature
of the natural world and is thus independent of the valuer.[9] Value is
nonanthropomorphic because it exists independent of the human valuer.
The problem with an objectivist approach is that the choice of a particular characteristic in qualifying something to be morally considerable is
left unexplained.[10] The claim that something with a given characteristic,
such as the capacity to reason, is of moral concern is to say that the
characteristic is good without really saying why. To justify one characteristic or another requires an appeal to a human preference or emotion,
contradicting the notion of an objective criterion for moral concern.

A subjectivist approach, on the other hand, relies directly on the human
capacity to emotionally identify with entities outside the self. Through
such identifications, external beings are brought into the realm of moral
concern.[11] While value in this case is anthropomorphic in the sense that
it lacks existence apart from the human valuer, it is not anthropocentric
because of the human capacity to value something in nature independent
of any instrumental values it may have. While choices of the objects of
moral concern are subjective, they will not be totally arbitrary. The
capacity to identify with something requires some sort of connection to
it, such as being a member of a particular family or society, belonging
to a particular species, being a member of a given biotic community, or
being a product of some biophysical process.

An environmental ethic can, in theory, be holistic in its focus with
species and ecosystems being the objects of moral concern, or be individualistic with individual organisms being morally considerable. While
there is a natural human tendency to identify with the individual organism in nature, the functioning of ecosystems raises problems for a strictly
individualistic environmental ethic. Natural processes often dictate the
sacrificing of individual organisms. Overpopulation of rabbits, for exam-

ple, may be resolved by increased predation by wolves. To protect individual organisms in many instances would require their removal from their ecological context. To do so for all organisms would be an overwhelming task.[12] On the other hand, ecosystems and species can be protected from human disturbances. Not all rabbits can be saved from premature death, but by preserving the ecosystem in which they are embedded, we can preserve them as a species. Even though human sentiments for wild animals are often individualistic, the actions that can be taken to preserve individuals are, for all practical purposes, restricted to protecting ecological wholes.

While ethical theory tends to focus on moral norms that apply to individuals, in practice there are dimensions of moral behavior that are holistic in their focus, such as patriotism and institutional loyalty. The human capacity for emotional identification is thus not totally individualistic. The human species evolved as a consequence of the interaction of geophysical and ecosystem evolution, and an understanding of this phenomenon can result in the human capacity to emotionally identify with other species as fellow life forms and with ecological wholes as creators of order and producers of life forms.[13] Such identifications make possible the human treatment of ecosystems and species as valuable for themselves. A holistic environmental ethic is thus reasonable on the grounds that human beings can emotionally identify with environmental wholes, and a holistic approach to ethical decisions on environmental issues may be the only feasible way of implementing an environmental ethic based on individualistic sentiments for organisms in nature.

To summarize, an environmental ethic that says nature is valuable in its own right can be justified philosophically. Given that the valuing of nature for itself is a logical possibility, the question of whether individuals actually value nature this way is a reasonable one to ask.

Valuing Nature in Practice

So far, the discussion has focused on theoretical possibilities for valuing nature. What about valuing nature in practice? How has nature in fact been valued by human beings and what have been the consequences for nature itself? These are the central questions this book addresses for the case of old-growth forests in the Pacific Northwest. Before turning to these questions, a brief overview of how nature has been valued in the United States historically will establish the kinds of attitudes that underlie the exploitation of natural resources generally and forests specifically in the nineteenth and twentieth centuries, and it will determine whether noninstrumentalist views of nature entered into the national debate on preserving natural areas by the time the modern movement to preserve wilderness that contains old-growth forests began in the 1950s and 1960s. As Aldo Leopold argues, "We can be ethical only in relation to something we can see, feel, understand, love, or otherwise have faith in." What is needed to foster an ethical view of the natural world is "an ecological conscience."[14] If Leopold is right, we should not expect such a consciousness to emerge and foster the view that nature has value in its own right until ecological understanding has taken root.

To understand values in reality is not an easy task. The real values motivating historical events are hidden in the minds of the participants and are not always expressed, and if they are, there is no assurance as to the honesty of their expression. The best one can do is analyze events to determine the logical possibilities for motives, discern the values expressed in writings by culturally influential thinkers, attempt to determine the content of popular attitudes expressed in correspondence or periodicals, and establish the values expressed in government legislation, documents, and public testimony. Only a small sample of writers who have addressed the question of attitudes toward nature can be considered here. This is, I hope, adequate to provide a reasonable background for the task at hand: to understand the complex of values underlying the decline and preservation of old-growth forests.

Early Attitudes

The dominant attitude toward nature in nineteenth-century American history, one that retains much popular strength to this day, can perhaps best be characterized as a tangible instrumentalism: nature is valued as an instrument for the tangible materials it provides to human beings. This attitude was clearly expressed in the nineteenth-century public debate over disposition of lands in the public domain. How were the vast landholdings of the U.S. government to be transferred to private hands, and what ends were to be served in the process? After an early period when the goal of land policy was to raise money for the purpose of financing government operations and retiring the government debt, public land laws were instituted that focused on the provision of cheap land for western settlers and land grants to promote western transportation development.[15] The land laws, on the one hand, were to promote the creation of a Jeffersonian society of small landowning farmers who would serve as the backbone of a democratic society and who would gain an unchallengeable right to the land in a Lockean fashion through working it and investing their labor in it.[16] Land was to be worked by smallholders to provide food and fiber for their own use as well as for commercial sales.

On the other hand, land laws were devised to promote western economic expansion. Corporations were provided large land grants in exchange for the development of both roads and railroads. The land received by the railroads was generally resold and served as a means for generating a flow of income for the railroads. Railroad grant lands were often purchased by land companies for resale to settlers at relatively high prices, and the railroads themselves charged settlers relatively high prices for land. Because railroads often gained control of the best lands, poorer settlers were forced to seek homesteads on less desirable tracts.[17] In some cases, railroads retained ownership of large blocks of land, and in some instances grant lands were sold in relatively large blocks to timber companies.[18] Grant lands consequently reduced the amount of cheap land available to settlers, and the respective goals of widely distributing cheap land to smallholders and rapid western economic expansion came into conflict.

Two fundamental views of the role of land in American society thus developed, one based on a political ideal, and one based on the reality of the modern business enterprise. Both were oriented to the material and instrumental use of nature, but their ultimate goals differed. A wide dispersion of landownership among smallholders, according to the political ideal, was to ensure a reasonably equitable distribution of wealth and political influence. Smallholdings would be worked by their owners and would provide for their owner's economic independence. By virtue of embodying their labor in improvements to the land, they would legitimize their title to it and would have full control over the use to which it was put. The philosophical roots of landownership were at once Jeffersonian and Lockean.[19] Land and the natural resources it contained were to serve as instruments by which to simultaneously achieve economic prosperity and social and political equity.

As a practical matter, however, vast amounts of the public domain came into the hands of speculators and large corporations that viewed land as an instrument by which to achieve the accumulation of wealth. Land, like labor, was thus an instrument, a means of production, to be used in the process of capital accumulation. The essence of modern capitalism is profit and capital accumulation, and everything including nature is instrumental to that end.[20] In many instances, land could be put to its highest-valued economic use through its combination into large tracts held not by smallholders but by large corporations. The scale of landownership needed for efficient use in the arid West[21] as well as the wet, forested Pacific Northwest was much above that specified by the Homestead Act and other land laws. Large-scale landownership turned out to be a central theme in the historical development of the Pacific Northwest timber industry. Large millowners accumulated vast tracts of forestland in order to assure a steady supply of timber for their mills.[22] The scale of landholding followed the scale of milling operations. Except for the floodplains of a few river valleys and a few scattered prairies, smallholder agriculture was infeasible in the mountainous, densely timbered forests of the Pacific Northwest.[23]

The Jeffersonian landholding vision thus went unrealized and probably was unrealizable in many parts of the country. The Lockean view of property ownership, giving full control over the use of nature on landed property to the owner, was nonetheless largely retained in American property law. This was done even though corporate property could never be justified and legitimized through the working and improvement of the land by the owner.[24]

Conservation Movement

The first serious reaction to the rapid transfer of the public domain to private hands came in the form of the conservation movement. Like smallholders or corporate property owners, participants in the conservation movement were clearly interested in the material instruments that nature could provide for human benefit, but they were especially concerned with the rapid and wasteful exploitation of public domain resources. They desired the use of nature's materials, but they wanted to see it accomplished on an efficient and sustainable basis. The conservationists, responding to the cut-and-run approach to timber harvesting and to fears of timber famines, the obtaining of resources in the public domain illegally, and the general decline in the amount of forested land, advocated the wise use of forest resources and favored the sustained-yield forest practices that had been developed in Germany and other European countries.[25] Taking a cue from George Perkins Marsh and his influential work *Man and Nature*, early conservationists were also concerned with the relationship between forests and water, and the preservation of forests was viewed by many as necessary to assure adequate water supplies for economic development in the relatively arid West.[26]

The leadership of the conservation movement was made up of a new breed of professional scientists from such fields as hydrology, forestry, and geology. Most were active in professional organizations that voiced concern about national resource policy and believed that resource problems could be resolved through application of science and technology.[27] The American Association for the Advancement of Science was one of the first organizations to stress the need for the preservation and management of forests.[28] While the American Forestry Association, founded in 1875, was originally composed mostly of botanists, landscape gardeners, and estate owners who were more interested in forest preservation than sustained-yield forestry, the nature of the organization began to change under the leadership of Bernard Fernow, a trained forester from Germany. Fernow became the head of the Division of Forestry in the Department of Agriculture, where he emphasized research work on forest management.[29] The Division of Forestry had been created in 1876 to study forestry problems, and under the leadership of Franklin B. Hough the division produced an extensive report on forests that recommended the creation of forest reserves. The American Forestry Association under Fernow shifted its central concern from the preservation of forests for preservation's sake to forest management practices that could obtain a sustainable maximum yield of wood products from American forests.[30]

Conservationists were interested in preservation of forests, as evidenced by their role in the passage of the Forest Reserve Act of 1891 permitting the president of the United States to establish forest reserves on public land. Their ultimate goal was the use of forests for the production of wood fiber and as watersheds for the purpose of providing municipal and irrigation water. The act marked a major shift in policy away from the transferring of forested land in the public domain to private ownership and toward public ownership and management.[31] The conservation movement reached its high point with the creation of the national forest system out of the reserves established under the 1891 law and the choice of the U.S. Forest Service as the national forests management agency, both the result of the efforts of Gifford Pinchot, the guiding light of the conservation movement in the first part of the twentieth century.[32]

Preservationists

At about the same time the conservation movement was forming and gaining momentum, alternative visions of human interactions with the natural world in the American setting were being formulated that were generally nonmaterial or intangible in their focus, but nonetheless instrumental. In this view, nature not only provides material sustenance but also sustenance for the human spirit. This idea was in direct conflict with the more popular attitude that wild nature is something to be feared and to be tamed or transformed into material objects that can serve human ends.[33] The goal of western settlement was not to preserve the beauty of the wild landscape but to convert it to arable land and to make use of the resources it contained. Yet the landscape itself symbolized to Americans their destiny of western conquest and settlement.[34] In particular, monumental features of the landscape, such as those found in the Yellowstone and Yosemite areas, symbolized western settlement and the uniqueness of American culture. For literary figures and eventually for the popular press, wilderness began to symbolize the great American heroic quest—

the settlement of the frontier—and wilderness itself was most easily represented by its great natural monuments and scenic wonders.

This is the central theme of Alfred Runte's important work on the history of the national park system.[35] He argued that the early national parks had to satisfy two basic criteria. First, they had to be worthless in the sense that they contained no marketable material resources and were not useable for agriculture, and, second, they had to have within their boundaries scenic wonders that could be held up as monuments rivaling the cathedrals and edifices of Europe for their splendor and beauty. Some felt, according to Runte, the natural beauty of the American continent provided one of the few criteria on which the United States could be compared positively with the older European societies.

At first, preservation efforts focused on geological curiosities as opposed to the preservation of wilderness itself. The justification for the preservation of Yellowstone was not founded on its wilderness qualities but rather on the unusual geysers and other geological features.[36] Later, once the idea of wilderness and the values associated with wilderness had been more extensively publicized by John Muir and other writers, preservation of wilderness landscape in addition to geologic features became a preservationist goal, one that was first accomplished with the creation of Yosemite National Park. Not only were the falls and cliffs preserved but surrounding forestlands as well.[37]

The notion of scenic monumentalism was thus broadened to include notions that wilderness as a whole, including its flora and fauna, can provide raw material for aesthetic enjoyment and spiritual reflection. Although Muir in his unpublished writings often argued that nature had value in its own right, in his published works he emphasized the aesthetic attractions of natural areas for the purpose of widening the appeal of the idea of wilderness preservation.[38] Defense of wilderness must be couched in instrumentalist terms where society is concerned primarily with the fulfillment of individual human needs and does not yet accept the radical idea that something other than human beings can be objects of moral concern. Many, including Muir, were influenced by Henry David Thoreau's transcendentalism and his idea that nature reflects universal spiritual truths and that the experience of wild nature can provide a setting for the transformation and improvement of human values.[39] In addition, the wilderness was seen as a setting in which the frontier experience could be replayed and key elements of the American character reaffirmed.[40] Without wilderness, the opportunity for spiritual reflection and improvement and testing of abilities to replay the frontier quest would not be possible.

The materially oriented conservationists and the nonmaterial preservationists at the turn of the century were both relatively small groups of people without any real base of political support. They were nonetheless influential figures capable of using their positions in society to achieve their goals. John Muir and Robert Underwood Johnson, with some backing from the Southern Pacific Railroad, which undoubtedly had an eye to the profitable tourist trade that Yosemite might generate, were able to successfully lobby for passage of the Yosemite Act in 1890, creating a national park.[41] Preservationists and conservationists together were largely responsible for the passage of the Forest Reserve Act.[42] Gifford Pinchot, who had the ear and cooperation of President Theodore Roosevelt, was successful in his efforts to create the U.S. Forest Service and the national forest system and institute sustained-yield management principles in the national forests.[43]

A Split in the Movement

The preservationists, who wanted to preserve the forests and associated landscapes from economic use, ultimately broke with the conservationists, who were primarily interested in utilizing the resources of nature efficiently and on a sustained-yield basis. The break came with a fundamental disagreement over the disposition of the Hetch Hetchy Valley in Yosemite National Park. The city of San Francisco considered damming the river to be the best possible solution to the city's chronic water shortage problem, one that was vividly brought to the public's attention by insufficient water supplies during the San Francisco earthquake and fire in 1906.[44] The split in the debate was represented by John Muir's intense opposition to the proposed dam and Gifford Pinchot's support of the project. Although President Roosevelt expressed sympathy for preserving areas of natural beauty and wanted to keep the conservationists and preservationists together in a single movement, he deferred to the views of Pinchot and other conservationists and gave his support to the project in the spring of 1908.[45] Advocates for the project included San Francisco politicians and business interests and western irrigationists and water power developers.[46] However, in the face of intense preservationist opposition to the dam, Roosevelt ultimately withdrew his support.[47] Despite heavy preservationist pressure by a lengthy list of prominent individuals and organizations against a bill in Congress authorizing the dam, it was approved by Congress and President Woodrow Wilson in 1913.[48]

Although the preservationists lost the Hetch Hetchy battle, in the process they gained sufficient political strength to win congressional authorization of the National Park Service, which was to be devoted to the preservation of natural areas as opposed to their exploitation for extractable resources. Despite strong opposition from the U.S. Forest Service, which considered itself to be fully capable of managing national parks, a bill authorizing the National Park Service was signed into law in 1916.[49] This set the stage for a competitive struggle between the forest and park services over the control of natural areas in the public domain, a struggle that was to play a role in the history of forestland preservation in the Pacific Northwest. The outlook of the U.S. Forest Service epitomized the values of its conservationist supporters, while the outlook of the Park Service initially was preservationist in orientation. However, the Park Service quickly shifted in the direction of promoting commercial tourism, as it searched for wider political support in Congress. The transportation revolution brought forth by the automobile provided the perfect means for increasing political support. Auto touring was the new fashion, and the national parks with their scenic wonders provided an obvious destination. By encouraging this trend with the construction of auto-oriented facilities, the National Park Service could increase visitors and thus a base for support of park expansions and acquistions.[50]

The Modern Preservationists

Prior to World War II, membership-based wilderness advocacy groups had played only a limited role in major decisions on wilderness and forest preservation. The key participants in wilderness preservation political conflicts were the U.S. Forest Service, the U.S. Park Service, various economic interests, and a small but influential group of amateur and professional preservationists and conservationists who most oftened acted individually rather than on the behalf of some group. After World War II, this began to change. Wilderness advocacy groups became a central force in the setting of forest preservation policy, with the Wilderness Society and Sierra Club taking the leading role.

The Sierra Club, the older of the two groups, was founded in San Francisco by John Muir and others interested in preserving the Sierra Nevada Mountains in 1892. Throughout the remainder of Muir's life, the club was politically active in efforts to preserve the Sierra range, and also became famous for its mountain outings. After Muir's death, it essentially became a social club organized around its outings and avoided participation in preservationist politics. The rebirth of the Sierra Club as a force in preservationist politics did not take place until younger members, such as Ansel Adams, Richard Leonard, and David Brower, took over the club, increased its political activities, and established a professional staff. By 1950, membership had increased to 7,000 from 3,000 a decade earlier, a figure that had been stable for many years. By 1959, under David Brower's direction, membership had doubled again.[51]

The Wilderness Society was founded in 1935 in Washington, D.C., by Robert Marshall, Aldo Leopold, and others for the general purpose of preserving wilderness and with the immediate task of protecting the Appalachian Trail. It was initially a small Washington-based organization under the tight control of Marshall and a few others. By the 1950s, Wilderness Society membership had expanded to 5,000 despite tight control of the club by its leadership, and it had developed an influential and competent staff under the leadership of Olaus J. Murie, a highly respected mammalogist, and Howard Zahniser.[52]

In the early years of the postwar wilderness movement, the leadership of the Sierra Club and Wilderness Society argued for preservation of wild areas on primarily aesthetic grounds, as had their predecessors, such as Muir and Marshall. The central preservationist issue of the 1950s was the proposed Echo Park Dam in northwest Colorado on the border of Utah, which would have inundated hundreds of miles of wild and isolated canyons in the Dinosaur National Monument along the Green and Yampa rivers. Brower and Zahniser brought together a coalition of preservationist groups to fight the proposed dam in Congress, arguing that the area constituted an important scenic resource in addition to being a precedent setting infringement on a national park.[53] The controversy served to focus arguments made over the years for wilderness preservation. The central theme was that wild areas like the Dinosaur National Monument were needed to provide human beings the opportunity to reestablish contact with nature and to experience the original pioneer wilderness.[54] The success of the preservationists in preventing the construction of Echo Park Dam set the stage for the proposing and eventual passage of the Wilderness Act in 1964.[55]

The opponents of Echo Park Dam predominantly used standard preservationist arguments, emphasizing the need to preserve wilderness for its scenic beauty, its historical significance, and the opportunity it provides as a respite from the complexities of modern life. However, the Dinosaur dam controversy is of special interest because ecological arguments were suggested as a justification for wilderness preservation, and the idea of nature having intrinsic value was implied by at least one advocate of preservation.[56] Bernard De Voto, a well-known writer, argued that wilderness, such as that included in Dinosaur National Monument, needed to be preserved for the purpose of studying "the balances of Nature, the web of life, the interrelationships of species."[57] With the continuous march of resource development, there would soon be few such areas left. Charles C. Bradley, a Sierra Club activist, argued for the preservation of Dinosaur as a "gesture of human respect for the biotic community," and Howard Zahniser suggested in connection with Dinosaur that wilderness provides the opportunity for us to come to "know ourselves as the dependent members of a great community of life."[58] We have here the beginning of an ecological consciousness on the part of Bradley, De Voto, and Zahniser, and the extension of moral concern to the world of nature by Bradley, illustrating Leopold's view that ecological understanding can lead to moral concern for nature.

In the forums where these arguments were made, however, the authors were in effect preaching to the converted. With the exception of De Voto's article in the *Saturday Evening Post*, they were not trying to convince a larger public of the need for preservation. They were attempting rather to appeal for support to those who were already oriented toward preservation. Preservationists may well hold ecological or noninstrumental attitudes toward nature but not use them in arguments for preservation in the larger public and political arenas because such views carry little weight in a society that has little understanding of ecological ideas and has a strong instrumental orientation in its values. Instead, they will argue that wilderness ought to be preserved for its intangible values that are instrumental to human well-being. Only after a general shift in public attitudes toward acceptance of the idea that nature should be valued noninstrumentally for itself would it make political sense to employ noninstrumental values in arguing in public forums for the preservation of wilderness.

This point is substantiated by an analysis of the testimony given before Congress by opponents to the Echo Park Dam (Table 1-1). The content of this testimony for each individual who testified was analyzed and coded according to the list of possible arguments that one could make in favor of preserving natural areas (Table 7-1).[59] The argument most commonly made in testimony was that the canyon floors of the Dinosaur National Monument ought to be preserved in their natural state because of their unparalleled natural beauty. This argument is by implication instrumental, suggesting that those who visit the monument will be able to enjoy this natural beauty. The next most common argument was that Echo Park was not especially valuable as a dam site and that the same water storage and electricity generation goals could be accomplished at the same or even less cost at alternative sites. This is akin to the worthless lands argument suggested by Runte in his work on the national parks.[60] As for many national parks in the past, the preservation of Dinosaur National Monument was justified on the grounds that the scenery was unique and monumental and that the area was essentially worthless for other purposes. The third most popular argument was that the monument preserved in its natural condition could provide significant recreational opportunities, particularly in the form of river rafting and camping along the shores in the canyon bottoms. Other arguments made referred to instrumental but intangible benefits and included preserving the monument in its natural condition as a place for spiritual reflection, solitude, preserving Indian artifacts, and scientific research. Some also argued that the monument should be preserved for future generations, for its wildlife, and because of the tourist business it would generate. Only in one case did the testimony seem to approach the notion of valuing nature for itself when David Brower suggested the following:

I would say that every inch of the ground is sacred in a philosophical sense of the ground, the soil and the life it produces. We have been rather rough with that which is sacred in that sense.[61]

In sum, the arguments made by preservationists were predominantly rooted in the view that nature provides to human beings values that are intangible but are at the same time instrumental. That is, they are of benefit to human individuals. The ideas of an ecological consciousness and that nature is valuable in its own right make an appearance in the debate, but only in a tangential fashion. Center stage continued to be held by values that bring benefits to human beings. At this point in the wilderness preservation movement, the idea of an ecological consciousness and that nature had value in itself was beginning to enter preservationist thinking, but it had yet to significantly penetrate public discourse on wilderness issues.

Instrumentalism vs. Noninstrumentalism

The emphasis on instrumental values by preservationists in the Dinosaur debate occurred even though the spiritual fathers of wilderness preservation, Thoreau, Muir, and Leopold, all argued in one form or another that nature is valuable in its own right independent of benefits it provides to human beings. To take this position by no means precludes the idea that nature is also of value instrumentally for aesthetic reasons. All three argued in their writings that wild nature provides important nonmaterial human benefits. But they also each argued that nature is noninstrumentally valuable as well.

Thoreau, the transcendentalist, saw nature as providing the opportunity for human beings to move beyond their material selves and discover the ultimate truths by discovering the presence of divinity in the whole of the natural world. Wild nature for Thoreau was the raw material for transforming human values onto a higher plane.[62] But Thoreau seemed also to believe that nature should be valued for more than its instrumental role in shaping the human spirit. A nature suffused with divinity has value in its own right. In Thoreau's view, "the Earth I tread on is not a dead, inert mass; it is a body, has a spirit, is organic and fluid to the influence of its spirit."[63] He argued further for a parallel between those who abuse children and those who maltreat the natural landscape, suggesting prosecution for both.[64] As Roderick Nash notes Thoreau's attitude toward nature was virtually unprecedented in American intellectual circles.[65]

John Muir, who was strongly influenced by Thoreau, was even more direct and fervent in his view that wild nature and its constituent beings were to be valued for themselves. In Muir's view, "Nature's object in

Table 1-1
Arguments Made by Advocates of Preserving Dinosaur
National Monument in Congressional Testimony

Argument	Percentage of advocates making argument
1. Natural beauty, monumental scenery	78.9
2. Place for spiritual reflection	21.1
3. Place for solitude, escape	15.8
4. Preservation of cultural resources	21.1
5. Outdoor recreation	57.9
7. Preservation of wildlife, plantlife	10.5
13. Preservation for future generations	31.6
14. Area has no resource value	63.2
15. Preservation for scientific purposes	26.3
16. Preservation for economic purposes	15.8

Note: The total number of advocates testifying at all hearings was 19. Some testified more than once. For coding purposes, their testimony at separate hearings was combined. Arguments in Table 7-1 not made by advocates are not included in Table 1-1. The testimony can be found in U.S. House of Representatives, Subcommittee on Irrigation and Reclamation, Committee on Interior and Insular Affairs, *Colorado River Storage Project: Hearing on H.R. 4449, H.R. 4443, and H.R. 4463,* 83rd Congress, 2d. Session, Washington, D.C., January 18-23, 25-28, 1954 (Washington, D.C.: U.S. Government Printing Office, 1954); U.S. Senate, Subcommittee on Irrigation and Reclamation, Committee on Interior and Insular Affairs, *Colorado River Storage Project: Hearing on S. 1555,* 83rd Congress, 2d. Session, Washington, D.C., June 28-30, July 1-3, 1954 (Washington, D.C.: U.S. Government Printing Office, 1954); U.S. Senate, Subcommittee on Irrigation and Reclamation, Committee on Interior and Insular Affairs, *Colorado River Storage Project: Hearing on S. 500,* 84th Congress, 1st Session, Washington, D.C., February 28, March 1-5, 1955 (Washington, D.C.: U.S. Government Printing Office, 1955).

making animals and plants might possibly be first of all the happiness of each one of them, not the creation of all for the happiness of one."[66] In other words, nature was not created just as an instrument to promote the happiness of human beings. Muir, in his integrated view of the natural world, exhibited an ecological consciousness before the term was in popular usage, arguing that "when we try to pick out anything by itself, we find it hitched to everything else in the universe."[67] Because such attitudes were not very popular in Muir's day, he kept them to himself, expressing them in his private journals rather than in his published works and public statements arguing for the preservation of wilderness.[68]

Perhaps the single most influential work on the relationship between ecology and environmental ethics is Aldo Leopold's "Land Ethic." This work appears as a chapter in Leopold's widely read *A Sand County Almanac* and suggests there is a fundamental link between ecological understanding and the ethical treatment of nature.[69] Leopold argues for the extension of ethics to "man's relationship to the land and to the animals and plants which grow upon it."[70] In Leopold's view,

> All ethics so far evolved rest upon a single premise: that the individual is a member of a community of interdependent parts. His instincts prompt him to compete for his place in the community, but his ethics prompt him also to co-operate. . . . The land ethic simply enlarges the boundaries of the community to include soils, waters, plants, and animals, or collectively: the land.[71]

Leopold sees the ethical realm evolving over historical time to encompass first human individuals and then communities, and he holds out the land ethic as a possible next step in the process. He argues against a conservation ethic based strictly on the instrumental use of the land. Noting that "we can be ethical only in relation to something we can see, feel, understand, love, or otherwise have faith in," Leopold suggests that an ecological conscience leads to a "conviction of individual responsibility for the health of the land."[72] Ecological knowledge leads to an understanding of plants and animals as part of a living community and to the idea that biotic communities have ethical standing.

Leopold's land ethic provided a coherent, noninstrumental argument for the preservation of natural ecosystems contained within wilderness. The interesting question is whether, in the history of wilderness and forest preservation, an ecological consciousness manifests itself and whether it leads to the use of noninstrumental arguments in public forums. We have already seen that John Muir avoided arguing for the intrinsic value of wild nature because he feared such arguments would be ridiculed and might even hurt his cause. When those who advocate wilderness come out of the closet and begin to argue that nature should be preserved for its own sake, then it most probably indicates a broadening of the acceptance of such ideas, one preceded by a higher degree of ecological understanding. A central task of this book is to discern whether such is the case for the old-growth preservation movement.

Summary

A dominant theme in American history is that the function of the natural landscape is to provide material wealth for the purpose of furthering human ends. This materialist view underlay the strivings of large business enterprises seeking to carve out substantial landholdings from the public domain, the desires of Jeffersonian democrats who wanted to see a more socially equitable landholding system created from the public domain, and the conservationists who were concerned about excessive exploitation of natural resources. While the materialist view of nature remains strong, the view that nature possesses intangible, nonmaterial values for human beings emerged relatively early in American history. It served as a stimulus for the creation of a national park system and gained sufficient acceptance by the 1950s when the modern wilderness preservation movement gained its first major victory in preventing dam construction that would have inundated much of the Dinosaur National Monument. At this point in time, the notion of an ecological consciousness and the idea that nature is valuable in its own right were only just beginning to take hold in the wilderness preservation movement.

What constellation of values underlie the exploitation and decline of old-growth forests? Have value shifts away from the materialist view that sees forests as valuable only for the wood fiber they contain and toward the view that nature is valuable for nonmaterial or intangible reasons played a role in the preservation of old-growth forests? Did an ecological consciousness emerge within the old-growth preservation movement and did it foster the view that old-growth forests are valuable in their own right? Did such noninstrumental values get expressed in the public debate on old-growth preservation? Have economic changes, such as a declining economic dependency on old-growth forests, preceded such value shifts? Finally, given the ways in which old-growth forests are valued in practice, how should contemporary questions of preserving old-growth forest ecosystems be addressed? What is the appropriate framework for analysis and what does it imply about current policies to preserve old-growth forests? These are the key questions that remain to be addressed in the pages to follow.

After describing the basic ecology of Pacific Northwest forests in

Chapter 2, the aboriginal use and treatment of forests will be discussed in Chapter 3. The goal will be to determine, to the greatest extent possible, the impact of aboriginals on forests and the role that their values and attitudes may have played in their use of the natural world. Did aboriginal attitudes toward nature restrain the degree to which they exploited it? While a definitive answer to this question is probably impossible, speculation about it provides an interesting prelude to considering the impact of European settlers and their values on the forest environment.

In Chapter 4 the value system brought to the Pacific Northwest by Europeans will be addressed as well as the consequences of that value system for the treatment of forests. In Chapter 5, the ecological consequences of the exploitation of old-growth forests will be outlined and the extent of the decline in old growth will be estimated. In Chapter 6, the relative decline of the Pacific Northwest forest products industry will be documented and analyzed for the purpose of showing that this decline preceded and may have played a significant role in the increase of efforts to preserve old-growth forest landscapes in recent years. Chapter 7 will document the evolution of values and attitudes that underlie the parkland, wilderness, and old-growth preservation movements in the Pacific Northwest. The preservation of old growth up through the early 1980s, we will see, occurred primarily as a by-product of movements to create national parks and preserve wilderness areas. Beginning in the 1980s, however, a growing consciousness of the uniqueness of old-growth ecosystems increasingly played a role in the debate over preserving forestlands along with the issue of preserving endangered species and biotic diversity. In Chapter 8, the value foundations of what can be truly called an old-growth preservation movement with its focus upon an endangered species, the spotted owl, are investigated. The final chapter will summarize the key findings on the relationship between values and the preservation of old-growth forests and end with a discussion of how old-growth forests ought to be valuated. In this chapter, the cost-benefit approach to evaluating old-growth preservation issues will be given critical scrutiny, and it will be explicitly contrasted with alternative ethical criteria.

Notes

1. For an argument that a true environmental ethic requires a moral commitment extending beyond human beings to other types of organisms, see Tom Regan, "The Nature and Possibility of an Environmental Ethic," *Environmental Ethics* 3 (1981): 19-34.

2. Stephen J. Pyne, *Fire in America: A Cultural History of Wildland and Rural Fire* (Princeton: Princeton University Press, 1982), pp. 88-99; Richard White, *Land Use, Environment, and Social Change: The Shaping of Island County, Washington* (Seattle: University of Washington Press, 1980), pp. 14-34.

3. For an economic analysis of the process of converting old growth to managed stands, see William F. Hyde, *Timber Supply, Land Allocation, and Economic Efficiency* (Washington, D.C.: Resources for the Future, 1980).

4. For a more extensive treatment of the variety of instrumental evaluations that may be placed on nature, see Holmes Rolston, III, *Environmental Ethics: Duties to and Values in the Natural World* (Philadelphia: Temple University Press, 1988), pp. 1-44; and Warwick Fox, *Toward a Transpersonal Ecology: Developing New Foundations for Environmentalism* (Boston and London: Shambhala Publications, 1990), pp. 154-61.

5. For a work focusing on the idea of transformative values see Bryan B. Norton, *Why Preserve Natural Variety?* (Princeton: Princeton University Press, 1987).

6. A large number of authors deal with this issue, including Tom Regan, "Nature and Possibility"; J. Baird Callicott, "Intrinsic Value, Quantum Theory, and Environmental Ethics"; *Environmental Ethics* 7 (1985): 257-73; Kenneth E. Goodpaster, "On Being Morally Considerable," *The Journal of Philosophy* 75 (1975): 168-76; Rolston, *Environmental Ethics*; and Paul W. Taylor, *Respect for Nature* (Princeton: Princeton University Press, 1986).

7. Norton, *Why Preserve*, and "Intergenerational Equity and Environmental Decisions: A Model Using Rawls' Veil of Ignorance," *Ecological Economics* 1 (1989): 137-59.

8. Fox, *Transpersonal Ecology*, pp. 161-96.

9. Regan, "Nature and Possibility," pp. 19-34; Holmes Rolston III, "Values in Nature," *Environmental Ethics* 3 (1981): 113-28.

10. Callicott, "Intrinsic Value," pp. 258-59.

11. Ibid., pp. 260-66; Andrew Brennan, *Thinking about Nature* (London: Routledge, 1988), pp. 186-200.

12. Norton, *Why Preserve*, pp. 166-68.

13. For a discussion of the view that ecosystems are creators of new life forms, see Rolston, *Environmental Ethics*, pp. 186-89. For consideration of the human capacity to identify with ecological wholes, see Max Oelschlaeger, *The Idea of Wilderness: From Prehistory to the Age of Ecology* (New Haven: Yale University Press, 1991), pp. 281-353.

14. Aldo Leopold, *A Sand County Almanac: With Essays from Round River* (New York: Ballantine Books, 1966), p. 251.

15. Roy Robbins, *Our Landed Heritage, 1776-1936* (Lincoln: University of Nebraska Press, 1976), pp. 8-10, 50-90; Paul W. Gates, *History of Public Land Law Development* (Washington D.C.: U.S. Government Printing Office, 1968), pp. 219-47.

16. Robbins, *Our Landed Heritage*, pp. 206-9; Eugene C. Hargrove, "Anglo-American Land Use Attitudes," *Environmental Ethics* 2 (1980): 121-48.

17. Robbins, *Our Landed Heritage*, pp. 255-56.

18. Ibid.; Bureau of Corporations, *The Lumber Industry, Part I* (Washington, D.C.: U.S. Government Printing Office, 1913-1914), pp. 99-100; Edmond S. Meany, Jr., "The History of the Lumber Industry in the Pacific Northwest to 1917," Ph. D. diss., Harvard University, 1935, pp. 215-26.

19. Hargrove, "Ango-American Land Use Attitudes," pp. 131-43.

20. Karl Polanyi, *The Great Transformation* (Boston: Beacon Press, 1957).

21. This was a key theme in John Wesley Powell, *Report on the Lands of the Arid Region of the United States*, Wallace Stegner, ed. (Cambridge: Belknap Press, 1962).

22. James N. Tattersall, "The Economic Development of the Pacific Northwest to 1920," Ph. D. diss., University of Washington, 1960; Thomas R. Cox, *Mills and Markets: A History of the Pacific Coast Lumber Industry to 1900* (Seattle: University of Washington Press, 1974), pp. 122-26, 280-81.

23. So-called stump farms were attempted in cutover areas, but they failed miserably. Besides the problem of the stumps themselves, Pacific Northwest soils were not very fertile (White, *Land Use*, pp. 113-41).

24. Moreover, the Lockean justification for property in nature on further examination can be shown to be fundamentally flawed. Locke's clearest statement of his views basing property rights on labor is the following:

> Though the Earth, and all inferior Creatures be common to all Men, yet, every Man has a *Property* in his own *Person*. This no Body has any Right to but himself. The *Labour* of his Body, and the *Work* of his Hands, we may say, are properly his. Whatsoever then he removes out of the State that Nature hath provided, and left in, he hath mixed his *Labour* with, and joyned to it something that is his own, and thereby makes it his *Property*.

> As much land as a Man Tills, Plants, Improves, Cultivates, and can use the Product of, so much is his *Property*. He by his Labour does, as it were, inclose it from the Common.

While a normative basis exists for the human ownership of the products of the human hand, none of a similar sort exists for the ownership of nature. Locke argues that individuals have a right to the ownership of the products of their labor, but because nature is not a product of human labor, this justification fails even though Locke tries to argue that those who work the land and mix their labor with it own it and all the products of nature on it. Because nature is not a product of the human hand, this kind of justification cannot really be used. The Lockean foundation of property in nature, which in many respects is at the foundation of American property law, lacks a clear normative basis, apart from the notion that property rights may be necessary for an economically efficient use of resources. [John Locke, *Two Treatises of Government*, ed. Thomas I. Cook (New York and London: Hafner Press, 1947), secs. 27, 32; David P. Ellerman, "On the Labor Theory of Property," *Philosophical Forum* 16 (1985): 293-326].

25. Samuel T. Dana and Sally K. Fairfax, *Forest and Range Policy: Its Development in the United States*, 2d ed. (New York: McGraw-Hill, 1980), pp. 40-55.

26. Ibid., pp. 39, 41.

27. Samuel Hayes, *Conservation and the Gospel of Efficiency* (Cambridge: Harvard University Press, 1959), pp. 2-3.

28. Dana and Fairfax, *Forest and Range Policy*, pp. 41-42.

29. Ibid., p. 43; Hayes, *Conservation*, pp. 27, 50-55; Harold K. Steen, *The U.S. Forest Service: A History* (Seattle: University of Washington Press, 1976), pp. 23-26.

30. Hayes, *Conservation*, pp. 27-30.

31. Ibid., pp. 36, 114-18; Dana and Fairfax, *Forest and Range Policy*, pp.57-70; Roderick Nash, *Wilderness and the American Mind*, 3d ed. (New Haven: Yale University Press, 1982), pp. 133-34.

32. Hays, *Conservation and the Gospel of Efficiency*, pp. 39-55; Steen, *U.S. Forest Service*, pp. 71-78.

33. Nash, *Wilderness*, pp. 23-43.

34. Ibid., pp. 141-60.

35. Alfred Runte, *National Parks: The American Experience*, 2d ed. (Lincoln: University of Nebraska Press, 1987), pp. 11-64.

36. Ibid., p. 46; Nash, *Wilderness*, p. 112.

37. Ibid., p. 132; Stephen Fox, *The American Conservation Movement: John Muir and His Legacy*, (Madison: University of Wisconsin Press, 1985), p. 128.

38. Roderick Nash, *The Rights of Nature: A History of Environmental Ethics* (Madison: University of Wisconsin Press, 1989), pp. 40-41.

39. Nash, *Wilderness*, pp. 84-95, 125-27.

40. Ibid., pp. 141-60.

41. Nash, *Wilderness*, p. 132; Fox, *American Conservation Movement*, pp. 127-8. Muir knew E. H. Harriman, the president of the Southern Pacific, and apparently used his relationship with Harriman to further the Yosemite cause.

42. The measure was introduced by Secretary of the Interior Noble under the influence of two conservationists, Fernow and Edward A. Bowers. There is also some evidence that Noble was influenced by Muir and Johnson, two preservationists. (Hays, *Conservation*, p. 36, 114-18; Dana and Fairfax, *Forest and Range Policy*, pp. 56-57; Nash, *Wilderness*, pp. 133-34; Steen, *U.S. Forest Service*, pp. 26-27).

43. Ibid., pp. 69-78.

44. Nash, *Wilderness*, p. 161.

45. Ibid., pp. 162-164; Fox, *American Conservation Movement*, pp. 139-46; Runte, *National Parks*, pp. 78-81.

46. Dana and Fairfax, *Forest and Range Policy*, pp. 109-11.

47. Nash, *Wilderness*, p. 168.

48. Ibid., pp. 170-81.

49. Ibid., pp. 180-81; Dana and Fairfax, *Forest and Range Policy*, pp. 108-9; Fox, *American Conservation Movement*, p. 146; Runte, *National Parks*, pp. 82-105; Steen, *U.S. Forest Service*, pp. 114-18.

50. Dana and Fairfax, *Forest and Range Policy*, pp. 109-11; Robert Shankland, *Steve Mather of the National Parks*, 3d. ed. (New York: Knopf, 1970), pp. 145-50.

51. Fox, *American Conservation Movement*, pp. 272-81.
52. Ibid., pp. 266-72.
53. Ibid., pp. 281-86.
54. Nash, *Wilderness*, pp. 209-19.
55. Ibid., pp. 220-37.
56. Ibid., pp. 209-14.
57. Bernard DeVoto, "Shall We Let Them Ruin Our National Parks," *Saturday Evening Post* 223 (1950): 44.
58. Charles C. Bradley, "Wilderness and Man," *Sierra Club Bulletin*, 37 (December, 1952): 5-9, 67; Howard Zahniser, "The Need for Wilderness Areas," *National Parks Magazine* 29 (1955): 166.
59. The coding system presented in Table 7-1 is a general one, intended for use in later chapters of the book as well as in this chapter. It includes the full range of arguments that possibly can be presented for preserving natural areas and is based on arguments presented in all the congressional testimony investigated in this book as well as material in Rolston, *Environmental Ethics*. The arguments are subdivided by general categories. Whether a particular category involves arguments based on tangible or intangible resources or instrumental or noninstrumental values is indicated. Content analysis as practiced in journalism generally uses more than one coder in order to test for consistency in coding. Usually, in such, cases interpretations of meaning are required, and significant errors are a possibility. [See Charles E. Osgood, George J. Suci, and Percy H. Tannenbaum, *The Measurement of Meaning* (Urbana: University of Illinois Press, 1957).] However, in the case of congressional testimony, there is little doubt when someone is arguing that a given area ought to be preserved because it has significant natural beauty, or provides recreational opportunities, or contains significant wildlife and plant resources. Consequently, the author did his own coding in analyzing the content of congressional testimony. There are cases where arguments are based on circumstances unique to the particular area. For example, the constructing of a dam in Dinosaur National Monument was viewed by preservationists as a dangerous precedent that could affect development elsewhere in the national park system. Such arguments were not considered in the general coding system. Arguments based on the fulfillment of needs are clearly instrumental in character. However, advocates for the preserving of natural areas often justify preservation on the grounds that it will protect certain ecosystems, plants, or wildlife without explicitly claiming whether these are valued for instrumental or noninstrumental reasons. This is generally the case for arguments made under category C. If, however, the area is recommended for preservation explicitly for the purpose of hunting, then the argument would enter under category B.
60. Runte, *National Parks*, pp. 48-64.
61. U.S. Senate, *Colorado River Storage Project*, Hearings before the Subcommittee on Irrigation and Reclamation, Committee on Interior and Insular Affairs, 84th Congress, 1st Session on S. 500, February 28, March 1-5, 1955 (Washington D.C.: U.S. Government Printing Office, 1955).
62. Nash, *Wilderness*, pp. 85-95.

63. *The Writings of Henry David Thoreau*, vol. 3, Bradford Torrey, ed. (Boston: 1906), vol. 3, p. 165. Quoted in Nash, *Rights of Nature*, pp. 36-37.

64. Ibid., p. 37.

65. Ibid.

66. John Muir, *A Thousand-Mile Walk to the Gulf*, William F. Bade, ed. (Boston: 1917), pp. 354-56. Quoted in Nash, *Rights of Nature*, p. 40.

67. John Muir, *My First Summer in the Sierra* (Boston: 1911), p. 211. Quoted in Nash, *Rights of Nature*, p. 40.

68. Ibid., p. 41.

69. Leopold, *Sand County Almanac*.

70. Ibid., p. 238.

71. Ibid., p. 239.

72. Ibid., pp. 251, 258.

2

Natural History of Old-Growth Forests

Pacific Northwest forests have been ecologically altered by human activity through a shift in their age structure in the direction of youth. To put it more bluntly, exploited forests in the modern era are not allowed to grow old. Human history alters natural history. This alteration in the "natural" age structure of a forest is called "seral shifting." A "sere" is a particular phase of a successional process through which one plant community and its associated wildlife is replaced by another. The notion of ecological succession is central to understanding both the natural and economic history of Pacific Northwest forests and, in particular, the old-growth component of those forests.

A successional process begins with a disturbance to the landscape, such as a fire, that opens soil to direct sunlight and permits colonization by herbs and shrubs that thrive in the open. Eventually, young saplings of trees that grow rapidly in the open sunlight gain a foothold and, after a period of time, form a dense forest. As time passes, a natural thinning process occurs, opening up the forest floor. This allows the colonization of shade-tolerant species, which progressively gain dominance over the pioneer tree species whose saplings are usually intolerant to shade.[1]

In the successional process, the early seres usually add biomass at a rapid rate, while the later seres generally achieve a comparatively stable level of total biomass. Basically, as the biomass increases, more and more biological production goes to the maintenance of existing levels of biomass than to the production of added biotic material, or net biological production. The total biomass and total productivity in a mature forest can be substantial, but because of respiration needs, net productivity can be very low or even zero. Because early seres typically have a high level of net productivity, they are normally favored where humans intensively exploit forests. Forests are allowed to grow only so long as they are achieving a certain rate of net productivity before they are harvested, and the successional process is begun anew. The seral profile in exploited forests will thus be shifted in the direction of younger stands having smaller trees with higher rates of net productivity. Universal exploitation would mean the disappearance of old-growth stands.

One determining characteristic of the ecological structure of a forest is its seral phase in the successional process. Another is the basic climatic conditions faced by a particular forest. Climatic conditions in forests, specifically moisture and temperature, determine the species composition at any seral phase including the climax. A climatic climax is a plant community that would remain unaltered given the absence of a major disturbance under a given climatic regime. It is the final step in the successional process. A climatic climax community is used in the case of Pacific Northwest forests to define vegetational zones. Because vegetational zones vary according to temperature and moisture, and because both of these are at least partly dependent on geographic characteristics, such as elevation and orientation to prevailing weather patterns, the first step in understanding the natural history of Pacific Northwest forests is to consider the physical setting of the area.

The Geographic Setting

The geographic area referred to here as the Pacific Northwest includes western Washington and Oregon, the area between the crest of the Cascade Mountains and the Pacific Ocean bordered on the north by Canada and the south by California. In the early forest surveys, this was often called the Douglas fir zone. Its dominant visual geological features are high, rugged mountains, many with glaciers, relatively flat river valleys, and extensive estuarine waters.

The mountainous areas can be roughly divided into two mountain ranges running north to south, one along the coast and one inland roughly bisecting Washington and Oregon. These mountain ranges can be further divided into six distinct geological provinces (Fig. 2-1). From north to south on the coast, the divisions include the Olympic peninsula, the coast ranges, and the Klamath Mountains, and inland the divisions include the northern Cascades, the southern Washington Cascades, the western Cascades, and the Oregon high Cascades. The Cascades and coast ranges are cut horizontally by the Columbia River, which flows through a comparatively narrow gorge in the Cascades and widens out into a broad estuary as it enters the Pacific. In western Washington, the Olympic peninsula and the coast range are separated from the Cascades by the glacially

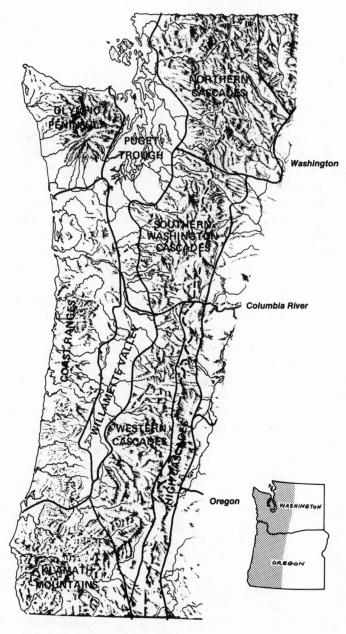

Figure 2-1: Physiographic and Geological Provinces of Western Oregon and Western Washington [Adapted from J. F. Franklin and C. T. Dyrness, *Natural Vegetation of Oregon and Washington*, Portland, Ore.: USDA Forest Service, GTR, PNW-8, 1973], p. 6.

carved Puget trough, part of which is Puget Sound. The Willamette River valley in Oregon is a southern extension of the Puget trough separating the coast ranges from the western Cascades.[2]

Mountains

The mountains of the Pacific Northwest were formed through a combination of uplifting and folding of geologic strata and volcanic action, both connected to the meeting of the Pacific and continental plates along the Pacific coast. The northern Cascades is a rugged mountain range composed of a series of jagged, often glaciated, peaks roughly equal in height of between 6,000 and 8,500 feet. The notable exceptions to this uniformity of height are two volcanic peaks, Mount Baker and Glacier Peak. The mountains are intersected by steep-sided, deep valleys with streams and rivers at relatively low elevations close to the mountain divide. The mountains are composed primarily of uplifted sedimentary rock, some of which has been metamorphosed and invaded here and there by granitic rock.[3]

The southern Washington Cascades, ranging between Snoqualmie Pass to the north and the Columbia River to the south, in contrast to the northern Cascades, were formed primarily through volcanic action and contain three major volcanic peaks—Mount Rainier, Mount Adams, and Mount St. Helens. Apart from the volcanic peaks, ridge heights tend to be similar at approximately 6,500 feet in the northern part of the area and gradually decline to around 4,000 feet in the southern part. Volcanic deposits have been extensively altered by faulting and folding, and, as in the north, the southern Washington Cascades are dissected by steep river valleys.[4]

The Cascades in Oregon can be divided into two distinct geologic provinces, the high Cascades to the east, containing all the high peaks, and the western Cascades to the west, containing older volcanic flows at lower elevations. The ridges of the western Cascades seldom exceed 5,000 feet and are relatively uniform in height; evidence of glaciation in the area is fairly extensive. The high Cascades, in contrast, are characterized by rolling terrain cut at intervals by glaciated channels that carry westward flowing streams and are punctuated by a number of volcanic peaks and cones rising as much as 5,000 feet above the surrounding area, which itself is about 5,000 to 6,000 feet in elevation.[5]

The Olympic peninsula, the northern limit of the coastal mountains in the Pacific Northwest, is dominated by the rugged, snowcapped Olympic Mountains, which are surrounded on three sides by relatively flat coastal lowlands. The interior of the mountains, a rugged area made up mostly of sedimentary rock, is ringed by ridges of volcanic origin on the north, east, and south, most of which reach altitudes of 4,000 to 5,000 feet. Extensive rainfall on the western side of the mountains and the resulting cutting action of mountain streams have resulted in relatively steep slopes. Active glaciers and evidence of glacial activity in the past are common.[6]

Extending south from the Olympics are the coast ranges starting with the Willapa Hills in Washington and ending at the Coquille River in Oregon. The coast ranges are much lower in elevation than other mountains in the Pacific Northwest, running anywhere from 1,500 feet to 2,500 feet in elevation with a few peaks that are slightly higher. The geology of the coast ranges is a mixture of sedimentary rock, rock of volcanic origin, and intrusive igneous rock. The Klamath Mountains to the south of the coast ranges (often referred to as the Siskiyou Mountains) in southwest Oregon is a rugged, extensively dissected area of folded and deformed metamorphic, sedimentary, and intrusive rock formations. The altitude of these mountains tend to exceed those of the coast range, reaching 2,000 feet near the coast and 4,000 feet inland.[7]

Between the coastal and inland mountains, as already noted, extends the Puget trough to the north and the Willamette valley to the south. The northern part of the Puget trough was glaciated by a lobe of the cordilleran ice cap in the Pleistocene epoch, which extended south of Olympia, Washington, approximately 12 miles. A significant portion of the northern Puget trough is taken up by Puget Sound. The unglaciated portion of the trough extends to the Columbia River. The Willamette valley is a broad, alluvial flat bordered by groups of low hills. It is approximately 125 miles long and ends where the Cascade and Klamath mountains merge to the south.[8]

Climate

Weather interacts with the physiography and geology of the Pacific Northwest to provide the environmental setting for its forests. The area has a marine climate characterized by wet, mild winters and cool, relatively dry summers, heavy precipitation, most of which occurs in the fall and winter months, prolonged cloudy periods, a long frost-free season, and modest temperature differentials between night and day. Precipitation ranges from 70 to 120 inches per year on the coast and from 31 to 47 inches in the Puget trough and Willamette valley. Most precipitation is the result of low-pressure systems approaching from the Pacific on the dominant westerly winds. The mountains of the area have a significant effect on the distribution of precipitation. The coastal ranges intercept substantial amounts of moisture and are responsible for unusually dry areas, called rain shadows, immediately to their east and for limitations on rainfall in the Willamette valley and Puget trough. While very little winter precipitation falls as snow in the lowland areas because of mild temperatures, winter temperatures decrease rapidly with elevation, and a significant amount of the annual precipitation at higher elevations occurs as snow. Precipitation also tends to increase somewhat over the region moving from south to north.[9]

Prevailing weather patterns are the primary explanation for the unique character of Pacific Northwest forests. The forests of western Washington and northwest and coastal Oregon are unusual because of the size and longevity of their trees, the magnitude of their total biomass accumulation at maturity, and the extreme dominance by conifers as opposed to deciduous hardwoods so prevalent in other temperate forests. If allowed to grow undisturbed, a typical Douglas fir will live 750 years or more, attain a diameter of 60 to 85 inches, and reach a height of 250 feet. The biomass per acre achieved by the Douglas fir is the largest known for any plant species in the world. The mild wet winters and relatively dry summers are probably the primary reason for the large biomass accumulations and the dominance of conifers. These conditions prolong the growing season for coniferous tree species that retain their needles year-round and can thus carry out biological production through photosynthesis whenever conditions warrant it. Deciduous trees are adapted to the opposite weather pattern of cold winter temperatures, resulting in limited availability of water and warm, wet summers, and thus cannot compete as effectively in the Pacific Northwest as elsewhere.[10]

Vegetational Areas and Zones

The Pacific Northwest can be divided into three comparatively unique, broad vegetational areas: (1) the forests of western Washington and northwest and coastal Oregon, (2) the interior valleys of western Oregon, and (3) the interior forests of southwest Oregon.[11] Within each area, forests can be subdivided into vegetational zones identified by their climax species, those that would ultimately dominate in the forests in the absence of disturbance. In many forests of the area, however, a pioneer species, the Douglas fir, is often dominant in fact because of periodic disturbances such as fire and because it is relatively long-lived. Even though Douglas fir may be dominant, it is not the climax species because its saplings are shade intolerant and do best in sunny open areas. Given enough time and the absence of disturbances that expose the forest floor to open sunlight, shade-tolerant tree species will succeed the Douglas fir.

There are differing views over the importance of the climax notion in and the character of the successional process. While there may be a general tendency in the successional process towards a climax, disturbance may be so pervasive that the climax is seldom achieved in reality. As will be discussed later, the central disturbing element in the prehistorical Pacific Northwest forests was fire, and it was fire that helped to maintain the dominance of the pioneering Douglas fir. The other issue of debate is the general nature of the successional process itself. The organic approach, emphasized by one of the founders of ecology, Frederick Clements, is that one successional stage prepares the way for another. Plant species in earlier successional stages alter soil, temperature, and moisture conditions to the benefit of species in later successional stages. This occurs in the Northwest, for example, when the nitrogen-fixing red alder invades a burned-over site devoid of nitrogen and is succeeded by shade-tolerant species incapable of producing their own nitrogen. The alternative approach, one that is more atomistic in its orientation, is that succession can be simply explained by variations along ecological gradients, such as temperature, light, and moisture, and that dominant species in early successional stages either do not alter conditions or else alter conditions to their own disadvantage, but not necessarily to the advantage of other species.[12] Douglas fir forests, for example, create a shady understory in which their own seedlings cannot flourish. Whatever the view on successional theory, the notion of succession and climax is important in the analysis of Pacific Northwest forests. Forests in the Northwest are generally classified according to their dominant climax species, and the species composition of a forest will depend largely on its successional stage for a given set of climatic and other environmental conditions.

Forests

At the time of the arrival of the first white settlers, western Washington and northwestern and coastal Oregon were almost entirely forested with the exception of comparatively small prairie areas near the southern end of Puget Sound. With a few exceptions, the forests of the area can be classified into the Sitka spruce, western hemlock, Pacific silver fir, or mountain hemlock types on the basis of their climax dominant species. These different forest types are found in zones that are differentiated primarily by moisture and elevation. In general, the Sitka spruce zone is confined to a relatively narrow strip along the coast stretching from the northern tip of the Olympic peninsula into southwestern Oregon, the western hemlock zone covers the remaining lowland areas up to anywhere from 1,500 to 3,500 feet elevation depending on local weather conditions, the Pacific silver fir zone extends from approximately 2,000 to 4,000 feet with variations also related to local weather patterns, and the mountain hemlock zone extends beyond the Pacific silver fir zone up to anywhere from 5,500 to 6,500 feet.[13]

The Sitka spruce zone has the wettest and mildest climate of any of the Pacific Northwest forest zones, receiving up to 120 inches of precipitation per year in addition to moisture from summer fog that condenses in the tree crowns and drips to the forest floor. The major tree species found in this zone includes the Sitka spruce, Douglas fir, western hemlock, western red cedar, and red alder, the latter species being most commonly found on recently disturbed sites. Shore (lodgepole) pine is commonly found along the coast, while California laurel, Port-Orford-cedar, and coast redwood are found in southwestern Oregon. Other minor species include Pacific silver fir, grand fir, and bigleaf maple.[14] Typical understory plant species are listed in Table 2-1 and generally form a rich ground cover in the mature forests of this zone.[15]

Table 2-1
Principal Overstory and Understory Plants:
Sitka Spruce Zone

Common name	Scientific name
Major overstory species	
Douglas fir	*Pseudotsuga menziesii* (Mirb.) Franco.
Red alder	*Alnus rubra* Bong.
Sitka spruce	*Picea sitchensis* (Bong.) Carr.
Western hemlock	*Tsuga heterophylla* (Raf.) Sarg.
Western red cedar	*Thuja plicata* Donn.
Minor overstory species	
Bigleaf maple	*Acer macrophyllum* Pursh.
California laurel	*Umbellularia californica* (Hook & Arn.)
Coast redwood	*Sequoia sempervirens* (D. Don.) Endl.
Grand fir	*Abies grandis* (Dougl.) Lindl.
Lodgepole pine	*Pinus contorta* Dougl. ex Loud.
Pacific silver fir	*Abies amabilis* (Dougl.) Forbes.
Port-Orford-cedar	*Chamaecyparis lawsoniana* (A. Murr.) Parl.
Understory species	
Modal sites	
Evergreen violet	*Viola sempervirens* Greene.
False lily-of-the-valley	*Maianthemum dilatatum* (Wood.) Nels. & Macbr.
Oregon oxalis	*Oxalis oregana* Nutt. ex T. & G.
Red huckleberry	*Vaccinium parvifolium* Smith.
Rustyleaf	*Menziesia ferruginea* Smith.
Smith's fairybells	*Disporum smithii* (Hook.) Piper.

Sword fern	*Polystichum munitum* (Kaulf.) Presl.
Three-leaved coolwort	*Tiarella trifoliata* L.
Western springbeauty	*Montia sibirica* (L.) How.
Wood violet	*Viola Glabella* Nutt.

Dry sites

Evergreen huckleberry	*Vaccinium ovatum* Pursh.
Pacific rhododendron	*Rhododendron macrophyllum* G. Don.
Salal	*Gaultheria shallon* Pursh.

Wet sites

Deer fern	*Blechnum spicant* (L.) With.
Devilsclub	*Oplopanax horridum* (J.E. Smith.) Miq.
Lady fern	*Athyrium filix-femina* (L.) Roth.
Mountain woodfern	*Dryopteris austriaca* (Jacq.) Woyner ex Schinz & Thell.
Red elderberry	*Sambucus racemosa* L. var. *arborescens* (T. & G.) Gray.

Note: The source for this table is Franklin and Dyrness, *Natural Vegetation of Oregon and Washington*, pp. 59-60. Epiphytes, mosses that hang from trees, are also abundant as well as a variety of cryptogams, a type of fern. Wet and dry sites often include some of the modal site species.

The western hemlock zone is also characterized by a damp, mild, maritime climate but is subject to greater moisture and temperature extremes than the Sitka spruce zone because it is located further inland farther from the moderating influence of the ocean, is subject to greater variations in elevation, and contains a greater variety of mountainous terrain. Precipitation is concentrated in the winter months and ranges from 60 to 120 inches, although the figures tend to be lower (31 to 35 inches) in the Puget Sound area lying behind the Olympic Mountain rain shadow. The major forest species in this zone are Douglas fir, western hemlock, and western red cedar. Minor species include grand fir, Pacific silver fir in higher elevations, Sitka spruce near the coast, and white and lodgepole pine on glacial drift in the Puget Sound area. Red alder is commonly found on disturbed sites and in riparian areas along with bigleaf maple. In the southern portion of the zone in Oregon, incense cedar, sugar pine, and ponderosa pine are found as well. The overstory and understory composition varies considerably from dry to wet sites. On very dry sites, western hemlock may be completely absent and Douglas fir will be the dominant and even the climax species, while on damper sites, both will be present. As already noted, the Douglas fir is in great abundance in the western hemlock zone even though it is not the climax species. The understory also varies extensively according to dampness, with ocean spray and salal dominating the dry sites and sword fern and Oregon oxalis dominating damp sites. Common understory species are listed in Table 2-2. Understory composition is similar for younger, seral stands and old-growth forests. Forest composition also varies from north to south because of diminishing precipitation in the western hemlock zone as a whole.[16]

Table 2-2
Principal Overstory and Understory Plants:
Western Hemlock Zone

Common name	Scientific name
Major overstory species	
Douglas fir	*Pseudotsuga menziesii* (Mirb.) Franco.
Red alder	*Alnus rubra* Bong.
Western hemlock	*Tsuga heterophylla* (Raf.) Sarg.
Western red cedar	*Thuja plicata* Donn.
Minor overstory species	
Bigleaf maple	*Acer macrophyllum* Pursh.
California laurel	*Umbellularia californica* (Hook. & Arn.)
Coast redwood	*Sequoia sempervirens* (D. Don.) Endl.
Golden chinkapin	*Castanopsis chrysophylla* (Dougl.) A. DC.
Grand fir	*Abies grandis* (Dougl.) Lindl.
Incense cedar	*Libocedrus decurrens* Torr.
Lodgepole pine	*Pinus contorta* Dougl. ex Loud.
Oregon white oak	*Quercus garryana* Dougl.
Pacific silver fir	*Abies amabilis* (Dougl.) Forbes.
Pacific madrona	*Arbutus menziesii* Pursh.
Ponderosa pine	*Pinus ponderosa* Dougl. ex Loud.
Port-Orford-cedar	*Chamaecyparis lawsoniana* (A. Murr.) Parl.
Sitka spruce	*Picea sitchensis* (Bong.) Carr.
Sugar pine	*Pinus lambertiana* Dougl.
Tanoak	*Lithocarpus densiflorus* (Hook. & Arn.) Rehd.
Western yew	*Taxus brevifolia* Nutt.
Western white pine	*Pinus monticola* Dougl. ex D. Don.
Understory species	
Modal sites	
Cutleaf goldthread	*Coptis laciniata* Gray.
Evergreen violet	*Viola sempervirens* Greene.
Oregon grape	*Berberis nervosa* Pursh.

Pacific rhododendron   *Rhododendron macrophyullum* G. Don.
Rattlesnake plantain   *Goodyera oblongifolia* Raf.
Red huckleberry   *Vaccinium parvifolium* Smith.
Salal   *Gaultheria shallon* Pursh.
Sword fern   *Polystichum munitum* (Kaulf.) Presl.
Trailing blackberry   *Rubus ursinus* Cham. & Schlecht.
Twinflower   *Linnaea borealis* L.
Vine maple   *Acer circinatum* Pursh.

Dry sites

Common bear grass   *Xerophyllum tenax* (Pursh.) Nutt.
Creambush ocean spray   *Holodiscus discolor* (Pursh.) Maxim.
Creeping snowberry   *Symphoricarpos mollis* Nutt. var. *hesperius* (G. N. Jones.) Cronq.
Golden chinkapin   *Castanopsis chrysophylla* (Dougl.) A. DC.
Oregon iris   *Iris tenax* Dougl.
Pacific rhododendron   *Rhododendron macrophyllum* G. Don.
Salal   *Gaultheria shallon* Pursh.
Snowqueen   *Synthyris reniformis* (Dougl.) Benth.
Twinflower   *Linnaea borealis* L.
Western fescue   *Festuca occidentalis* Hook.
Western hazel   *Corylus cornuta* Marsh.
Whipple vine   *Whipplea modesta* Torr.
White hawkweed   *Hieracium albiflorum* Hook.

Wet Sites

Cutleaf goldthread   *Coptis laciniata* Gray.
Deer fern   *Blechnum spicant* (L.) With.
Deerfoot vanilla leaf   *Achlys triphylla* (Smith.) DC.
Lady fern   *Athyrium filix-femina* (L.) Roth.
Oregon grape   *Berberis nervosa* Pursh.
Oregon oxalis   *Oxalis oregana* Nutt. ex T. & G.
Red huckleberry   *Vaccinium parvifolium* Smith.
Sword fern   *Polystichum munitum* (Kaulf.) Presl.
Twinflower   *Linnaea borealis* L.
Vine maple   *Acer circinatum* Pursh.
Western coolwort   *Tiarella unifoliata* Hook.
White inside-out-flower   *Vancouveria hexandra* (Hook.) Morr. & Dec.
Wild ginger   *Asarum caudatum* Lindl.

Note: This table is adapted from Franklin and Dyrness, *Natural Vegetation of Oregon and Washington*, pp. 72-78.

    The Pacific silver fir zone is wetter and cooler than the adjacent western hemlock zone, receiving much of its precipitation in the form of snow in the winter months as a result of its higher elevation. The forest composition in this zone varies widely and typically includes Pacific silver fir, western hemlock, noble fir, Douglas fir, western red cedar, and western white pine. At its upper limit, mountain hemlock and Alaska cedar occur. Typical understory species are listed in Table 2-3. Understory and over-story composition of forests in this zone vary extensively as the result of moisture and elevation differences.[17]

Table 2-3
Principal Overstory and Understory Plants:
Pacific Silver Fir Zone

Common name	Scientific name
Overstory species	
Alaska cedar	*Chamaecyparis nootkatensis* (D. Don.) Spach.
Douglas fir	*Pseudotsuga menziesii* (Mirb.) Franco.
Mountain hemlock	*Tsuga mertensiana* (Bong.) Carr.
Noble fir	*Abies procera* Rehd.
Pacific silver fir	*Abies amabilis* (Dougl.) Forbes.
Western hemlock	*Tsuga heterophylla* (Raf.) Sarg.
Western red cedar	*Thuja plicata* Donn.
Western white pine	*Pinus monticola* Dougl. ex D. Don.
Understory species	
Alaska huckleberry	*Vaccinium alaskaense* How.
Big huckleberry	*Vaccinium membranaceum* Dougl. ex Hook.
Bunchberry dogwood	*Cornus canadensis* L.
Common bear grass	*Xerophyllum tenax* (Pursh.) Nutt.
Deerfoot vanilla leaf	*Achlys triphylla* (Smith.) DC.
Devilsclub	*Oplopanax horridum* (J. E. Smith.) Miq.
Dwarf blackberry	*Rubus lasiococcus* Gray.
Lady fern	*Athyrium filix-femina* (L.) Roth.
Oakfern	*Gymnocarpium dryopteris* (L.) Newm.
Oregon grape	*Berberis nervosa* Pursh.
Queencup beadlily	*Clintonia uniflora* (Schult.) Kunth.
Red huckleberry	*Vaccinium parvifolium* Smith.
Salal	*Gaultheria shallon* Pursh.
Starry solomonplume	*Smilacina stellata* (L.) Desf.
Twinflower	*Linnaea borealis* L.
Vine maple	*Acer circinatum* Pursh.
Western prince's pine	*Chimaphila umbellata* (L.) Bart.
Western coolwort	*Tiarella unifoliata* Hook.
White trillium	*Trillium ovatum* Pursh.

Note: This table is adapted from Franklin and Dyrness, *Natural Vegetation of Oregon and Washington*, pp. 94-96.

Table 2-4
Principal Overstory and Understory Plants:
Mountain Hemlock Zone

Common name	Scientific name

Overstory species

Alaska cedar	*Chamaecyparis nootkatensis* (D. Don.) Spach.
Douglas fir	*Pseudotsuga menziesii* (Mirb.) Franco.
Engelmann spruce	*Picea engelmannii* Parry. ex Engelm.
Lodgepole pine	*Pinus contorta* Dougl. ex Loud.
Mountain hemlock	*Tsuga mertensiana* (Bong.) Carr.
Noble fir	*Abies procera* Rehd.
Pacific silver fir	*Abies amabilis* (Dougl.) Forbes.
Shasta red fir	*Abies magnifican* Murr. var. *hastensis* Lemm.
Subalpine fir	*Abies lasiocarpa* (Hook.) Nutt.
Western red cedar	*Thuja plicata* Donn.
Western hemlock	*Tsuga heterophylla* (Raf.) Sarg.
Western white pine	*Pinus monticola* Dougl. ex D. Don.
Whitebark pine	*Pinus albicaulis* Engelm.

Understory species

Dry sites

Big huckleberry	*Vaccinium membranaceum* Dougl. ex Hook.
Blueleaf huckleberry	*Vaccinium deliciosum* Piper.
Common bear grass	*Xerophyllum tenax* (Pursh.) Nutt.
Dwarf blackberry	*Rubus lasiococcus* Gray.
One-sided wintergreen	*Pyrola secunda* L.
Red mountainheath	*Phyllodoce empetriformis* (S.W.) D. Don.

Wet sites

Avalanche fawn lily	*Erythronium montanum* Wats.
Big huckleberry	*Vaccinium membranaceum* Dougl. ex Hook.
Cascade azalea	*Rhododendron albiflorum* Hook.
Dwarf blackberry	*Rubus lasiococcus* Gray.
Evergreen violet	*Viola sempervirens* Greene.
Ovalleaf (blue) huckleberry	*Vaccinium ovalifolium* Smith.
Rustyleaf	*Menziesia ferruginea* Smith.
Sitka or Pacific mountain ash	*Sorbus sitchensis* Roemer var. *grayi* (Wenzig) C. L. Hitchc.
Sitka valerian	*Valeriana sitchensis* Bong.
Strawberry-leaf blackberry	*Rubus pedatus* J. E. Smith.
Western twayblade	*Listera caurina* Piper.

Note: This table is adapted from Franklin and Dyrness, *Natural Vegetation of Oregon and Washington*, pp. 104-106.

The highest, coolest, and wettest forested zone in the Cascade, Olympic, and Klamath mountains is the mountain hemlock zone. A dominant feature of this zone is its massive winter snow accumulations of up to 25 feet in depth. Typical tree species in this zone include mountain hemlock, subalpine fir, and lodgepole pine, the latter two species occurring on the dry sites. Pacific silver fir also is present in the northern portion of the zone along with Alaska cedar. Minor species include Douglas fir, subalpine fir, and western white pine on the wetter sites. A wide variety of understory species are typically found in the zone, some of which are listed in Table 2-4. Much of this zone has been burned over in the last 150 years resulting in rather poor forest development and a predominance of areas in early seral species. Indians often set fires in this zone in order to maintain fields of huckleberry as a food source.[18]

Successional Patterns

A question of central interest in later chapters will be successional patterns in the forests of western Oregon and Washington. Disturbance from wildfire, and in some cases fires set by aboriginal peoples, were common in all the forest zones, even the relatively wet areas on the Olympic peninsula. The extent of fire disturbance tended to increase, however, from north to south along a declining precipitation gradient. In modern times, fire disturbance has been partially replaced and significantly expanded by clearcut logging. Although successional patterns are widely variable in detail, the general pattern is fairly consistent throughout the Sitka spruce and western hemlock forest zones, the two zones that will be of central interest in analyzing the impact of postsettlement economic activity on forests.

Immediately after site disturbance, the plant cover is composed of residual species and various invading herbaceous species, such as fireweed and woodland groundsel. By the second year, invading species become dominant, including fireweed, bracken fern, and common thistle, and build up their populations into the fourth and fifth year. After this weed stage, shrubs begin to dominate, including vine maple, trailing blackberry, Oregon grape, rhododendron, ceanothus, and various species of willow. These dominate the site until overtopped by Douglas fir saplings. Dense stands of Douglas fir then often develop and suppress much of the understory vegetation until mortality begins to open the stands up at 100 to 150 years of age, permitting invasion by understory species and western hemlock seedlings.

Although full successional patterns of disturbed areas have not been studied, because of the inability of Douglas fir to reproduce in the shaded understory, and because of western hemlock's shade tolerance, the latter species will ultimately dominate if there is no further disturbance. Within this successional pattern, there is substantial variation. In the coastal Sitka spruce zone, for example, dense shrub communities composed of salmonberry, red elderberry, and huckleberry often develop after disturbance. Red alder frequently invades disturbed areas in this zone, dominates for a comparatively short period of time because it is short-lived, and can be succeeded by semipermanent brushfields or previously suppressed Sikta spruce, western red cedar, or western hemlock. More generally, species composition following disturbance depends on the extent of burning, and understory and overstory composition depends on the extent of moisture and the available seed sources.[19] Again, disturbance and succession are important phenomena in determining the ecological structure of Pacific Northwest forests. Prior to white settlement, the principle disturbing agent was fire, either naturally occurring or resulting from the activities of local aboriginal populations. With white settlement timber harvesting has become the principle disturbing agent, and, as we will see in Chapter 5, it has caused a substantial transformation of the ecology of northwest forests.

Prairie Areas

While the Northwest landscape is stereotypically described as forested, there are some areas that were unforested and had been that way for many years at the time of white settlement. Within the forests of western Washington, there are prairie areas located at the southern end of the Puget trough and even in the damp coastal Sitka spruce zone. These prairies were maintained free of forests apparently because of the presence of droughty, gravelly soil and because of fire from natural and human sources. As a consequence of human settlement and reduced fire activity, these areas have been partially invaded by forests.[20] The Quillayute prairie on the Olympic peninsula apparently never has been forested, suggesting that its existence cannot be traced to fire, although fire may have played a role in its maintenance as a prairie.[21] The prairies in the Puget trough resisted invasion by Douglas fir because of droughty, infertile soil and the closed nature of the prairie plant community and, possibly, because of periodic burning. Invasion accelerated once the soil was disturbed by grazing.[22] These prairie areas were not large, constituting approximately 168,000 acres in the Puget trough and perhaps 1,000 acres on the Olympic peninsula.[23]

The most extensive areas of prairie are to be found in the interior valleys of western Oregon. These include the Willamette, Umpqua, and Rogue river valleys and are the driest areas west of the Cascades, receiving from 20 to 40 inches of rain each year. The winters are mild and damp, but the summers are hot and dry. These climatic conditions are attributable primarily to the rain shadow provided this area by the coastal mountain ranges.

Prior to white settlement, these valleys were composed primarily of prairie and oak savannas, with dense forests lining the valleys in the foothills. The prairies were apparently maintained by fire set primarily by aboriginal populations prior to white settlement.[24] Unlike the Quillayute prairie on the Olympic peninsula, the Willamette valley apparently was forested at one time, according to an analysis of pollen in sediment samples.[25] In the absence of fire or other disturbance, most of these prairie areas would probably return to forest, although some grassland communities appear to be at a climax. Since white settlement, some of the prairie areas have been invaded by forests, although forestlands have been cleared in other areas of these valleys for agricultural use. The successional pattern is apparently from grassland to oak savanna to oak woodland to a mixed conifer-hardwood forest. Oregon white oak and California black oak dominate the savanna and woodlands, while Douglas fir, grand fir, ponderosa pine, and incense cedar are common conifers in the woodlands and dense forests, the latter two being more common towards the southern end of the region. Other important hardwoods include Pacific madrona and bigleaf maple.[26]

Southern Interior Forests

At the southern end of the interior valley area lies the forest zones of southwestern Oregon including the Siskiyou Mountains (the northernmost range in the Klamath Mountains group) and the west side of the southern Cascades. This area is ecologically complex and thus not easily described with any brevity. It basically covers the east side of the Siskiyou Mountains, where from low elevations to high there is a mixed-evergreen zone, a white fir zone, a Shasta red fir zone, and a mountain hemlock zone, and the west side of the Cascades with the same zonal structure, except that the mixed-evergreen zone is replaced by a mixed-conifer zone. The area is wet and damp in the winter and extremely hot and dry in the summer with annual precipitation running between 24 and 67 inches depending on elevation and distance from the coast. Natural and anthropogenic fire played an important role in the area previous to white settlement because of the prolonged, hot, dry summers.[27]

The dominant trees in the mixed-evergreen zone are Douglas fir and tanoak, while other species that may be present are Pacific madrona, golden chinkapin, and various species of oak. Other conifers found in the zone include sugar pine, ponderosa pine, and incense cedar. The mixed-conifer zone is typically composed of Douglas fir, sugar pine, incense

Table 2-5
Principal Overstory and Understory Plants:
Mixed-Evergreen and Mixed Conifer Zones

Common name	Scientific name
Overstory species	
Canyon live oak	*Quercus chrysolepis* Liebm.
Douglas fir	*Pseudotsuga menziesii* (Mirb.) Franco.
Golden chinkapin	*Castanopsis chrysophylla* (Dougl.) A. DC.
Incense cedar	*Libocedrus decurrens* Torr.
Pacific madrona	*Arbutus menziesii* Pursh.
Ponderosa pine	*Pinus ponderosa* Dougl. ex Loud.
Sugar pine	*Pinus lambertiana* Dougl.
Tanoak	*Lithocarpus densiflorus* (Hook. & Arn.) Rehd.
White fir	*Abies concolor* (Gord. & Glend.) Lindl.
Understory species	
Baldhip rose	*Rosa gymnocarpa* Nutt.
Bear bush	*Garrya fremontii* Torr.
Big huckleberry	*Vaccinium membranaceum* Dougl. ex Hook.
Bigleaf sandwort	*Arenaria macrophylla* Hook.
Bracken fern	*Pteridium aquilinum* (L.) Kuhn.
California hazel	*Corylus cornuta* Marsh. var. *californica* (D.C.) Sharp
California honeysuckle	*Lonicera hispidula* (Lindl.) Dougl. ex T. & G. var. *vacillans* (Benth.) Gray.
Columbia brome	*Bromus vulgaris* (Hook.) Shear.
Creeping snowberry	*Symphoricarpos mollis* Nutt. var. *hesperius* (G. N. Jones.)
Deerfoot vanilla leaf	*Achlys triphylla* (Smith.) DC.
Evergreen violet	*Viola sempervirens* Greene.
Golden chinkapin	*Castanopsis chrysophlla* (Dougl.) A. DC.
Green manzanita	*Arctostaphylos patula* Greene.
Harford melic	*Melica harfordii* Boland.
Hooker's fairybells	*Disporum hookeri* (Torr.) Nicholson.
Low dogbane	*Apocynum pumilum* Greene.
One-sided wintergreen	*Pyrola secunda*
Oregon boxwood	*Pachistima myrsinites* (Pursh.) Raf.
Oregon grape	*Berberis nervosa* Pursh.
Pacific poison oak	*Rhus diversiloba* T. & G.
Pine-mat manzanita	*Arctostaphylos nevadensis* Gray.
Rattlesnake plantain	*Goodyera oblongifolia* Raf.
Slender gaultheria	*Gaultheria ovatifolia* Gray.
Slender-tubed iris	*Iris chrysophylla* How.

Snow dewberry	*Rubus nivalis* Dougl. ex Hook.
Spreading dogbane	*Apocynum androsaemifolium* L.
Squawcarpet	*Ceanothus prostratus* Benth.
Starflower	*Trientalis latifolia* Hook.
Threeleaf anemone	*Anemone deltoidea* Hook.
Trailing blackberry	*Rubus ursinus* Cham. & Schlecht.
Twinflower	*Linnaea borealis* L.
Vine maple	*Acer circinatum* Pursh.
Western prince's pine	*Chimaphila umbellata* (L.) Bart.
Western fescue	*Festuca occidentalis* Hook.
Western yew	*Taxus brevifolia* Nutt.
Whipple vine	*Whipplea modesta* Torr.
White hawkweed	*Hieracium albiflorum* Hook.

Note: This table is adapted from Franklin and Dyrness, *Natural Vegetation of Oregon and Washington*, pp. 134-142.

cedar, and white or grand fir, with Douglas fir being the most abundant species. Common understory species are listed in Table 2-5 for the mixed-evergreen zone and the mixed-conifer zone.[28]

Little is known about succession in the mixed-conifer zone, although it is apparent that brushfields, dominated by ceonothus, are commonly established after fires and can be perpetuated by frequent reburning. Also, the climax species appears to be white or grand fir, although fires have apparently limited these species from obtaining overstory dominance. On dry sites Douglas fir and incense cedar appear to be the climax species. Frequent openings in the mixed-conifer forest permit the regeneration of shade-intolerant species, such as sugar pine, Douglas fir, incense cedar, and ponderosa pine.[29]

The white fir zone is a narrow belt located above the mixed-conifer and mixed-evergreen zones and is dominated by white fire, with Douglas fir, sugar pine, ponderosa pine, and white pine as associates. Above this lies the Shasta red fir zone extending from roughly 5,000 to 7,000 feet elevation with Shasta red fir dominant, with white fir, white pine, lodgepole pine, and mountain hemlock as associates, and above the red fir zone is found the highest forested area, the mountain hemlock zone already discussed above.[30]

Summary

Generally speaking, the ecological characteristics of Pacific Northwest forests can be aligned along three key gradients: successional stage, temperature, and moisture. The successional stage of a forest is determined by the length of time that has passed since its last major distur-bance. As time passes, dominance shifts from pioneer species, such as the Douglas fir, to the climax species such as the western hemlock. Because the Douglas fir is a long-lived species, it will maintain a substantial presence for up to several hundred years in a typical Pacific Northwest forest. The primary disturbing element in Northwest forests prior to white settlement was fire.

The composition of forests also varies according to temperature, which is largely a function of elevation and secondarily of latitude. The various forest zones identified by their climax species are primarily defined by elevation and thus temperature. Moisture also plays a role in determining forest composition and varies according to distance from the coast, el-evation, and location with respect to mountain ranges.

Notes

1. For a general discussion of ecological succession, see Robert Leo Smith, *Ecology and Field Biology*, 3d ed. (New York: Harper and Row, 1980), pp. 612-43. For an interesting historical treatment of the concept of a climax community, see Donald Worster, *Nature's Economy: A History of Ecological Ideas* (Cam-bridge: Cambridge University Press, 1984), pp. 205-20.

2. Jerry F. Franklin and C. T. Dyrness, *Natural Vegetation of Oregon and Washington*, (Portland, Ore.: USDA Forest Service, Pacific Northwest Range and Experiment Station, 1973), pp. 5-9. The descriptive material on the natural history of Pacific Northwest forests in this first chapter as well as in the rest of the book relies heavily on Franklin and Dyrness, a work that is highly rec-ommended for those desiring a more detailed treatment.

3. Ibid., pp. 17-20.

4. Ibid., pp. 21-22.

5. Ibid., pp. 23-26.

6. Ibid., pp. 9-11.

7. Ibid., pp. 11-15.

8. Ibid., pp. 15-17.

9. Ibid., pp. 38-42.

10. Ibid., pp. 53-55.

11. Ibid., p. 44.

12. Smith, *Ecology*, pp. 624-27.

13. Franklin and Dyrness, *Natural Vegetation of Oregon and Washington*, pp. 55-57.

14. Ibid., pp. 58-60.

15. For a layman's guide to Pacific Northwest plants, see Eugene N. Ko-zloff, *Plants and Animals of the Pacific Northwest* (Seattle: University of Washington Press, 1976).

16. Franklin and Dyrness, *Natural Vegetation of Oregon and Washington*, pp. 70-82.

17. Ibid., pp. 93-98.
18. Ibid., pp. 101-8.
19. Ibid., pp. 61-63, 82-88.
20. Ibid., pp. 69-70, 88-89.
21. Frederick B. Lotspeich, Jack B. Secor, Rose Okazaki, and Henry K. Smith, "Vegetation as a Soil-forming Factor on the Quillayute Physiographic Unit in Western Clallam County, Washington," *Ecology* 42 (1961): 53-68.
22. Frank Alexander Lang, "A Study of Vegetation Change on the Gravelly Prairies of Pierce and Thurston Counties, Western Washington," MS thesis, University of Washington, 1961, pp. 84-92.
23. Ibid., p. 6.
24. Franklin and Dyrness, *Natural Vegetation of Oregon and Washington*, pp. 110-29.
25. Henry P. Hansen, "Postglacial Forest Succession, Climate, and Chronology in the Pacific Northwest," *Transactions of the American Philosophical Society, New Series* 37, pt. 1 (1947): 84-86.
26. Franklin and Dyrness, *Natural Vegetation of Oregon and Washington*, pp. 110-29.
27. Ibid., pp. 130-32.
28. Ibid., pp. 133-43.
29. Ibid., pp. 143-48.
30. Ibid., pp. 150-58.

3

Aboriginal View of Nature and Old-Growth Forests

Although the first explorers and settlers of European stock marveled at the size and age of trees in the Pacific Northwest, they did not find on their arrival an undisturbed primeval forest. Aboriginal peoples had been living in the area and utilizing its forest for centuries. To what extent did the aboriginal Indian populations make use of the forests, and how did this use change the ecology of the forests? This is the first question that must be addressed in gaining an understanding of both the prehistory and history of old-growth forests. The benchmark for judging the historical impact of modern industrial society on old-growth forests will not be a forest devoid of human activity—this would be a hypothetical setting rather than a prehistorical one—but, rather, the forests as utilized by Pacific Northwest Indians.

We will see that the use of forest resources by aboriginal peoples, and therefore their propensity to modify the ecology of forests, was comparatively moderate. This moderation suggests further questions about the aboriginal use of forests. Was the exploitation of forests by Pacific Northwest Indians limited simply because of an inadequate technology, or were there cultural elements, or what can be called "cultural restraints," that inhibited the use of forest resources and thus the alteration of the ecology of forests? Were these "cultural restraints" the consequence of how Indians valued nature? The answer to this question marks the starting point for a general discussion in upcoming chapters of possible attitudes human societies can have toward forests and the consequences of those attitudes for the exploitation of forest resources.

The Use of Forests by
Pacific Northwest Indians

The native Indian populations living in the Pacific Northwest at the time of the arrival of settlers of European background enjoyed an abundance of material resources and a standard of living that permitted an accumulation of material goods beyond that necessary for basic subsistence.[1] The primary sources of food and fiber for Pacific Northwest Indians were the ocean and estuarine waters, rivers and streams, and forestlands. The single most important food was salmon, which was caught in such abundance that the average daily consumption of salmon was a full pound or more. The total Indian catch along the Pacific coast, according to one estimate, was approximately equal to 21 percent of the modern catch in the 1940s.[2] The Indians caught several varieties of salmon, including the chinook, coho, sockeye, steelhead, pink, and chum.

The salmon are fishes uniquely adapted to the Pacific Northwest ecology and geography. Mature salmon ready to spawn ascend the rivers of their birth to lay their eggs in the gravel beds of relatively fast-flowing streams containing cool, clean, highly oxygenated waters. After their birth, the juvenile salmon, or smolt, remain in streams or lakes for a period of time before migrating to the ocean waters of the Pacific and adjoining saltwater estuaries, where they range widely in search of food sources for the remainder of their adult life. With the exception of the steelhead, salmon spawn once and then die.

This life cycle is an adaption to ecological conditions that has resulted in significant breeding success and is highly dependent on the character and quality of spawning and rearing areas. The availability of such areas can be traced to the presence of glaciated rocky peaks, which serve as a source of gravel for stream beds, abundant rain and snow that feed mountain streams, and large, old-growth forests that limit mass soil movements and siltation of streams and provide large woody debris in the form of fallen logs in streams, creating the pool and riffle habitat that is favored by salmon smolt. The periodic runs of large populations of salmon into the rivers and streams of the Northwest and the resulting ease of harvesting salmon in relatively confined stream and river waters made them an ideal food source for the native populations. Forestlands, the resource of primary interest here, played a role in the ecological success of the salmon.[3]

The use of marine resources by native populations was not confined entirely to the salmon. Coastal tribes fished such species as the halibut, herring, smelt, and pilchard, gathered a variety of mollusks and other marine life in the intertidal zone, and hunted various marine mammals, such as seals, whales, and sea otters, for both food and skins.[4]

While salmon served as the primary source of protein for virtually all Pacific Northwest Indians, the forests and prairie areas were an important sources of the relatively small amounts of plant food that was available. The diet of the Pacific Northwest Indian was extraordinarily rich in protein but deficient in vegetable foods and starches. Forestlands were not only important for food gathering but also were the central source of fiber and materials used for clothing, houses, weaponry, fishing gear and facilities, canoes, and household implements. A variety of plant species were gathered for medicinal and ceremonial purposes as well. The hunting and trapping of various mammals in the forests and prairie lands provided an additional source of protein and skins and bones for clothing and tools.[5]

The variety of plant species used by western Washington Indians alone is rather amazing (Table 3-1). The Indians of western Washington were most heavily concentrated in the Sitka spruce and the western hemlock forest zones discussed in Chapter 2. Of the principle species in a mature old-growth forest of the Sitka spruce zone (Table 2-1), 67 percent were species used by Indians (Table 3-1). A comparable figure for western hemlock zone species (Table 2-2) that were utilized by Indians is 53 percent. If differences in scientific names used by Gunther and Franklin and Dyrness were reconciled, the figures would probably be somewhat higher. To put it simply, Pacific Northwest Indians extensively utilized the range of plant species available in old-growth forests. They also utilized species found on disturbed sites, the early seres, such as the bracken fern, trailing blackberry, thimbleberry, salmonberry, red elderberry, huckleberry, vine maple, and salal.

Of all the trees found in the old-growth forests of western Washington, the most important for the Indians was the western red cedar. It was used in house construction for posts, planks, and roof boards. Houses constructed by western Washington Indians were relatively large, sometimes housing several families, and were usually permanent, although in some cases they could be disassembled and moved. Cedar was also extensively used in the construction of dugout canoes, ranging from relatively small canoes used inland along the rivers to very large seagoing canoes used by coastal tribes for long-distance transportation as well as the hunting of large marine mammals. Cedar was also used for the construction of storage boxes. The bark of the cedar tree was a most important resource used for a variety of purposes including padding for infants' cradles; as a raw material for plaiting, braiding, or weaving into clothing, containers, and mats; and as a lining for cooking pits. The limbs of the cedar tree were stripped of their bark and braided into rope, and the roots were used widely in basketry. The buds and inner bark of the cedar tree were

Table 3-1
Plants Used by Aboriginal Populations
in Western Washington

Common name	Scientific name

Overstory species

Bigleaf maple	*Acer macrophyllum*
Douglas fir	*Pseudotsuga menziesii*
Grand fir	*Abies grandis*
Hazelnut	*Corylus californica*
Lodgepole pine	*Pinus contorta*
Oregon white oak	*Quercus garryana* Dougl.
Oregon ash	*Fraxinus oregana* Nutt.
Pacific madrona	*Arbutus menziesii*
Red alder	*Alnus rubra*
Rocky Mountain juniper	*Juniperus scopulorum*
Sitka spruce	*Picea sitchensis*
Western hemlock	*Tsuga heterophylla*
Western red cedar	*Thuja plicata*
Western white pine	*Pinus monticola*

Understory species

Alumroot	*Heuchera micrantha* Dougl.
American vetch	*Vicia americana* Muhl.
Baneberry	*Actaea aguta* Nutt.
Bedstraw	*Galium aparine*
Bellwort	*Disporum smittii* (Hook.) Piper.
Blackcap	*Rubus leucodermis* Dougl.
Blue huckleberry	*Vaccinium ovalifolium* Sm.
Blue elderberry	*Sambucus cerulea* Raf.
Bracken fern	*Pteridium aquilinum* (L.) Kuhn.
Bunchberry dogwood	*Cornus canadensis* L.
Burdock	*Arctium minus* (Hill.) Bernh.
Buttercup	*Ranunculus flammula* L.
Camas	*Camassia quamash* (Pursh.) Greene.
Cascade azalea	*Rhododendron albiflorum* Hook.
Cascara	*Rhamnus purshiana* DC.
Coast strawberry	*Fragaria chiloensis* (L.) Duch.
Columbine	*Aquilegia formosa* Fisch.
Common gooseberry	*Ribes divaricatum* Dougl.
Common bear grass	*Xerophyllum tenax* (Pursh.) Nutt.
Common coltsfoot	*Petasites speciosus* (Nutt.) Piper.
Cow parsnip	*Heracleum lanatum* Michx.
Crab apple	*Pyrus diversifolia* Bong.

Cranberry	*Vaccinium oxycoccus* L., var. *ovalifolium* Michx.
Creambush ocean spray	*Holodiscus discolor* (Pursh.) Maxim.
Deer fern	*Blechnum spicant* (L.) Roth.
Deerfoot vanilla leaf	*Achlys triphylla* (Smith.) DC.
Devilsclub	*Oplopanax horridum* (J. E. Smith.) Miq.
Dewberry	*Rubus macropetalus* Dougl.
Dogwood	*Cornus pubescens* (Nutt.) Coville.
Douglas spirea	*Spiraea douglassii* Hook.
Evergreen huckleberry	*Vaccinium ovatum* Pursh.
Fairy bells	*Disporum oreganum* (Wats.) Benth. & Hook.
False lily-of-the-valley	*Maianthemum dilatatum* (Wood.) Nels.& Macbr.
False hellebore	*Veratrum viride* Ait.
Fawn lily	*Erythronium oregonum*
Fireweed	*Epibolium angustifolium* L.
Fool's huckleberry	*Menziesia ferruginea* Sm.
Fringe-cup	*Tellima grandiflora* (Pursh.) Dougl.
Giant vetch	*Vicia gigantea* Hook.
Goat's-beard	*Aruncus sylvester* Kostel.
Hedge nettle	*Stachys ciliata* Dougl.
Indian paintbrush	*Castilleja angustifolia* (Nutt.) G. Don.
Kinnikinnick	*Arctostaphylos uva-ursi* (L.) Spreng.
Labrador tea	*Ledum groenlandicum* Oeder.
Lady fern	*Athyrium filix-femina* (L.) Roth.
Larkspur	*Delphinium menziesii* DC.
Licorice fern	*Polypodium vulgare* L.
Maidenhair fern	*Adiantum pedatum* L.
Mock orange	*Philadelphus gordonianus* Lindl.
Nettle	*Urtica lyallii* Wats.
Ninebark	*Physocarpus capitatus* (Pursh.) Kuntze.
Nootka rose	*Rosa nutkana* Presl.
Orange honeysuckle	*Lonicera ciliosa* (Pursh.) Poir.
Oregon oxalis (wood-sorrel)	*Oxalis oregana* Nutt.
Oregon grape	*Berberis nervosa* Pursh.
Oso berry	*Osmaronia cerasiformis* (T. & G.) Greene.
Oxeye daisy	*Chrysanthemum leucanthemum* L.
Pacific dogwood	*Cornus nuttallii* Audubon.
Pearly everlasting	*Anaphalis margaritacea* (L.) Benth. & Hook.
Poison hemlock	*Conium maculatum* L.
Queencup beadlily	*Clintonia uniflora*
Rattlesnake plantain	*Goodyera oblongifolia* Raf.
Red elderberry	*Sambucus racemosa* L. var. *arborescens* (T. & G.) Gray.
Red-flowering currant	*Ribes sanguineum* Pursh.
Red huckleberry	*Vaccinium parvifolium* Smith.

Rose	*Rosa pisocarpa* Gray.
Salal	*Gaultheria shallon* Pursh.
Salmonberry	*Rubus spectabilis* Pursh.
Scented bedstraw	*Galium triflorum* Michx.
Self heal	*Prunella vulgaris* L., var. *lanceolata* (Barton.) Fern.
Serviceberry	*Amelanchier florida* Lindl.
Silvergreen	*Adenocaulon bicolor* Hook.
Silverweed	*Potentilla pacifica* Howell.
Skunk cabbage	*Lysichitum americanum* Hult. & St. John.
Skunk currant	*Ribes gracteosum* Dougl.
Snowberry	*Symphoricarpos albus* (L.) Blake.
Spring beauty	*Claytonia sibirica* L.
Stonecrop	*Sedum* sp.
Swamp currant	*Ribes lacustre* (Pers.) Poir.
Swamp honeysuckle	*Lonicera involucrata* (Richards.) Banks.
Sweet cicely	*Osmorhiza chilensis* (H. & A.)
Sword fern	*Polystichum munitum* (Kaulf.) Presl.
Tall Oregon grape	*Berberis aquibolium* Pursh.
Thimbleberry	*Rubus parviflorus* Nutt.
Thistle	*Cirsium* sp.
Three-leaved coolwort	*Tiarella trifoliata* L.
Tiger lily	*Lilium columbianum*
Trailing currant	*Ribes laxiflorum* Pursh.
Twinflower	*Linnaea borealis* L.
Twisted-stalk	*Streptopus amplexifolius* (L.) DC.
Vine maple	*Acer circinatum* Pursh.
Water parsley	*Oenanthe sarmentosa* Presl.
Western yew	*Taxus brevifolia* Nutt.
Western wood strawberry	*Fragaria vesca* L. var. *bracteata* (Heller.)
White trillium	*Trillium ovatum* Pursh.
Wild bleeding heart	*Dicentra formosa* (andr.) DC.
Wild cherry	*Prunus emarginata* (Dougl.) Walp.
Wild ginger	*Asarum caudatum* Lindl.
Wild strawberry	*Frageria cuneifolia* Nutt.
Wood fern	*Dryopteris dilatata* (Hoffm.) Gray.
Woolly sunflower	*Eriophyllum lanatum* (Pursh.) Forbes.
Yarrow	*Achillea millefolium* L.
Youth-on-age	*Tolmiea menziesii* (Pursh.) T. & G.

Note: This table is adapted from Erna Gunther, *Ethnobotany of Western Washington: The Knowledge and Use of Indigenous Plants by Native Americans* (Seattle: University of Washington Press, 1981). The table includes mostly species found in western Washington forests, although a few species found mostly in open areas are included.

used for medicinal purposes, and cedar boughs were used for scouring the body in ceremonial baths prior to a guardian spirit quest.[6]

Numerous other trees provided materials, medicines, and, in some cases, foods for Indians in western Washington. The western yew was valued for the strength of its wood and was used for weapons and implements, such as bows, arrows, harpoons, and dip nets. The western white pine was sometimes used for small dugout canoes, and its pitch was used for medicinal purposes. The root of the Sitka spruce was extensively used in basketry and rain hats, the pitch was used for caulking canoes and chewing gum, and the young shoots were eaten raw. The bark of the western hemlock was used in the making of dye, the wood was used in the construction of fish traps and for firewood, and the pitch was used as a medicine. The ubiquitous Douglas fir was not used for woodwork because its wood did not split evenly, but it was employed in shafts for harpoons and salmon spears and handles for dip nets. It was also a major source of firewood, and its bark was used to make a light brown dye for the purpose of making fishnets invisible to the fish. The red alder was next to cedar as the most widely used species in woodworking and was extensively employed in the making of spoons, dishes, platters, and paddles. Alder was also a preferred wood for smoking salmon.[7]

A variety of understory species was also gathered in the forests for use as food, medicine, or fiber in weaving, basketry, and mat making. Berries that were gathered for immediate consumption or preservation included Oregon grape, gooseberry, skunk currant, trailing currant, thimbleberry, salmonberry, blackcap, wild blackberry, evergreen blackberry, strawberry, serviceberry, salal, evergreen huckleberry, blue huckleberry, red huckleberry, cranberry, red elderberry, and blue elderberry. Ferns were gathered for their leaves and rhizomes, which were used in cooking and for a variety of other purposes. Bear grass was gathered for use in the weaving of mats. A variety of plants in the lily family were gathered for their bulbs as well as their leaves. The leaves or roots of most of the herbaceous understory species used by aboriginal populations (Table 3-1) were gathered for medicinal purposes, to use in making various types of tea, or in some cases for food. The wood of some of the shrubs, such as ocean spray, was used for digging sticks or other implements. Although the major food sources for Pacific Northwest Indians indeed were marine in origin, the forests were nonetheless an important source of food and fiber, as Erna Gunther's fascinating work on western Washington ethnobotany documents.[8]

Even though western Washington was heavily forested, prairie areas were scattered along the coast, including the Forks and Quillayute prairies used by the Quileute Indians and the Baker's, Cook, and O'Tool prairies near the Quinault Indians, as well as large prairie areas near the south end of Puget Sound. As indicated in Chapter 2, these prairies were maintained partly as the result of their soil composition, but were probably burned as well by local Indian groups. Prairies and similar open spaces were important sources of plant food, including tiger lily bulbs, which were steamed and eaten, camas bulbs, bracken fern, and acorns of the Oregon white oak.[9] The Skagit Indians apparently cultivated tiger lilies in burned-over areas. The prairies also provided a source of animal protein and were apparently burned over in order to lure elk and deer to feed on young fern shoots and thus be easy targets for the bow and arrow.[10]

While Gunther's work applies only to western Washington, its conclusions on the use of plants by Indians probably extend to northwest and coastal Oregon because of their ecological similarity to western Washington. The Tillamook Indians, for example, gathered a number of species of berries, roots, and greens mentioned by Gunther.[11] The Tilamook were a Salish-speaking people like the Indians of Washington, and were also heavily dependent on the salmon, marine mammals, and intertidal organisms.

Even though Pacific Northwest Indians got the bulk of their protein from marine sources, they still hunted land mammals for food and fiber. Animals utilizing forest habitats that were commonly hunted include the black tailed deer, elk, mountain goat, black bear, grizzly bear, beaver, snowshoe rabbit, fisher, raccoon, and otter.[12] Hunting was clearly of greater importance to the inland groups than it was to coastal Indians, although the latter also engaged in hunting. The bow and arrow as well as traps and snares were commonly used in hunting, and hunters often worked together to drive game over cliffs. Fire was a common aid to hunters and was used to burn away brush and small trees to make travel easy and to encourage new browse to attract deer and elk to the area. Fire was also sometimes used to flush game from a confined area.[13]

Use of Fire

Pacific Northwest Native Americans utilized forests resources extensively, but their limited numbers and limited ability to harvest large trees significantly diminished their potential for changing the ecology of forestlands. The one tool available to Indians that could cause major alterations of the landscape was fire. In the case of the Willamette valley, as much as 2 million acres of land were maintained in prairie and savanna as a consequence of aboriginally set fires. Grasslands, which were more productive of desired food resources, were thus substituted for forest-lands. After the fires, the Kalapuya Indians, who occupied much of the valley, apparently would gather wild honey, grasshoppers, and tarweed seeds. Fire also concentrated game animals and made hunting easier. The grasslands evidently regenerated rapidly after burning. Burning of the prairie areas was thus integral to the economy of the local Indian populations. After burning stopped with white settlement, the amount of woodland increased significantly, demonstrating the importance of fire in shaping the ecology of the valley.[14]

Fires were also set in the small prairie areas of western Washington, but involved, at most, no more than 200,000 acres.[15] Northwest Indians also may have set fires in forest openings to encourage thimbleberry, salmonberry, red elderberry, red and evergreen huckleberry, and bracken and sword fern crops.[16] These are early seral species in the successional process for Washington and Oregon forests and thus could be maintained through burning.[17]

The actual extent of such intentional burning in the forested areas of Washington and Oregon is unknown. White argues that in lowland areas around Puget Sound, fires set by Indians may have been important in restarting forest succession and insuring the dominance of the Douglas fir. In the absence of fire, Douglas fir does not reproduce because of its shade intolerance, and dominance would eventually shift to western hemlock. Because lightning as an ignition source was generally confined to mountainous areas, the only other source of combustion would be native Indian populations prior to white settlement. The dominance of Douglas fir in lowland areas thus implies that fires set by Indians must have significantly altered the local forest ecology.[18] If White is right, then fires in lowland areas were predominantly anthropogenic in origin. However, given the relatively limited overall use of forests by Indians and the generally coastal and riparian orientation of their hunting and gathering activities, fires started by Indians were probably confined to areas near villages. The large volumes of standing timber contained in relatively large diameter trees found by European settlers suggests that the impact of fires started by aboriginal peoples must have been restricted in its extent.[19] Although Stephen J. Pyne argues eloquently and vigorously in his landmark work on the history of wildland fire that Indians in many areas on the American continent substantially altered the forests and extended grasslands as the result of their use of fire, his argument applies somewhat less forcefully in the Pacific Northwest, at least outside of the Willamette valley and coastal lowlands.[20]

Aboriginal Culture and
the Exploitation of Nature

Human beings, including aboriginal peoples, are by nature manipulators and modifiers of their environment. Whether Pacific Northwest Indians fully utilized the resources available to them given their technological capacities, or whether they exercised restraint in their use of resources is the central question to be addressed in this section. If they did exercise such restraint, what were the possible reasons? This is the question to be addressed in the next section.

Pacific Northwest Indians utilized wood fiber taken from the forests for firewood and materials for building and woodworking, but much of that was gathered as fallen timber and only a limited amount was cut, partly because of the lack of efficient tools for felling live timber. Cut timber was extensively used in the construction of houses and canoes, but the amount used in comparison to the standing stock was relatively small. A rough figure for cut-timber utilization can be calculated using population data and an estimate of the total board feet of timber per person in the typical Northwest Indian winter house. The total amount of timber in a winter house measuring 40 by 100 feet was approximately 22,000 board feet. Assuming an average occupancy of four families with five persons each, the approximate board footage per capita would be 1,100.[21] To account for waste in construction and the use of cut timber for canoes and other artifacts, a doubling of this figure seems reasonable for a rough total estimate per capita. The resulting figure can then be multiplied by aboriginal population estimates for the area to get an idea of the total board feet of timber in use at any point in time.

Population and Timber Consumption

Aboriginal population estimates are themselves subject to debate. The whole issue of aboriginal population estimates, such as those made by James Mooney, has been taken up in considerable detail in a landmark article by Henry F. Dobyns.[22] Because Mooney and others vastly underestimated the negative impact on aboriginal populations of diseases, warfare, and economic displacement caused by European contact, Dobyns claims that aboriginal population estimates should be adjusted upwards by substantial amounts. Herbert C. Taylor believes that the aboriginal population of the lower northwest coast, stretching from Vancouver Island and lower British Columbia to northwestern Oregon, was approximately 26 percent greater than Mooney's estimates.[23] An analysis of Indian disease mortality and population data in a more recent study by Robert T. Boyd suggests that Mooney's population estimates for the Columbia

River basin should be adjusted upwards by as much as 67 percent. Because the lower Columbia River basin suffered more from introduced disease than other areas in the Pacific Northwest, increasing Mooney's estimates by 67 percent for the entire region should avoid underestimation of the precontact aboriginal population.[24]

The original population estimate for western Washington and Oregon by Mooney was 62,900.[25] Using the 67 percent upward adjustment, the population estimate would increase to approximately 105,000. Given this figure, the total board feet of timber required by the Indians would have been approximately 231 million board feet, most of which was cedar. The total standing stock of western red cedar in 1933 after a considerable amount of harvesting had been undertaken was approximately 25 billion board feet.[26] The total aboriginal requirement for cedar at a given point in time would therefore be approximately 0.9 percent of the total standing stock, an insignificantly small figure. The harvest in any given year would be much less than this, depending on the typical life span of a winter house and other wood objects. If it was 30 years, the annual harvest would be approximately 7.7 million board feet, or 73 board feet per capita.[27] This would amount to about 0.03 percent of the standing stock. The modern day lumber production figure per capita for the United States is approximately 480 board feet per capita.[28] Aboriginal consumption was thus approximately 15 percent of today's consumption figure, but because the aboriginal population was so small compared to current population, the aboriginal harvest of timber was relatively infinitesimal.

Population and the Salmon Harvest

As the calculation on cut-timber consumption suggests, a central reason that forests were not more fully exploited was the comparatively small size of the Indian population and the resulting limited level of timber consumption relative to the total standing stock potentially available. While the per capita consumption level was significantly less than that experienced in modern industrial societies, it was still fairly substantial. The issue that needs to be considered, then, is the source of limitations on the level of prehistorical Indian population in the Pacific Northwest. Since forest resources were apparently not a binding constraint on population growth, attention must be directed to the key food resource that served as the underpinning of Pacific Northwest Indian material wealth, the salmon. Did limitations on the ability to catch salmon or to preserve and store it for winter use place restrictions on Indian population levels? If the harvesting and preserving of salmon were not binding constraints, then what were the other possible restrictions on the utilization of resources and, therefore, population levels? Were there cultural restraints on the use of key food resources that in turn led to limitations on population and thus the use of forests?

The apparent abundance of resources in the Pacific Northwest, particularly the large salmon runs, suggests, at first glance, that a comparatively large Indian population could have been sustained. This perception is further supported by the common practice of accumulating material wealth beyond biological need among Pacific Northwest Indians, suggesting an ability to sustain a population larger than the actual level.[29] This pre- sumes that the production of a surplus indicates a potential for devoting a portion of existing resources to the production of necessities as opposed to wealth goods.

Wayne Suttles, an anthropologist who has extensively studied the culture and economic foundation of northwest coastal Indians, argues that the apparent material abundance is deceiving, and that the ecology of the area dictated a periodic scarcity of resources.[30] All groups potentially suffered an annual period of scarcity in the winter or early spring when fresh salmon was unavailable if their stores of preserved food were limited. Local groups, however, could also suffer a periodic scarcity resulting from the failure of a particular food resource to materialize. Salmon runs are notorious for their variability in timing and magnitude from year to year, and their migratory route in riparian waters can change significantly from one year to the next.[31] Such annual variability can be traced to a host of factors, including stream flow, temperature, and the extent of siltation on spawning grounds, as well as weather conditions on the ocean feeding grounds. Abundance in forest wildlife and berry crops could also vary from year to year in relationship to the extent of forest fire activity. Certain berry crops often prosper on recent burns, and open burned-over areas provide feed for deer.[32] While abundance was the norm, any given local group could expect to face a limitation on its resources at some undetermined point in time, a limitation that could place restrictions on population.

Wealth Accumulation

As Suttles and others have pointed out, because wealth goods served as the foundation of the status system for Pacific Northwest Indian cultures, the striving to accumulate them was strong.[33] The wealth drive was not an individual one but was focused rather on the family grouping. The ability to give wealth goods to guests at potlatches and guardian spirit dances brought prestige and honor to the family grouping sponsoring the celebrations. The potlatch was a great celebration given for a special event, such as the death of an important person, the inheritance of a particular position or status, a marriage of an important family member, or the birth of a potential heir to an important family position, and involved inviting many guests, providing a great feast, and giving wealth goods, such as blankets, woven mats, or carved articles, as gifts. Individual family members worked hard to accumulate such goods so that family prestige could be enhanced by giving them away.[34]

Another ceremony that required the giving away of wealth goods to guests was the guardian spirit dance. In many Pacific Northwest Indian societies, each individual sought out a guardian spirit through a quest involving fasting, rites of purification, and spending time alone in the woods. The guardian spirit provided special powers to the possessor, particularly powers needed to successfully accumulate wealth goods and to live in reasonable comfort. In the winter, the guardian spirit sometimes visited the individual and signified the visit to the possessor by causing him or her to become ill. If this happened, the individual was required to engage in a guardian spirit dance. The immediate family would provide gifts to guests invited to observe the dance, and if the dance was not performed, the belief was, at least for one tribal grouping, that the individual involved would die as a result.[35]

Thus, the driving force in the accumulation of wealth goods was the striving for status by the local family group. The wealth goods accumulation and redistribution system, Suttles argues, was also a functional part of the subsistence system.[36] The basic economic unit in Pacific Northwest society was the kinship group composed of families related through siblings, and separate kinship groups had ties to other groups in other locations through marriage. It was members of these affinal groups who were invited to the potlatch and other ceremonial events and who were endowed with gifts of wealth goods. These groups also exchanged visits in which the visiting group would bring food as a gift and receive wealth goods as gifts in return. Consequently, one group could exchange wealth goods for food with another, an arrangement that would be advantageous during a period of local scarcity. Moreover, the system of status achievement through the giving away of wealth goods would assure a reasonably wide distribution of such goods among local groups so that even the poorest groups would have some to trade for food in times of local resource scarcity. The effects of local scarcity were thus at least partially mitigated by the ability to ceremonially exchange wealth goods for food. This pushed back the barrier to larger population levels somewhat, but did not necessarily eliminate it.

Because the accumulation of wealth goods for the purpose of exchange through gift giving was an integral element of the subsistence system, the large accumulations of such goods did not as such indicate a real ability to support an expanded population. The procuring of food resources for subsistence was a seasonal activity. Salmon were caught and dried or smoked in the spring and summer months for use during the winter period when fresh fish or other meats were not readily available. The production of wealth goods was predominantly confined to the winter months and did not compete with food gathering activities. A local Indian group could have fully utilized its salmon resource at a maximum sustainable level and thus have been unable to support a larger population level even though it possessed the capacity to produce wealth goods. Wealth goods are thus not a reliable indicator of a potential capacity to produce more subsistence goods and support a larger population.

Resource Exploitation and Population

Since the presence of wealth goods is consistent with use of food resources at or below maximum sustainable levels, the question of whether Pacific Northwest Indians had the capacity to exploit their resources to a greater extent than they actually did must be addressed more directly. The question that needs to be considered is whether the salmon resource could have been exploited more extensively in the aggregate to support a larger total aboriginal population in the prehistorical Pacific Northwest.

A fuller exploitation of the salmon resource to support a larger Indian population would not only have involved an increase in the total catch without a significant reduction in the catch per person but also an increase in the capacity to dry or smoke the salmon. If Hewes's figures on the aboriginal salmon harvest are accepted, then it seems clear that the salmon resource was underutilized. Hewes estimated that Indians in a region stretching from northern California to southeastern Alaska harvest approximately 128 million pounds of salmon annually. This figure is 21 percent of the approximately 600 million pounds of salmon that were being harvested in the late 1930s in a comparable area.[37] Since a portion of the 1930s harvest was taken by ocean trollers whose fish would not have generally reached their full adult weight, the harvest should be adjusted upwards for the purpose of comparison to the aboriginal catch. Also, the late 1930s catch includes the harvest of runs that had been severely depleted over time because of overfishing and spawning habitat deterioration.[38] The point is, a sustained annual inriver catch somewhat larger than 600 million pounds was probably possible prehistorically.

For several reasons, however, Hewes's estimates cannot be accepted as they stand. In a discussion of estimates of the aboriginal salmon harvest in the Columbia River basin, analysts point out that Hewes's estimates need updating to account for new ethnographic information on per capita salmon consumption by particular tribal groups, the fact that approximately 80 percent of the salmon is edible, and the fact that the caloric value of the salmon diminishes when it quits feeding as it enters fresh water and expends calories migrating up stream.[39] Hewes's procedure was to first estimate the per capita salmon consumption based on an annual caloric requirement figure, and then to multiply the per capita estimate times population to derive the total level of consumption. Hewes did not take into account the 20 percent waste factor in calculating per capita consumption nor the loss in caloric value of a pound of salmon for Indians who harvested salmon at distances well upstream from the mouth of the river.

For the Columbia River basin, analysts suggest that Hewes's estimates need to be adjusted upwards by approximately 50 percent to account for new ethnographic data and caloric loss from migration and another 25 percent to account for the proportion of a salmon that is inedible. The result is an increase in the aboriginal Columbia River basin harvest to approximately 42 million pounds. Adjusting for caloric loss and inedibility for the Fraser River harvest, the Hewes harvest estimates should be increased from approximately 20 million pounds to 34 million pounds.[40] Because other rivers along the Pacific Coast with salmon runs are much shorter in length than the Fraser or Columbia, the freshwater caloric loss is insignificant in those rivers. Also, for many of these rivers, harvesting is concentrated heavily in the lower reaches. Consequently, adjusting Hewes's figures for rivers other than the Fraser or Columbia for caloric loss is unnecessary. However, the inedibility adjustment needs to be made. Once this is accomplished and the adjusted Fraser and Columbia catches are added, the new aboriginal harvest estimate is approximately 182 million pounds.

Hewes's estimates are also problematic because of his use of Mooney's aboriginal population figures. As already noted, Mooney's population estimates need to be adjusted upwards. Increasing Mooney's population estimates by the 67 percent figure suggested above, the aboriginal salmon harvest estimate would increase to approximately 304 million pounds, a figure that is slightly over one-half of the late 1930s harvest level.[41]

Could the Indians have increased their harvest on a sustained-yield basis given that they were already catching approximately 300 million pounds of salmon? The late 1930s harvest figure suggests a run of at least 705 million pounds assuming an 85 percent exploitation rate, a rate suggested as likely for this period by a fisheries biologist.[42] If this run prevailed in aboriginal times, then the exploitation rate would have been approximately 44 percent for the 304-million-pound harvest figure. Estimated optimal exploitation rates that would maximize the sustained-yield harvest on the Columbia River are 77 percent for the coho, 62 percent for the sockeye, 68 percent for the chinook, 69 percent for the steelhead, and 30 percent for the chum.[43] The aggregate exploitation rate by the Indians was well below these figures with the exception of the chum. This suggests that Indians could have substantially increased their harvest of salmon in the Pacific Northwest on a sustained-yield basis.

Could Northwest Indians have increased the harvest without a significant reduction in the catch per person? If an increase in the catch served to sustain a larger Indian population, it is a possibility that the catch per person would decline and as a result threaten the survival of the existing population in the long run. While there is no way of determining for sure what would have happened to the catch per person if the aboriginal harvest had been increased, there is a distinct possibility that catch per person could have actually increased as the total harvest increased. If the rate of exploitation for salmon was initially fairly low, as indicated by the above analysis of the data on aboriginal harvests, the classic spawner-return curves from biological theory suggest that the run over some range could actually be increased by increasing the harvest.[44] The explanation for this phenomenon is that large runs that are subject to modest harvesting pressure would result in congestion on the spawning ground and reduced smolt productivity. If in these circumstances the spawning population were reduced through increased harvests, the congestion would be relieved and smolt production would increase. Hence, there is at least a theoretical possibility that the salmon run could have been increased through an increase in the harvest. Since a larger run would tend to make fish easier to catch, the amount of fish harvested per person would tend to rise. Also, it is possible that the existing catch per person was more than enough on average to sustain the population and there was some room for a reduction in catch per person caused by an increase in the harvest and a movement down the spawner-return curve toward a lower run level. Again, these are just possibilities, but possibilities that seem fairly probable in light of the relatively low utilization rate for salmon runs.

Also, the technology used by aboriginal peoples to harvest salmon was, in many respects, fairly sophisticated and did not differ extensively from more modern fishing practices, and in all likelihood did not serve as a barrier to increasing the harvest.[45] In some ways, the Indians used more efficient techniques than are used today. The weirs built across streams to trap migrating salmon were much more efficient than, for example, the modern troller in catching salmon. Traps and similar devices in the modern period were outlawed because they were too efficient and could easily damage runs, a problem that apparently did not arise in the aboriginal period. The Kepel fish dam in northern California, for example, was constructed and operated by Indians for a period of approximately ten days even though the run lasted several times longer than that.[46] At the end of ten days, the dam was removed so the fish could pass freely. Apparently, Indians did not need to operate the dam longer to fulfill their requirements for salmon.

Suttles suggests that the bottleneck in salmon harvesting and preparation for winter use may have been a limited capacity to smoke or dry salmon in order to preserve and store it.[47] Because sunny stretches in the Northwest tend to be limited in duration, outdoor drying was restricted to the summer months. On the outer coast, outdoor drying may have been possible only for brief stretches because of frequent rain. Consequently, the preserving of salmon was often done by smoking it inside the cedar houses in which the Indians lived. This placed a potential limitation on the amount of salmon that could be preserved. The amount of drying and smoking capacity was limited by the amount of housing space. As Suttles notes, the limitation on the exploitation food resources may have been determined not by the capacity to harvest the resource in the case of the Pacific Northwest Indians but rather to preserve it and store it.[48] Suttles seems to downplay the possibility that less elaborate structures could have been built and used for smoking even though there are some references that seem to indicate that this was a practice occasionally used on the northwest coast.[49] Possibly, the reason separate structures for smoking salmon were not built was because the winter houses provided sufficient capacity.

In any case, the capacity for drying and smoking salmon was sufficient to support the population level that in fact prevailed on the northwest coast. Because drying and smoking were labor-intensive activities, and because the forest resources used for constructing drying racks and houses and to keep smoking fires burning were abundantly available, drying and smoking was an activity characterized by what economists call "constant returns to scale." What this means is that the capacity for drying and smoking could be increased in proportion to population. A larger population would simply provide the added labor supply needed to carry on the extra drying and smoking required. While drying and smoking could be a barrier to increasing the amount of salmon preserved per capita, it would not be a barrier to increasing the total amount of salmon preserved through an increase in the total population.

In sum, there is a strong likelihood that Pacific Northwest Indians did not fully utilize the principle food resource available to them. As a result, their population was smaller than it could have been and the exploitation of the forests was less extensive than otherwise. If resources were underutilized by Pacific Northwest Indians, what are the possible reasons? What elements of Indian culture could have restrained resource utilization?

Cultural Restraints on Resource Exploitation

Leisure Societies

A popular conception of Stone Age hunter-gatherers is that their technology rendered them impoverished, and, if they were capable of doing so, they would have increased their standard of consumption. Anthropological research on primitive peoples suggests, however, that many groups were in fact highly efficient at exploiting their environment but limited their consumption as well as their population levels as a matter of choice. Marshall Sahlins suggests that these were the first true leisure societies, and they were borne of relatively limited wants. Production in the form of hunting and gathering was engaged in only to the extent necessary to fulfill basic material needs. Sahlins cites evidence that much of the typical day for primitive hunting and agricultural societies was spent in leisure.[50] Sahlins also points out that primitive hunter-gatherers employed stringent measures to control population levels, such as sexual abstinence, infanticide, and senilicide, in order to avoid the problem of diminishing returns to productive efforts. The motivation in such societies did not seem to be the modern one of maximizing the accumulation of material wealth but, rather, the minimizing of time spent in the activities of material production.

Sahlins also implies, however, that the intensification of labor tends to increase with social complexity and that complex social relationships beyond the immediate family unit are necessary for economic survival in a world of uncertainty.[51] Because the individual family can experience productive catastrophe in any given year, more extensive economic and social ties are needed. Where social relationships become more complex, one basic family unit will produce a surplus that is given as a gift to other family units related through kinship ties. The giving of such gifts demonstrates the powers and enhances the community status of the giver. While Northwest Indian societies relied on hunting, fishing, and gathering, they were culturally rather complex, suggesting a reasonable intensification of labor. Because they had comparatively permanent winter dwellings, and because they had relatively large canoes available, it was possible for them to accumulate and transport a fairly large amount of wealth goods. Gift giving and wealth accumulation was not constrained by the need to migrate in the seeking of food resources. Northwest Indians had a fairly strong propensity to accumulate material wealth for the purpose of gift giving to achieve social status, and larger families would mean a larger capacity to produce wealth goods and thus a greater social status. Hence, the inclination to leisure in primitive hunter-gatherer societies discussed by Sahlins seems to apply with less force to more culturally developed societies, such as those in the prehistoric Pacific Northwest.

This does not mean, however, that leisure was unimportant in Northwest Indian societies. James Swan reports on the rather carefree approach taken by the Indians he observed toward accomplishing their material goals. Nothing was done with any great haste.[52] In an ethnographic study of the Tlingit Indians of southeastern Alaska, a tribe with an even higher level of cultural complexity than those of the Pacific Northwest, Kalvero Oberg reports extensive amounts of time devoted to leisure and a rather casual attitude toward work.[53] Even though there was a striving for status through the accumulation and giving away of wealth goods among Northwest Indians, there was also a countervailing tendency to approach daily life at a leisurely pace. Under such a regime, the amount of material wealth taken from nature would be necessarily restricted.

Spiritual Views of Nature

Another possible explanation for restraint in the exploitation of the salmon resource by Pacific Northwest Indians comes from Calvin Martin's fascinating work *Keepers of the Game*.[54] American Indians viewed all objects in nature as enspirited beings living lives that are not fundamentally different than those of humans.[55] According to Indians, the natural world was populated by nonhuman persons. All objects in nature, human and nonhuman, were viewed as having an immortal spirit, including the species of game most commonly pursued by the Indians. These animals willingly sacrificed their worldly material existence so that the Indians would have food to live. For their part, the Indians had to subscribe to a system of taboos and rituals in order to assure the continued cooperation of the prey species. In other words, there was a compact between the Indian and the prey, and if the compact was broken, Indians would lose their means of subsistence. According to Martin, the motivation for maintaining the compact was partly fear of retaliation, but also in some instances affection. Martin claims that the hunter would in time gain a sense of great affection and respect for the hunted.[56] In a sense, the hunted prey became a part of the Indian's immediate community. One of the taboos that the Indian hunter obeyed was not to overkill the prey or to waste its meat. This taboo, supported by attitudes of fear and affection, thus restrained the exploitation of game species. Martin goes on to suggest that this sort of behavior likely applied to a large cross-section of the American Indian population.[57]

Did there exist among Pacific Northwest Indians attitudes and taboos toward their principle food source, the salmon, that could have resulted in restrictions on consumption? Discussions of ceremonies, mythologies, and cosmologies in the ethnographic literature suggests a commonality in the Pacific Northwest Indian view of nature and that of the Indian tribes discussed by Martin. Pacific Northwest Indian mythologies generally suggest that there was a period of time when humans and animals were very similar and that a "transformer" changed animals into their present form. These same mythologies argue that animals lead lives that are much like those of humans, and that animals have immortal souls much the same as humans.[58] The nonhuman world of nature, in the eyes of the aboriginal Pacific Northwest Indians, was thus populated by what can be referred to as "nonhuman persons."

The clearest manifestation of veneration for the salmon was the first salmon ceremony carried out by many of the Pacific Northwest Indian tribes. While the content of the ceremony varied from tribe to tribe, it basically involved a ceremonial eating of the first salmon caught from a major run of salmon, usually the first run in the spring. The salmon was treated in some cases as an honored guest, and the cooking and carving of the salmon had to be conducted according to a specified formula. In most instances, the bones had to be disposed of in a certain way, usually by returning them to the water with the expectation that the salmon would revive and return again next year. Some tribes viewed the first salmon as the chief of the salmon people who had to be treated with special care in order to assure his return the next year as the leader of the run. Most Indians believed that salmon lived much of the year in a distant place carrying on lives that were like those of humans and that once a year they left their home, changed into their salmon form, and ran into the rivers. In some tribes, prayers were said to the salmon in which it is referred to as a friend and a supernatural being, thanked for the giving of its substance to the Indian, and asked to keep illness and death away.[59]

There were also certain taboos surrounding the salmon, such as the prohibition of ceremonially "unclean" persons, for example persons in mourning or menstruating women, from eating the salmon or participating in the first salmon ceremony. Children were admonished to not make fun of salmon or play with them after they were caught.[60] The consequence of doing so would be a taking of the child's soul by the salmon. Some tribes also had admonitions against wasting meat in general and salmon in particular, and ethnographers report that in some cases only enough salmon were taken to fulfill immediate consumption and winter storage needs, after which the screens in fish weirs were removed so that salmon could pass freely.[61] Some fish traps had permanent holes in them to permit a certain number of fish to escape upstream continuously.[62]

Generally speaking, Pacific Northwest Indians treated the salmon with respect, observed certain ceremonies and taboos, and in return expected the salmon to cooperate by returning each year and allowing themselves to be caught and eaten. There thus existed a compact between the Indian and the salmon of the type described by Martin. While there was no explicit provision or taboo against overharvesting, it seems to be implicit in various admonitions against waste and in the veneration of the salmon. If this was indeed the case, it could at least partly explain why the Pacific Northwest Indians did not fully exploit the salmon resource and, in the process, increase their population levels and more extensively utilize and ecologically alter the forests. The Indians did seem to exercise cultural restraint in the use of resources, a restraint rooted in the view that animals are enspirited beings that must be treated with respect. Whether this was a respect born of fear or affection cannot be said for sure. Certainly, fear played a major role where the loss of a salmon run would mean starvation. Also, the end result of a failure to obey taboos in many instances was believed to be illness and death. On the other hand, the veneration for the salmon implicit in the solemnity of the first salmon rite also suggests a certain amount of affection for a being that sacrificed its material existence so that the Indian could live the good life.

Conclusion

If the above arguments hold true, the valuation of nature by Indians in the Pacific Northwest went beyond a strictly materialist form of instrumentalism. Indians apparently treated the natural world with a respectful attitude and as a consequence may have exercised restraint in their use of nature's resources. They may have done this to alleviate feelings of guilt and fear or out of feelings of affection. Restraint of this sort would have been undertaken for instrumental reasons, but not for material reasons if the motivation of affection or the fear of some sort of nonmaterial reprisal was the driving force. To claim, however, that nature was viewed by Indians as valuable in itself, an idea which is a product of a rather modern form of abstract ethical reasoning, may be going too far.[63]

Notes

1. Philip Drucker, *Cultures of the North Pacific Coast* (New York: Harper and Row, 1965), pp. 1-8; June McCormick Collins, *Valley of the Spirits: The*

Upper Skagit Indians of Western Washington (Seattle: University of Washington Press, 1980), p. 3; Wayne Suttles, *Coast Salish Essays* (Vancouver: Talon Books, 1987), pp. 26-28.

2. Gordon Winant Hewes, "Aboriginal Use of Fishery Resources in Northwestern North America," Ph.D. Diss., University of California, Berkeley, 1947, pp. 222-27. As will be argued later, this figure is probably too low.

3. Anthony Netboy, *The Columbia River Salmon and Steelhead Trout: Their Fight for Survival* (Seattle: University of Washington Press, 1980), pp. 37-54.

4. Drucker, *Cultures of the North Pacific Coast*, pp. 5, 17-19.

5. Ibid., pp. 19-45.

6. Ibid.; Collins, *Valley of the Spirits*, pp. 59-70; Erna Gunther, *Ethnobotany of Western Washington: The Knowledge and Use of Indigenous Plants by Native Americans* (Seattle: University of Washington Press, 1973), pp. 19-21.

7. Ibid., pp. 16-19, 27.

8. Gunther, *Ethnobotany of Western Washington*.

9. Ibid., pp. 15, 25; Franklin and Dyrness, *Natural Vegetation of Oregon and Washington*, pp. 69, 88-9.

10. Gunther, *Ethnobotany of Western Washington*, p. 15; Lotspeich et al., "Vegegation as a Soil-forming Factor," pp. 53-68; Lang, "A Study of Vegetation Change," pp. 84-92; White, *Land Use, Environment, and Social Change*, pp. 18-23. White notes that Indians on Whidbey Island maintained prairie areas through burning for the purpose of encouraging growth of the nettle and bracken fern and to provide an area where camas could be cultivated. White suggests that encouragement of game, such as deer and elk, was probably not the primary reason for burning prairie areas because neither animal grazes on grasses that burning would encourage. If fires spread to adjacent forests, however, it would tend to open up the forest floor and encourage the growth of herbs and shrubs on which deer did browse.

11. John Sauter and Bruce Johnson, *Tillamook Indians of the Oregon Coast* (Portland: Binfords and Mort, no date), pp. 101-03.

12. Collins, *Valley of the Spirits*, pp. 52-53; Drucker, *Cultures of the North Pacific Coast*, pp. 19-20.

13. Sauter and Johnson, *Tillamook Indians*, p. 76.

14. William G. Morris, "Forest Fires in Western Oregon and Western Washington," *Oregon Historical Quarterly* 35 (1934): 313-39; James R. Habeck, "The Original Vegetation of the Mid-Willamette Valley, Oregon," *Northwest Science* 35 (1961): 65-77; Jerry C. Towle, "Changing Geography of Willamette Valley Woodlands," *Oregon Historical Quarterly* 83 (1982): 67-87; Carl L. Johannessen, William A. Davenport, Artimus Millet, and Stephen McWilliams, "The Vegetation of the Willamette Valley," *Annals of the Association of American Geographers* 61 (1971): 286-302; C. Melvin Aikens, "Archaeological Studies in the Willamette Valley, Oregon," *University of Oregon Anthropological Papers* no. 8 (1975): 3-13. The latter reference provides a general overview of Kalapuya culture. Also see Lloyd R. Collins, "The Cultural Position of the Kalapuya in the Pacific Northwest," MS thesis, University of Oregon, 1951, pp. 37-57.

15. The Quillayute prairie was quite small, amounting to little more than 3,000 acres (Lotspeich et.al., "Vegetation as a Soil Forming Factor," p. 53). The prairies near southern Puget Sound contained approximately 168,000 acres (Lang, "A Study of Vegetation Change," p. 1).

16. Gunther, *Ethnobotany of Western Washington*, p. 15; Collins, *Valley of the Spirits*, p. 57. References in the anthropological literature on intentional burning are rare. According to Marian Smith, berry fields were purposely burned by the Puyallup and Nisqually Indians [Marian W. Smith, *The Puyallup-Nisqually* (New York: Columbia University Press, 1940), p. 273].

17. Franklin and Dyrness, *Natural Vegetation of Oregon and Washington*, pp. 61, 85-86.

18. White, *Land Use, Environment, and Social Change*, pp. 23-25.

19. See Chapter 5 for estimates of the original amount of land in old-growth forests by tree diameter. The combined anthropogenic and natural fire cycle for western Washington Douglas fir forests suggests that approximately 0.3 percent of the total land area in forests was burned annually.

20. Pyne, *Fire in America*.

21. The actual size of Indian winter houses varied extensively from the very large potlatch house, with dimensions of up to 50 by 200 feet to comparatively small dwellings occupied by the less prosperous families. Gunther lists six houses ranging in size from a low of 20 by 30 feet to a high of 50 by 200 feet, the latter being a potlatch house [Erna Gunther, "Klallam Ethnography," *University of Washington Publications in Anthropology* 1 (1927): 186-190]. House sizes mentioned by Collins, Pettitt, and Olson, respectively, are 18 by 120 feet, 50 by 70 feet, and 60 by 40 feet [Collins, *Valley of the Spirits*, p. 61; George A. Pettitt, "The Quileute of La Push: 1775-1945," *Anthropological Records* 14 (1950): 4; Ronald L. Olson, "The Quinault Indians," *University of Washington Publications in Anthropology* 6 (1936): 61]. Excluding the potlatch house, the square footage per person for the houses mentioned by Gunther ranged from 100 to 200 square feet. To insure that the board footage is not underestimated, a figure of 200 square feet per person is used. A 40-by-100-foot dwelling would then be capable of housing four families with five persons each at 200 square feet per person. For a discussion of the various house types in the Puget Sound area, see T. T. Waterman and Ruth Greiner, "Indian Houses of Puget Sound," *Indian Notes and Monographs*, 1921. To simplify the calculation of board footage in the typical Indian winter house, it is assumed that the roof is flat, the walls are 10 feet in height, and that all boards used were 2.5 inches thick. A shelf 3.5 feet wide around the periphery of the house is also included in the calculation as well as six upright posts 3 feet wide and 8 inches thick and three cross beams 17 inches in diameter. These dimensions are taken from Waterman and Greiner, pp. 27-28, 37.

22. James Mooney, "The Aboriginal Population of America North of Mexico," *Smithsonian Miscellaneous Collections* 80 (1928); Henry F. Dobyns, "Estimating Aboriginal American Population: An Appraisal of Techniques with A New Hemispherical Estimate," *Current Anthropology* 7 (1966): 395-416.

23.   Herbert C. Taylor, Jr., "Aboriginal Populations of the Lower Northwest Coast," *Pacific Northwest Quarterly* 54 (1963): 158-165.

24.   Northwest Power Planning Council, *Appendix D of the 1987 Columbia River Basin Fish and Wildlife Program, Compilation of Information on Salmon Steelhead Losses in the Columbia River Basin* (Portland, Ore.: March 1986), pp. 72-73; Robert T. Boyd, "The Introduction of Infectious Diseases among the Indians of the Pacific Northwest, 1774-1874," Ph.D. diss., University of Washington, 1985, pp. 267-294, 324-372. The Columbia River basin and coastal areas immediately adjacent to the mouth of the Columbia apparently suffered smallpox epidemics in about 1775 and again in about 1801. While the 1775 epidemic evidently extended along the entire north Pacific coast, the 1801 epidemic was confined to the Columbia basin and the central coast. Thus, the 67 percent upward adjustment to Mooney's population estimates would result in an overstatement of precontact aboriginal population numbers for much of western Washington and points north. (See Boyd, pp. 73-111.)

25.   Mooney, "The Aboriginal Population of America," pp. 15-18.

26.   H. J. Andrews and R. W. Cowlin, *Forest Resources of the Douglas-Fir Region*, USDA Forest Service, Pacific Northwest Forest and Range Experiment Station (Washington, D.C.: U.S. Government Printing Office, 1940), p. 32.

27.   Winter houses were sometimes burned at the death of their owner. (See Gunther, "Klallam Ethnography," p. 194.) If this were the case generally, the life of a winter house could be as short as 30 years, given that this is a reasonable figure for the average Indian life span. Since all houses were not destroyed in this manner, and since cedar is a wood that is highly resistant to deterioration, then a winter house would last much longer than 30 years and the annual harvest of cedar would be correspondingly much lower.

28.   Marion Clawson, "Forests in the Long Sweep of American History," *Science* 204 (June 1989): 1172.

29.   Drucker, *Cultures of the North Pacific Coast*, pp. 49-51.

30.   Suttles, *Coast Salish Essays*, pp. 26-63.

31.   For statistical data that illustrate the variability of salmon runs, see George A. Rounsefell and George B. Kelez, "The Salmon Fisheries of Swiftsure Bank, Puget Sound, and the Fraser River," *Bulletin of the Bureau of Fisheries* 48 (1938): 693-823. Also, see J. A. Crutchfield and G. Potecorvo, *The Pacific Salmon Fisheries: A Study of Irrational Conservation* (Washington D.C.: Resources for the Future, 1969).

32.   Suttles, *Coast Salish Essays*, pp. 34-35.

33.   Ibid., pp. 26-29; Drucker, *Cultures of the North Pacific Coast*, pp. 15-25.

34.   Ibid., pp. 55-56; Collins, *Valley of the Spirits*, pp. 131-43.

35.   Ibid., pp. 171-89.

36.   Suttles, *Coast Salish Essays*, pp. 15-25.

37.   Hewes, "Aboriginal Use of Fishery Resources, " pp. 212-44. Later data on salmon harvests include hatchery fish and reflect habitat decline from dam construction on the Columbia River and thus would not serve as a very good basis for determining the size of prehistorical salmon runs. Earlier data on salmon harvests are incomplete.

38. Rounsefell and Kelez, "The Salmon and Salmon Fisheries of Swiftsure Bank," pp. 754-815.

39. Northwest Power Planning Council, *Appendix D of the 1987 Columbia River Basin Fish and Wildlife Program*, pp. 66-75.

40. The procedure used in making the adjustment was identical to that employed in Northwest Power Planning Council's *Appendix D*. The basic assumption is that salmon lose an average of 75 percent of their caloric content when they migrate the full length of the Fraser River. To meet daily caloric requirements, this would mean that the catch estimated by Hewes would have to be adjusted up by dividing his estimate by 1 minus the caloric loss percentage. To arrive at the caloric loss for each tribe, the distance of the tribe from the mouth of the river was estimated using information from Bruce Hutchinson, *The Fraser* [(New York: Rinehart and Co., 1950), pp. 3-7]. This distance was divided by the total length of the Fraser, and this ratio was multiplied by the 75 percent caloric loss figure for the full length of the river. The resulting adjusted estimates of consumption were then adjusted to account for inedibility of part of each fish.

41. See note 22.

42. Pacific Northwest Power Planning Council, *Appendix D of the 1987 Columbia River Basin Fish and Wildlife Program*, pp. 11-12.

43. Ibid.

44. Crutchfield and Potecorvo, *The Pacific Salmon Fisheries*, pp. 23-25.

45. Joseph A. Craig and Robert L. Hacker, "The History and Development of the Fisheries of the Columbia River," *Bulletin of the Bureau of Fisheries* 49 (1940): 139-47.

46. Hewes, "Aboriginal Use of Fisheries Resources," p. 84.

47. Suttles, *Coast Salish Essays*, pp. 54-61.

48. Ibid., p. 56.

49. For example see Gunther, "Klallam Ethnography," p. 190; Erna Gunther and Hermann Haeberlin, "The Indians of Puget Sound," *University of Washington Publications in Anthropology* 4 (1930): 22.

50. Marshall Sahlins, *Stone Age Economics* (Chicago: Aldine-Atherton, 1972), pp. 1-99.

51. Ibid., pp. 101-48.

52. James B. Swan, *The Northwest Coast; or, Three Years' Residence in Washington Territory* (New York: Harper and Brothers, 1857; reprinted, Seattle: University of Washington Press, 1972), pp. 135-36.

53. Kalervo Oberg, *The Social Economy of the Tlingit Indians* (Seattle: University of Washington Press, 1973), pp. 77, 88-89.

54. Calvin Martin, *Keepers of the Game: Indian-Animal Relationships and the Fur Trade* (Berkeley: University of California Press, 1978). Martin's book has been controversial. For a critique of it see Shepard Krech III, ed., *Indians, Animals, and the Fur Trade: A Critique of Keepers of the Game* (Athens: University of Georgia Press, 1981).

55. Ibid., pp 33-35; J. Baird Callicott, "Traditional American Indian and

Western European Attitudes Toward Nature: An Overview," *Environmental Ethics* 4 (1982): 300-306.

56. Martin, *Keepers of the Game*, pp. 113-49.

57. Ibid., 157-88. Others have also suggested that Indian attitudes toward prey species and even plants serve as a restraint on consumption and overexploitation. For example, see J. Donald Hughes, *American Indian Ecology* (El Paso: Texas Western Press, 1983), pp. 34, 50, and Christopher Vecsey, "American Indian Environmental Religions," in Christopher Vecsey and Robert W. Venables, *American Indian Environments: Ecological Issues in Native American History* (Syracuse: Syracuse University Press, 1980), pp. 19-37.

58. Collins, *Valley of the Spirits*, pp. 211-13; June McCormick Collins, "The Mythological Basis for Attitudes Toward Animals Among Salish-Speaking Indians," *Journal of American Folklore* 65 (1952): 353-59; Barbara Savadkin Lane, "A Comparative and Analytic Study of Some Aspects of Northwest Coast Religion," Ph. D. diss., University of Washington, 1953, pp. 72-73.

59. Erna Gunther, "An Analysis of the First Salmon Ceremony," *American Anthropologist* n.s. 28 (1926): 605-17; Erna Gunther, "A Further Analysis of the First Salmon Ceremony," *University of Washington Publications in Anthropology* 2 (1928): 133-73.

60. Collins, *Valley of the Spirits*, p. 224.

61. Smith, *The Puyallup-Nisqually*, pp. 272-73; Pettitt, "The Quileute of La Push," p. 7. In the case of the Quileute, the last Indian village upstream built a permanent dam, but one that all but the largest fish could jump over.

62. Gunther, "Klallam Ethnography," p. 199.

63. Callicott, in "Traditional American Indian and Western European Attitudes toward Nature," pp. 311-18, claims that Indian attitudes toward nature were moral in character, but he also rejects a strict Kantian interpretation of the idea of intrinsic value for one based on a more relativist notion of a moral sentiment. He argues further that the Indian attitude toward nature is in many respects consistent with the Leopoldian land ethic.

4

Valuing Forests in the Era of Exploitation

European cultures from which white settlers came had a rather different view of the natural and social world than Pacific Northwest Indians. Europeans saw objects in nature as things to be used for the creation of economic wealth rather than as enspirited beings requiring appeasement or commanding affection. They saw land and places as alienable objects to be bought and sold rather than as locales to which cultural attachments are formed. They sought to influence the natural world directly through its physical transformation rather than indirectly through ceremony and mythical practice. They believed that individuals ought not to be tied to the local group and that they should change social attachments and localities when necessary for the earning of income and accumulating of wealth. The alienability of both land and labor and a rationalistic outlook toward nature were key premises required for the functioning of the new market economy that was at the foundation of the European industrial revolution and, as we will see, the economic development of the Pacific Northwest.[1]

The European instrumentalist and materialist view appears to have been a root cause of the dramatic transformation of the Pacific Northwest forests, which has occurred in the last 125 years. As will be shown in Chapter 5, the exploitation of timber and industrial forest management practices have resulted in the replacement of forests in the full range of seral development, from young stands of saplings on disturbed sites all the way to old-growth stands with trees up to 700 or 800 years old, by forests that are no more than 60 to 100 years old. The central question to be addressed in this chapter is: What attitudes did European settlers have toward forests and how were these attitudes expressed in their actions?

The first step in answering this question is to provide evidence of the attitudes possessed by basically three groups of people: settlers who farmed or attempted to farm the land, capitalists who started timber harvesting and milling ventures, and laborers who came to the forests to find a means of earning a living. The next step is to establish how these attitudes manifested themselves, first in the creation of property in timber, and second in the searching out of markets for timber. If actions speak louder than words, it is the manifestation of attitudes rather than their expression that provides the critical evidence of human values and what they mean for the disposition of the natural world.

The Attitudes of Settlers toward the Forests

Three classes of settlers had a direct impact on the forests of the Pacific Northwest: those who settled the land and engaged in agriculture as their primary means of earning an income; those who established enterprises to generate income and wealth through the harvesting and processing of timber; and those who worked for wages in the forests and the lumber mills. Although each class of settler viewed the forests in instrumental terms, there were subtle differences in attitudes between them attributable to their different economic roles.

The first wave of settlers was attracted to the floodplains and prairies of the river valleys. In western Oregon, the expansive Willamette valley, kept free of timber as a consequence of aboriginally set prairie fires, attracted the most early settlers.[2] The Donation Land Act, passed in 1850, allowed an individual to claim 320 acres of land in the Oregon Territory and a husband and wife to claim up to 640 acres. Soon after passage of this act, most of the valley was quickly claimed, although much land stood idle as speculative holdings. Because of a lack of readily available hired labor, these large claims could not be fully worked by a single family.[3]

Those settlers who came after the best lands had been taken up had to clear the forestlands of timber in order to plant crops, a slow and laborious process that often yielded cropland of little value. In their struggle to extract income from the land, the forests were both an impediment and a supplementary source of income. In some cases, where there was a market, timber could be cut and sold.[4] Where there was no market or where harvesting was too difficult, burning the large trees was common. The settlers seemed awed by the size of the trees, but that did not stop them from clearing the land by whatever means necessary, as described by Silas Plimpton, a settler on the lower Columbia River in the 1850s:

> The old growth of trees are now lieing prostrate & cover a great portion of the land. I have traveled a greate distance upon ceder logs that were three & four hundred feet long & from 4 to 10 feet in diameter such trees as these would surprise you were you to see them. Most of the timber that is standing is very large & lofty. The way we clear this land is some what singular—we bore holes in the trees & set them on fire with a match & they will burn down in a few days & then after they are down they will burn the inside of the tree all out & leave nothing but the sap & bark.[5]

The few settlers who expressed their attitudes had little sentimental attachment to the forests. Their main objective was to "get the land subdued and wilde nature out of it."[6] The forests, in essence, were a barrier to the farmer. The lumberman in this setting was a heroic figure, as suggested by the biographers of Frederick Weyerhaeuser: ". . . society cried out to the lumbermen: 'Your job is to turn the forest into schools, churches, railway stations, factories, houses, fences; get on with it. At the same time, clear the land for the worthy farmer!'"[7]

Settlers soon discovered that much of Oregon and Washington west of the Cascades was inhospitable to the subsistence and limited commercial agriculture that provided an economic foothold in the frontier area west of the Mississippi. With the exception of the river valleys, the landscape was too rugged and heavily forested for agriculture, and the soil was generally unsuitable.[8] Significant economic growth had to await the creation of industrial employment and, therefore, the development of the forest products industry. Settlers in the Northwest could not hope to carve out an economically independent existence based on small-scale landholding and agriculture. Ezra Meeker, a pioneer settler on Puget Sound, looked upon the landscape with disappointment on first viewing:

> Had not the little wife and I made a solemn bargain or compact, before we were married that we were going to be farmers? Here, I could see a dense forest stretched out before quite interesting to the lumberman, and for aught I knew, channels for the ships, but I wanted to be neither a lumberman nor sailor, and so, my first camp on Puget Sound was not cheerful and my first night was not passed in contentment.[9]

Rather than the usual frontier economic complex of small farmers and supporting commercial enterprises, the Pacific Northwest economy was to be dominated early on by large-scale industrial enterprises, and most individuals would obtain their living by working for someone else rather than themselves.[10]

Lumberjacks and Timber Barons

Those individuals who organized the timber industry in the Pacific Northwest saw forestlands not as a barrier to economic prosperity but as an instrument for achieving positions of material wealth and power. Forests were measured by them not in terms of any intangible values but in terms of board feet of exploitable timber.

Among the first to arrive of those who became great timber barons in the Pacific Northwest were A. J. Pope and W. C. Talbot. After establishing a lumberyard in San Francisco, Pope and Talbot decided to take advantage of the vast supply of timber in the Puget Sound region and establish a waterside mill. From this mill they could transport lumber by ship to the burgeoning California market.[11] The goal was not to settle a new land but to establish a lumber production facility that could be controlled from afar in San Francisco and would serve distant markets. Once the mill was established, Pope and Talbot were to see little of the great forests in the area. Their singular interest was in obtaining timber and processing it into lumber:

> Talbot who had come in search of timber, sailed past thousands of acres of land so densely wooded that they could supply dozens of sawmills with logs fore generations. Upon going ashore, his down-Easters were aghast at the immense trunks stretching skyward a hundred feet and more without a limb. Wherever they looked, they saw only timber—tall-firs—straight as arrows, large as California redwoods they had heard about but never seen . . . Here was the spot for a mill.[12]

While this statement is an interpretation by the Pope and Talbot, Inc., historians, it more than likely describes actual attitudes. Talbot claimed that "we shall make more lumber than all the other Mills put together on the Sound."[13] His interest in the forests of the Pacific Northwest was for the lumber they contained.

George Emerson, a sawmill owner on Washington's coast at Gray's Harbor, exhibited an emotional attachment to trees uncharacteristic of his peers, exclaiming that he could not "watch an axe or a saw enter their flesh without a shudder."[14] This did not stop Emerson from building up a substantial business in lumber, nor did he exhibit similar sentimental feelings toward his employees.[15] During the depression of the 1890s, he looked forward to the day when a weakening of organized labor would permit him to again manage his workers "with a taut rein and whip in hand."[16] Someone who looks at human beings in instrumental terms would, in the end, probably have little difficulty doing the same for forests, despite public statements to the contrary.

Another great timber baron, Frederick Weyerhaueser did not enter the Pacific Northwest lumber industry until the turn of the century, but his company was destined to become the largest owner of forestland in the Pacific Northwest. This was made possible by the purchase of some 900,000 acres by Weyerhaeuser from the Northern Pacific Railway.[17] Apart from making this purchase, Frederick Weyerhaeuser himself had little to do with the development of the Weyerhaeuser Company lumber business in the Pacific Northwest. This was left largely to his descendants.[18]

Weyerhaeuser had accumulated his fortune in the lumber business of the upper Mississippi and the north woods of Wisconsin and Minnesota. What he thought about the disappearance of the great northern pinery is not revealed by his biographers. In his early days, Weyerhaeuser traveled extensively in the north woods seeking logging contracts, and his biographers claim that his "duties took him through a country of singular beauty" and that his "blue eyes must have kindled to the stands of lordly white pine rising straight up for a hundred and fifty feet or more."[19] But "singular beauty" again took second place to economic opportunity.

Those who labored for wages in the forests had little choice but to see the forests in instrumental terms. They needed to earn a living, and there were few alternative sources of employment available. The life of the lumberjack was impermanent, dangerous, and harsh. Conditions in the early logging camps were primitive, with few creature comforts. Logging was among the most dangerous of industrial activities, and logging operations were constantly on the move as timber resources were used up.[20] Lumberjacks were variously described by early observers as "debauched . . . indolent, intemperate, and dishonest," or as a "powerfully built race of men," who "though rude in manner, and intemperate, are quite intelligent," with "a passion for their wild and toilsome life."[21] They were viewed by their employers with contempt, and were seen as "things," "cattle," and "rif-raf."[22] "Men were just like tools, and you used them and threw them away if you didn't need them anymore," was the prevailing attitude according to Dow Beckham, a native of Coos Bay, Oregon, a lumbering center.[23]

Lumberjacks were nonetheless proud of their work. While written records of their attitudes are sparse, their pride and toughness are exhibited in the many photographs taken of lumberjacks atop the stumps of very large trees or standing on springboards aside large cuts in Douglas fir trunks 6 feet or more in diameter.[24] While their work in the timber industry brought them miserable standards of material comfort, it was nonetheless a vehicle through which they could meet the challenges of a vigorous outdoor life and exercise their ample physical skills. Whatever they thought about the destruction of the forests around them, when they first arrived in the Pacific Northwest, lumberjacks "were stunned at the first sight of the giant trees—Douglas firs up to ten feet across at the stump and two hundred feet tall."[25] At least one individual who worked in the logging industry now misses the landscape of an earlier era:

> The lower Columbia is a changed land today. Only in the minds of those who lived or traveled along the river fifty years ago does some echo remain of the silent, unbroken grandeur that clothed the rugged terrain when I found my way through devil's walking sticks and marsh from one head works to another.[26]

The attitudes toward the forests exhibited by early settlers were partly the result of the abundance of forests and timber they faced. One pioneer claimed that "the supply of logs for lumber will only be exhausted when the mountains and the valleys surrounding the Sound are destroyed by some great calamity of nature."[27] The view that the supply of timber was limitless prevailed beyond the turn of the century.[28] The old-growth forests were so vast in scale, it was difficult to imagine their ultimate destruction. Moreover, the early "bull team" method of logging was much less damaging to forests than later methods. Prior to the turn of the century, most logging in the Puget Sound area took place within 1 or 2 miles of the shoreline or along rivers where logs could be transported downstream during spring freshets. Because only marketable timber was cut, smaller trees and sometimes very large trees were left behind. Because logs were moved to waterside by oxen along skid roads, damage to the remaining vegetation was minimal. Although species composition may have shifted away from marketable species, such as Douglas fir, toward worthless trees that would be left standing such as western Hemlock, these forests regenerated fairly successfully. This occurred even though large amounts of waste left behind increased the incidence of fire.[29] Thus early logging in old-growth forests left little apparent damage.

Devastation of the Forests

Devastation of Pacific Northwest forests did not begin in earnest until use of the narrow-gauge railroad and steam donkey in logging operations became widespread around the turn of the century. The logging railroad brought access to previously untouched stands of timber.[30] The donkey, a steam engine that powered a winch, permitted more efficient removal of trees and resulted in the felling of entire stands. While a few defective trees might be left behind, these and any remaining smaller trees would often be destroyed in the yarding process. The result was that few seed trees would remain standing after the logging process, and if they did they would often be destroyed by subsequent fires. The fires would destroy, as well, any seedlings produced from germinating seeds remaining in the soil after logging. Forest regeneration was thus inhibited by early twentieth-century logging practices. Following the prevailing view that reforestation measures were too costly, timberland owners, the largest of which were the principle lumber mill owners, exhibited little apparent concern for the long-term fate of the forests.[31]

Valuing Forests: The Creation of Property in Timber

The economic development of the forest products industry in the Pacific Northwest required the acquisition of control over the timber resources through the creation of a property system in timberland and the development of external markets for lumber. Both processes provide us with further insight into the dominant attitudes of the day toward forests, not so much through the direct expression of attitudes as through the actual activities of those who developed the timber and lumber industry. The central thesis here is that actions often speak louder than words in the expression of motivation and attitude.

Legal property claims are generally established for the purpose of precluding nonowners from using something. The purpose of establishing property in timber stands would be to keep others from using them and to reserve them for the disposition of the owner. This disposition could be to preserve the timber stands in their natural state, but more than likely it would be to use them for material purposes. Establishing legal property claims in timber stands is costly and normally must be economically justified on the grounds that the property will yield an income flow in some form. Thus, if people value forests for material ends, they are likely to seek legal property claims in forests to ensure that they can realize that value. If people value forests for nonmaterial ends that lack a ready market, they will be incapable of seeking property rights on a large scale unless they happen to be very wealthy. Hence, the seeking of property claims in forestland will generally reflect a desire to use forests for material and instrumental purposes.

The Property Concept

There were propertylike relationships in Pacific Northwest Indian society, but such relationships were quite different from those found in the Western conception of property brought to the Northwest by white settlers. An individual Indian may have claimed to own a specific fishing spot on a river, but what that really meant was that the individual was a custodian of the particular locality with the right and responsibility to supervise the fishing that was to take place there. Members of the local group had to ask the owner for permission to use the spot, but the owner would not normally turn down such requests. Such property custodianships were inherited, were one of the determining elements of the custodian's status in the community, and were not alienable.[32] Aboriginal property, consequently, was not established for the purpose of enforcing exclusive use but rather to regulate communal use.

The European industrial view of property was rather different. Property was conceived fundamentally as an alienable object to be used as an instrument in the wealth creation process. Severing a relationship to an object of property in the process of production or through sale in a marketplace was readily undertaken if doing so increased the economic wealth of the individual property holder.

The normal means by which property is created in a market economy is through the process of commodity production. Commodity production of any sort involves the destruction or using up of inputs to create outputs. The producing agent, the one who organizes production, normally bears the liability of input destruction by making a contractual payment to the owners of the inputs used up. By doing so, that individual gains title to the resulting output. Production can thus be viewed as a process of asset and liability creation, with the agent who is willing and able to bear the liability of input destruction getting the title to the asset.[33] This, according to David Ellerman in his perceptive work on property, is the "laissez-faire" mechanism of appropriation which suggests, in Ellerman's words, that "when no law is broken, let the liabilities generated by an activity lie where they have fallen, and then let the party which assumed the liabilities claim any appropriable new assets resulting from the activity."[34]

Since objects in nature are not produced by human hands, the process of property creation is somewhat different. Property in nature is normally created by an act of appropriation and the willingness of the appropriator to bear the expense of defending the property claim. This, in turn, normally involves a prior collective appropriation of a given geographic area by a society as a whole and then a socially mediated individual appropriation of landed property and thus of objects in nature. This is the essence of the process by which property in timberland was created in the Pacific Northwest, although because of the peculiarities of U.S. land law the process was by no means smooth and without conflict. The ideological underpinnings of the land laws were to a significant degree

Jeffersonian in character—the land laws were intended to promote the creation of a society of small landowning farmers who, in Lockean terms, would gain an unchallengeable right to the land through working it and investing their labor in it.[35] In the Pacific Northwest, the Jeffersonian ideology was in direct conflict with the needs of large-scale industrial forestry. The result was the manipulation of land laws by timber barons so as to create the large scale landholdings needed by the forest products industry instead of the small scale holdings originally intended by Congress.

Creating Property in Timber

As already noted, the first step in creating individual property is its collective appropriation by a society. The United States initially gained control over the Oregon Territory, including the present states of Oregon, Washington, and Idaho, through the Oregon Compromise of 1846.[36] The treaty divided the Oregon country between the United States and Britain at the forty-ninth parallel, except for the southern tip of Vancouver Island, which was retained in British hands. The interest of the British government in the area had been primarily in the well-being of the Hudson's Bay Company and its extensive fur trade. By the 1840s, however, the population of fur-bearing animals in the Columbia River basin had been driven close to extinction, and attempts by the company to develop other resources, such as agricultural land, lumber, and salmon, met with only modest success.[37] By this time, settlement of the Oregon region by Americans was overwhelming the few British citizens residing in the area. Since the British government believed the region to be of little economic value with the decline of the fur trade and no longer wished to bear the costs of governmental administration, it was willing to cede much of the area to the United States.[38]

The other major claimants to the area were the native Indian populations, whose numbers, by this time, had been significantly reduced largely by the white settlers' diseases to which Indians lacked immunities.[39] By way of treaties and force of arms, Indians had been confined to reservations constituting a minute fraction of their original territories.[40] The remainder of the land in Oregon and Washington, including the timberlands of western Oregon and Washington, was then subject to individual appropriation under the prevailing public land laws.

There were several important methods used for the disposal of the public domain in Washington and Oregon (Table 4-1). While data are available on the different methods of disposal for all types of land use combined, they do not give a clear picture on the methods of acquisition used for forestlands specifically. Complete statistics for forestland acquisitions alone are not readily available, although some data do exist on

Table 4-1
Methods of Disposal of the Public Domain in
Oregon and Washington to 1923 (1,000 acres)

	Washington	%	Oregon	%
Grants to states				
Wagon roads	–	–	2,502	7.7
Educational purposes	3,000	10.2	4,230	13.1
Grants to railroad corporations	9,600	32.7	3,656	11.3
Homestead Act	7,000	23.8	6,000	18.6
Timber and Stone Act	2,158	7.3	3,791	11.7
Cash sale (preemption and other methods)	6,500	22.1	6,100	18.9
Other	1,142	3.9	6,021	18.7
Total	29,400	100.0	32,300	100.0

Source: Adapted from James N. Tattersall, "The Economic Development of the Pacific Northwest to 1920," University of Washington, Ph.D. diss., 1960, pp. 149-50.

the extent to which the various methods were used (Table 4-2). In the following discussion, four avenues to acquiring timberland will be the focus: the Homestead Act, the Timber and Stone Act, and land grants to states and railroads.

Homestead Act

In the early days of the timber industry in the Pacific Northwest, lasting from roughly 1860 to 1880, mills obtained much of their timber from independent loggers who in all likelihood cut a good portion of their timber illegally from the public domain. Local public tolerance for such practices was high because timber cutting was viewed as necessary for gaining an economic livelihood and standing forests were viewed as a hindrance to the expansion of agricultural cultivation. Timber appeared to be in great abundance, and the local settler could see no good reason for leaving it uncut on the public domain if there was something to be gained by cutting it. Prominent lumbermen were convicted for depredations of timber on the public domain but received inconsequential punishments from sympathetic courts and apparently suffered little loss of status.[41]

Most timber stealing from the public lands took place in the Puget

Sound area since that is where the timber industry was concentrated at the time. While the magnitude of such timber harvests cannot be documented, a government agent estimated that the value of timber taken between 1855 and 1869 amounted to not less than $40 million.[42] Because early enforcement efforts against timber depredations were relatively unfruitful, a policy of charging a stumpage fee was instituted, but the revenue that resulted was small because of the difficulty of enforcing payment.[43] Once the Northern Pacific Railroad received its land grant in 1864, it became heavily involved in the fight against timber depredations because timber was being harvested from lands it would ultimately receive once the railroad was complete.[44] The railroad's efforts eventually helped to bring timber depredations to an end, to the consternation of local loggers.

With the magnitude of the capital investment in mill machinery increasing over time as technological advances dictated a larger scale of operation—in the 1880s the number of sawmills declined by 12 percent while capital invested in the lumber industry increased 200 percent—mill owners increasingly looked upon getting their supply of logs from sometimes undependable independent loggers with disfavor and wanted an assured supply of logs that would last the life of their mills.[45] This could be best accomplished through the direct ownership of timberlands.[46] Although the intention of the Homestead Act was to create small farms, in the Pacific Northwest it was used to acquire timberlands from the public domain by large sawmilling enterprises. Lumbermen and speculators would simply pay individuals to enter claims under the Homestead Act, and the claimed land would then be turned over to the milling company or the speculator who initially financed the venture.[47] Puget Mill Company apparently utilized entire crews off its lumber schooners for the purpose of "dummy entry" on homestead claims, and the Washington Mill at Seabeck on Puget Sound only thinly disguised holdings acquired through dummy entry on its books.[48]

The extent to which dummy entry was used to acquire timberlands cannot be easily established. Meany does present some data, however, from a county assessor that show a large number of homesteads on forestlands without any land being cleared for a residence or cultivation.[49] The highest single decade of land acquisitions under the homestead law from 1900-1910 in Oregon coincided with a boom in timberland purchases by large mill owners as the center of timber production shifted from the Great Lakes area to the Pacific Northwest. Professional locators would assemble large plots of timberland, arrange for the entry of claims under the homestead law, and facilitate the eventual transfer of the land to the mill owner.[50]

At best, the forestlands of western Washington and Oregon were inhospitable for agricultural cultivation, and as a result the requirements of the Homestead Act were extremely difficult to satisfy. This suggests that most homestead lands in Pacific Northwest forestlands must have been illegally acquired. The absence of an alternative means for acquiring forest lands to an important extent invited violations of the land laws.

Timber and Stone Act

The difficulty of legally acquiring forestlands in the Northwest was partially alleviated by the passage of the Timber and Stone Act in 1878. Under the act, an individual could acquire 160 acres of forestland at $2.50 an acre provided that the timber was for the exclusive use and benefit of the acquirer. This provision of the law was liberally interpreted by the courts, and as a result forestland could be legally resold to a timber operator or speculator if the initial purchaser desired. This opened the way for professional locators to put together large tracts of timberland and arrange for their sale to large timber concerns. In Oregon, land sales through the Timber and Stone Act were especially heavy in the first decade of the century, the boom period for timberland acquisitions by large operators. Approximately 39 percent of private forestland in the state of Oregon was acquired through the Timber and Stone Act (Table 4-2).

In Washington, Timber and Stone Act sales were also particularly heavy between 1900 and 1910, the period of time during which timber operators from the Great Lakes area were establishing themselves in the Northwest in order to serve the national market opened up by the transcontinental railroads.[51] Ficken suggests, however, that compared to other avenues, the Timber and Stone Act did not play much of a role in the concentration of timber holdings in the hands of large operators in Washington, at least in comparison to railroad land grants.[52] Acquisitions of timber holdings in Washington through the Timber and Stone Act did, however, constitute 24 percent of the total of 9 million acres of privately owned timberland in the state (Table 4-2), a figure exceeded only by railroad grants. The real unknown in both states is the extent to which timberland was acquired using the Homestead Act. Approximately 38 percent of forestland acquisition in Oregon and 47 percent in Washington cannot be accounted for by known methods of acquisition (Table 4-2).

Land Grants

The concentration of land holdings in the hands of large mills in the Pacific Northwest can be attributed significantly to acquisitions from federal land grants to states and railroads. Upon admission to the union,

Table 4-2
Known Timberland Acquisitions for Washington and Oregon

	Acres	%
Washington		
Timber and Stone Act[1]	2,158,000	24.0
Northern Pacific grant[2]	2,415,788	26.8
Cash sale[3]	190,469	2.1
Subtotal	4,764,257	52.9
Total forestland[4]	9,000,000	
Oregon		
Timber and Stone Act[5]	3,791,000	38.8
Northern Pacific grant[6]	264,520	2.7
Oregon and California grant[7]	323,184	3.3
Wagon road grants[8]	265,720	2.7
State grant lands[9]	1,381,327	14.4
Subtotal	6,025,751	61.9
Total forestland[10]	9,768,000	

[1]Tattersall, "The Economic Development of the Pacific Northwest," p. 149.

[2]Eugene A. Brady, "The Role of Government Land Policy in Shaping the Development of the Lumber Industry in the State of Washington," University of Washington, MA thesis, 1954, pp. 64-65.

[3]Edmond S. Meany, "The History of the Lumber Industry in the Pacific Northwest to 1917," Harvard University, Ph.D. diss., 1935, pp. 180-83.

[4]Brady, p.55.

[5]Tattersall, p. 149.

[6]Jerry A. O'Callaghan, *The Disposition of the Public Domain in Oregon* (Washington, D.C.: U.S. Government Printing Office, 1960), p. 78.

[7]Ibid., p. 81.

[8]Ibid.

[9]Ibid., p. 61. These lands were sold during the timber boom period and were most likely all forestland.

[10]Ibid., p. 72.

states received 500,000 acres of land for internal improvements. In addition, states received land grants for the support of universities and agricultural colleges and also received two sections of each township for the establishment of a common school fund.

Oregon obtained a total of 4,345,230 acres from the federal government, of which 3,733,303 acres were dispersed by 1930. Much of this land was sold off cheaply during the timberland sale boom years in the

early part of the twentieth century and ended up in the hands of speculators. While a large share of it was undoubtedly timberland, exact estimates cannot be easily made.[53] Oregon, unlike many other states, had
not yet made specific claims for its school land grant in the public domain by the turn of the century. Oregon law permitted timber locators to
assemble timber tracts in the public domain, have the state make a claim
for them to the federal government, and then sell them to large timber
operators. Oregon also followed a policy of selling its school lands at the
minimum price of $1.25 per acre, a price well below the going market
figure for timberland in the first decade of this century. Between 1898
and 1905, sales of 1,381,327 acres of state land occurred in Oregon, most
of which was timberland.[54]

Washington, on the other hand, followed a more conservative policy,
retaining a significant share of its land grant rather than selling it off. A
law passed in 1909 precluded the state sale of timberlands having more
than 6,250 board feet per acre. Timber could be sold from these lands
only at auction and at prices at least as high as the appraised value.[55]

Aid to private enterprises through the public land laws, in both states,
took the form of land grants to road companies and railroads for the
purpose of transportation development. A total of 2,500,000 acres was
granted to the Oregon state government for distribution to wagon road
companies, while Washington did not receive any wagon road grants.[56]
A significant portion of the wagon road grants, occurred outside of timbered areas in Oregon and thus did not contribute substantially to the
private appropriation of timber holdings.[57] Two grants, one to the Oregon
Central Military Wagon Road and the other to the Willamette Valley and
Cascade Mountain Wagon Road resulted in the eventual carving out of
266,000 acres of private timberland.[58]

The role of railroad grants in bringing timberland into private hands
initially was substantial, especially in Washington. In a study published
in 1913, the three largest holders of timberland were the Southern Pacific
Company, the Weyerhaeuser Timber Company, and the Northern Pacific
Railway Company, and the vast bulk of their holdings were in the Pacific
Northwest.[59] Most of these holdings originated in railroad grants. The
Southern Pacific ultimately had to return much of its holdings (amounting to 1,934,580 acres in Oregon) to the federal government because of
a failure to fulfill the terms of its grant.[60] Prior to the return, however,
369,000 acres had already been sold to timber operators from the original grant and remained in the purchasers' hands. Another 265,000 acres
were acquired in Oregon as a result of the Northern Pacific grant in Washington. Because part of the Northern Pacific grant was in Mount Rainier
National Park, Northern Pacific could select in lieu tracts in Oregon,

most of which it sold to the Weyerhaeuser Timber Company.[61] Because of the recovery of the Southern Pacific holdings, railroad grants, in the end, played a modest role in transferring forestlands to private ownership in Oregon.

However, the situation was quite different in Washington State (Table 4-3). Almost half of the private commercial timberland holdings in the state entered private ownership as the consequence of land grants to the Northern Pacific railroad. These figures include only the study area defined by the Bureau of Corporations and exclude railroad grants elsewhere in the state.[62] The total land grant within Washington State amounted to 8,778,025 acres and included substantial timber holdings outside the Bureau of Corporations study area.[63] As already noted, the Northern Pacific was allowed to select 444,159 acres of land in lieu of its holdings in Mount Rainier National Park. Of this, 80,199 acres were selected in Washington and the rest in Oregon.

To satisfy the terms of its grant, Northern Pacific was required to dispose of much of its holdings as rapidly as possible. In the case of timberland, it did so by selling much of its holdings to large wood-products enterprises. Of the original 2,415,788 acres in southwestern Washington, the disposition of 1,926,118 acres could be accounted for in the Bureau of Corporations study. Of this, 355,781 acres were retained and the remainder was sold. Weyerhaeuser Timber Company purchased 1,231,857 acres of this portion of the land grant as well as 59,820 acres of the Rainier in lieu lands in Washington and 160,043 in Oregon.[64] The total holdings of Weyerhaeuser in Oregon at this point was 380,599 acres of timberland.[65] In short, Weyerhaeuser obtained extensive timber holdings through purchases from the Northern Pacific land grant and thus became a dominant force in the Pacific Northwest timber industry. As a result of railroad land grant sales, timberland ownership was heavily concentrated in the hands of a relatively few firms in Washington State (Table 4-3).

To summarize, despite the orientation of public land laws, such as the Homestead Act, to the creation of a Jeffersonian system of small-scale landholding agriculturalists, the land disposition system in the Pacific Northwest was reshaped to meet the needs of industrial forestry for large-scale landholdings. Because extensive small-scale agriculture was virtually an impossibility in the area, the settlers needed and supported the creation of a forest products industry and industrial forestry as a matter of economic survival. With the exception of the 1878 Timber and Stone Act, there was no law specifically designed for the disposal of timberland in the public domain. At first, settlers acquired timber by simply taking it from the public domain, a practice that was encouraged by the absence of significant law enforcement efforts against illegal timber

Table 4-3
Timberland Acquisitions and Holdings in Washington State

	Acres	% of total
Northern Pacific land grant (SW Washington)	2,415,788	42.3
Weyerhaeuser purchase from Northern Pacific (SW Washington)	1,231,857	21.6
Weyerhaeuser timberland holdings 1954	1,489,120	26.1
Timberland holdings of largest 10 owners 1954	3,819,920	66.9
Total private commercial timberland 1954	5,708,000	
Private forestland 1954	9,000,000	

Source: This table is adapted from Brady, "The Role of Government Land Policy in Shaping the Development of the Lumber Industry in the State of Washington," pp. 65-91.

depredations. As the scale of investment in milling operations increased in the 1880s, sawmill owners desired to have a more certain source of timber and moved to acquire property rights in standing timber. In the Northwest, this was accomplished either through illegal manipulation of public land laws or through acquisitions from state and railroad land grants. In short, timber barons did what they had to in order to obtain the raw materials they wanted to produce lumber to be sold in the marketplace to generate a return on money they invested in land and mills. Their goal was an instrumental one of wealth accumulation.

Valuing Forests:
Seeking Markets for Lumber

The creation of property in timberland was the necessary first step in the exploitation of standing timber. Exploitation of timber requires not only that millowners have access to the resource, but also that there exist a market for the end product. Consequently, the necessary second step in the exploitation of timber, or any natural resource, is finding a market for the final product. The rate at which exploitation of a natural resource takes place, and thus the rate at which the naturally occurring ecological system containing the resource is disturbed and transformed, will historically depend on the pace of the development of a market for the final product. The establishing of markets for Pacific Northwest forest products went through two definite stages, the first of which occurred prior to the development of transcontinental rail links and involved the opening of markets for lumber in California and various countries in the Pacific basin accessible by ship. The second involved the opening up of a national market based on rail shipments of forest products to the East.

Stage One: Maritime Markets

Prior to 1849 and the California gold rush, the lumber trade was modest on the West Coast, and lumber mills were few in number.[66] The Hudson's Bay Company did ship small amounts of lumber from a mill on the Columbia River to Hawaii and California in the 1820s.[67] Others soon entered the lumber trade in California and began serving a local market and undertaking intermittent shipments to South America as well as Hawaii.[68] Up to the 1840s, timber cutting was little more than an adjunct to other commercial enterprises. In 1844, the first mill of real importance was established at Bodega Bay in northern California and was operated as an independent enterprise. By this time, additional mills were also being established in Oregon and Washington.[69] The discovery of gold at Sutter's mill in 1849 marked the beginning of the first period of expansion in the timber industry. The influx of population into San Francisco induced by the gold rush set off a building boom that in turn resulted in a substantial growth in the demand for lumber. The gold rush set the stage for the exploitation of timber resources in the Pacific Northwest and the control of timber resources by San Francisco capitalists for the rest of the century, of which the Pope and Talbot Company was most prominent.

In 1850, the Pope and Talbot lumberyard was established in San Francisco by two Maine lumbermen, and in 1852 they decided to build a mill on Puget Sound. Oregon was bypassed by lumbermen at this time for two reasons—the great difficulty experienced by lumber schooners in safely navigating a sandbar at the mouth of the Columbia River to gain access to timber in the western Oregon interior and the lack of good harbors along the Oregon coast. In contrast, Puget Sound had numerous good waterside mill sites in protected harbors, and timber grew in abundance right down to the shoreline. Pope and Talbot and its Puget Mill Company set the industry pattern of backward vertical integration—from lumberyard to milling to logging. Because sawmilling was a relatively simple manufacturing process, merchants in a distant commercial center, such as San Francisco, could establish their own mills close to timber stands and still maintain adequate control.[70]

The boom in economic activity and the lumber trade induced by the gold rush did not last, and by 1855, a depression in the San Francisco lumber trade had set in. With the collapse of the San Francisco market, lumbermen began to seek other outlets for their timber. During the gold rush era, a few timber cargoes had been sent to the Orient and the Hawaiian Islands to fill the holds of cutters that were returning across the Pacific. With the decline of the San Franciso market, lumbermen began to seek out permanent markets in China, Latin America, Australia, and other countries in the Pacific basin. While these new outlets for lumber shipments were not large enough to fully offset the collapse of the California market, they did soften the blow, and they were to play a significant role in the Pacific Northwest lumber industry for the remainder of the century.[71]

Timber production growth accelerated rapidly in the 1880s (Table 4-4). In 1880, the lumber trade on the Pacific coast was dominated by relatively large mills located in the Puget Sound region and the Humboldt Bay area.[72] Although foreign markets were of great importance for these mills, San Francisco in particular and California generally continued to be the primary market and lumber continued to be shipped by water from waterside "cargo" mills to California and foreign ports.[73]

Stage Two: Rail Markets

While many thought the completion of transcontinental railroad links would immediately open up vast new markets for West Coast lumber in the East, this was not the case. In the 1880s, there were still many alternative sources of supply in the East and Midwest, and shipping rates on the transcontinental railroads were too high for West Coast lumber to successfully compete in eastern and midwestern markets. The Great Lakes lumber industry had yet to reach its zenith. Along with the southern pine region, it captured most of the market east of the Rockies. Rate wars between railroads eventually did permit market penetration as far east as Omaha for western lumber, but outside of Oregon, the effect on the lumber industry was relatively insignificant. Increases in shipments by water in the 1880s far outweighed the growth in shipments by rail.[74]

The boom in lumber production in the 1880s was primarily an indirect result of railroad construction. Prior to completion of the Northern Pacific's transcontinental link in 1883, railroad construction itself did generate a significant demand for bridge timbers and ties and stimulated the Oregon lumber industry. The Oregon industry was also helped by the growing transportation of Chinese coolie labor from Hong Kong for work on the railroad because lumber could be shipped on the reverse leg of the journey. However, with the completion of Northern Pacific construction in 1883, this source of demand faded away.[75]

Although railroads did not initially open up significant new markets in the East, railroads brought population growth and development to the West. This in turn caused an expansion of the market for timber to feed a boom in construction activity. In particular, a real estate development

Table 4-4
Timber Harvest Statistics for Western Washington
and Oregon (Millions of Board Feet)

Years	Western Washington		Western Oregon		Total	
	Average	% Change	Average	% Change	Average	% Change
1871-1880	126.7	–	106.9	–	233.6	–
1881-1890	510.1	302.6	256.4	139.1	766.5	228.1
1891-1900	1,127.9	121.1	484.5	89.0	1,612.4	110.4
1901-1910	2,876.1	155.0	1,193.4	146.3	4,069.5	152.4
1911-1920	4,133.0	43.7	1,880.0	57.5	6,013.0	47.8
1921-1930	6,453.2	56.1	3,122.0	66.1	9,575.2	59.2
1931-1940	4,352.3	-32.6	2,982.0	-4.5	7,334.3	-23.4
1941-1950	4,507.6	3.6	7,053.0	136.5	11,560.6	57.6
1951-1960	4,481.8	-0.6	8,773.6	24.4	13,255.4	14.7
1961-1970	6,057.1	35.1	8,301.6	-5.4	14,358.7	8.3
1971-1980	6,774.0	11.8	8,269.0	-0.4	15,043.0	4.8

Source: F. L. Moravets, *Lumber Production In Oregon and Washington, 1869-1948* (Portland, Ore.: USDA Forest Service, Pacific Northwest Range and Experiment Station, Forest Survey Report No. 100, December, 1949); Brian R. Wall, *Log Production in Washington and Oregon: An Historical Perspective* (Portland, Ore.: USDA Forest Service, Resource Bulletin, PNW 42, 1972); Washington Department of Natural Resources, *Timber Harvest Reports* (Olympia, Wa.: Department of Natural Resources, 1970-1980); USDA Forest Service, *Timber Resource Statistics for Non-Federal Forestland in Northwest Oregon* (Portland, Ore.: USDA Forest Service, Resource Bulletin, PNW-RB-140, September, 1986); USDA Forest Service, *Timber Resource Statistics for Non-Federal Forestland in West-Central Oregon* (Portland, Ore.: USDA Forest Service, Resource Bulletin, PNW-RB-143, March 1987); USDA Forest Service, *Timber Resource Statistics for Non-Federal Forestland in Southwest Oregon* (Portland, Ore.: USDA Forest Service, Resource Bulletin, PNW-138, September, 1986). Timber harvest or log production statistics were not collected until 1925. Timber harvest figures prior to 1925 are based on lumber production statistics for each state as a whole. The figures include lumber production for Douglas fir, western hemlock, Sitka spruce, the cedars, and true firs since these species were harvested primarily from western Washington and Oregon. In 1925, for example, only 1.9% of the Douglas fir harvest in Washington came from east of the mountains, and only 2.2% of the total for Oregon came from eastern Oregon. Prior to 1904, data on lumber production were available only for the census years (1869, 1879, 1889, 1899). Production data were estimated for noncensus years by first calculating an annual growth rate for production between census years and then using the annual growth rate to estimate yearly production figures. From 1925 on, the data are in terms of the international quarter-inch scale.

boom in southern California was an important new source of demand for northwest lumber. Railroads thus caused an expansion of lumber demand in the markets that the West Coast lumber industry had traditionally served rather than immediately opening up large new markets.[76]

Even though western timber did not significantly penetrate eastern markets in the 1880s, the future direction of the lumber business was clear. Great Lakes lumbermen, seeing the end of timber stands in that part of the country, started shifting their operations elsewhere by the end of the 1880s and began a massive investment in the purchase of timberlands and milling operations in the Pacific Northwest with the ultimate intention of serving the national market. The new mills they constructed were oriented primarily to rail rather than water shipment.[77]

The economic depression of the 1890s caused a collapse in the demand for Pacific Northwest lumber. The first sign of trouble was the end of the southern California real estate boom and a resulting sharp decline in lumber prices in the spring of 1888. Although a devastating fire in Seattle that burned much of the business district in 1889 created a temporary new market for lumber, by the early 1890s mill operations were either being curtailed or shut down in the Puget Sound area. The industry did not revive until the end of the 1890s with the help of increased demand caused by the gold rush in Alaska and the Yukon and the Spanish-American War.[78]

While foreign markets and the cargo trade still played a role in the lumber business, from the 1890s on, mills that shipped by rail to the East as well as to California markets increasingly dominated the industry. This meant modest growth for the cargo-oriented operations, such as Pope and Talbot, and rapid expansion for operations shipping mainly by rail, such as Weyerhaeuser.[79] The expansion of the market for Pacific Northwest lumber from the turn of the century on was driven by the growth demand in the interior of the North American continent. After this point in history, the amount of Pacific Northwest timber that could be sold in any given year was determined primarily by the extent of domestic building construction activity and the supply of timber available from alternative sources. Growth in the Pacific Northwest lumber industry slowed substantially over the period 1910 to 1916, and when growth rates in timber harvests accelerated again after World War I, they never again matched those experienced in the first decade of the century. Part of the explanation for slower growth can be found in the secular drop in the per capita consumption of wood products that began in 1906.[80]

A significant relative shift in production from Washington to Oregon occurred after 1929 (Table 4-4). In the 1930s, production declined in Washington and did not achieve production levels of the 1920s again until the 1980s. At the same time, production in Oregon dropped significantly during the Great Depression of the 1930s but achieved new record levels in the 1940s. The shift in production from Washington to Oregon can be explained by the historical pattern of timber exploitation. The exploitation of Washington timber commenced earlier because of its greater accessibility. Consequently, by the 1930s, timber stocks in Washington had been more extensively depleted than those in Oregon. The magnitude of original timber stocks before exploitation in the two states were comparable, according to the early timber surveys.[81]

The point of recounting this history of market seeking for Pacific Northwest lumber is simple. Market seeking was a necessary prerequisite to the economic exploitation of forests, and the exploitation of forests through the extraction of wood fiber was by its nature an instrumental activity—that is, instrumental to the earning of incomes and the creating of material wealth. Implicit in this activity was the attitude that forests are instruments and are valued as such.

Conclusion

This chapter says nothing surprising. Pacific Northwest forests in the late nineteenth and early twentieth centuries were perceived as a means of fostering economic development. Moreover, the successful creation of a timber industry in the Pacific Northwest was generally cheered by all as an important step on the way to material prosperity. The forests were a means to generate economic wealth, nothing less and nothing more. If there were many that were saddened by the destruction of the large, old trees, they kept their silence.

Notes

1. For a full discussion of the cultural foundation of the new market economy and its basis in rationality and the alienability of land, labor, and capital, see Karl Polanyi, *The Great Transformation*.
2. For a summary of the early settlement history of the Willamette Valley, see Jerry C. Towle, "Woodland in the Willamette Valley: An Historical Geography," Ph. D. diss., University of Oregon, 1974, pp. 45-90.
3. Ibid., pp. 72-77.
4. Ezra Meeker, *Pioneer Reminiscences of Puget Sound* (Seattle: Lowman and Hanford, 1905), pp. 34-35.
5. Helen Betsy Abbott, ed. "Life on the Lower Columbia, 1853-1866," *Oregon Historical Quarterly* 83 (1982): 254.
6. White, *Land Use, Environment, and Social Change*, p. 35.
7. Ralph W. Hidy, Frank E. Hill, and Allan Nevins, *Timber and Men: The Weyerhaeuser Story* (New York: Macmillan, 1963), p. 134.

8. For a discussion of problems faced by pioneer farmers, see White, *Land Use, Environment, and Social Change*, pp. 35-53. For an extensive discussion of the failure of farming on logged-off lands, see White, pp. 113-141.

9. Meeker, *Pioneer Reminiscences on Puget Sound*, pp. 37-38.

10. For a comprehensive treatment of the early economic development of the Pacific Northwest, see Tattersall, "The Economic Development of the Pacific Northwest to 1920." Tattersall's definition of the Northwest includes the states of Oregon, Washington, and Idaho. Agriculture was important to the economic development of the region as a whole, but it was largely confined to areas east of the Cascade Mountains, the Willamette valley being the only major exception. Tattersall notes the growing dominance of the timber industry in the economy after 1880 and points to the need for large scale landholdings in the Pacific Northwest for such economic activities as lumbering (pp. 126-31, 156-61).

11. Edwin T. Coman, Jr., and Helen M. Gibbs, *Time, Tide and Timber: A Century of Pope and Talbot* (New York: Greenwood Press, 1968), pp. 1-35.

12. Ibid., pp. 53-54.

13. William C. Talbot to Charles Foster, 4 September 1853, Josiah P. Keller Papers, Western Americana Collection, Beinechke Library, Yale University; quoted in Robert E. Ficken, *The Forested Land: A History of Lumbering in Western Washington* (Seattle: University of Washington Press, 1987), pp. 27-28.

14. Address to Pacific Coast Lumber Manufacturers Association, 28 February 1908, George H. Emerson Letterbooks, University of Washington Library; quoted in Ficken, *The Forested Land*, p. 4.

15. Ibid., p. 58.

16. Emerson to Simpson, 18 January 1894, Emerson Letterbooks; quoted in Ficken, *The Forested Land*, p. 80.

17. Hidy, Hill, and Nevins, *Timber and Men*, p. 212.

18. Ibid., pp. 207-45, 273-88.

19. Ibid., p. 60.

20. Ficken, *The Forested Land*, pp. 131-37; Vernon H. Jensen, *Lumber and Labor* (New York: Arno Press, 1971), pp. 3-23, 110.

21. Ibid., p. 22.

22. Ficken, *The Forested Land*, p. 133.

23. William G. Robbins, *Hard Times in Paradise: Coos Bay, Oregon, 1850-1986* (Seattle: University of Washington Press, 1988), p. 58.

24. Dennis A. Andersen, "Clark Kinsey: Logging Photography," *Pacific Northwest Quarterly* 74 (1983): 19-24.

25. Emil Engstrom, *The Vanishing Logger* (New York: Vantage Press, 1956), p. 7.

26. Oliver Greeley Hughson, "When We Logged the Columbia," *Oregon Historical Quarterly* 60 (1959): 208.

27. A. S. Mercer, *Washington Territory, the Great Northwest, her Natural Resources and Claims to Emigration. A Plain Statement of Things as they Exist* (Utica: 1865), p. 17. Quoted in Iva L. Buchanan, "Lumbering and Logging in the Puget Sound Region in Territorial Days," *Pacific Northwest Quarterly* 27 (1936): 34.

28. Robert E. Ficken, *Lumber and Politics: The Career of Mark E. Reed* (Seattle: University of Washington Press, 1979), p. 61.

29. White, *Land Use, Environment, and Social Change*, pp. 77-93; Thornton T. Munger, "Timber Growing and Logging Practice in the Douglas Fir Region," USDA Department Bulletin No. 1493 (Washington, D. C.: U.S. Government Printing Office, June 1927), pp. 14-15.

30. Cox, *Mills and Markets*, pp. 101-25, 207-12.

31. White, *Land Use, Environment, and Social Change*, pp. 94-112; Munger, "Timber Growing and Logging Practices in the Douglas Fir Region," pp. 13-15.

32. June McCormick Collins, *Valley of the Spirits*, pp. 80-81. Suttles, *Coast Salish Essays*, pp. 9-10.

33. For a discussion of property creation through production, see Ellerman, "On the Labor Theory of Property," pp. 293-326.

34. Ibid., p. 300.

35. Hargrove, "Anglo-American Land Use Attitudes," pp. 121-48.

36. Gates, *History of Public Land Law Development*, p. 84.

37. Tattersall, "The Economic Development of the Pacific Northwest to 1920," p. 35.

38. Ibid., p. 39.

39. Ibid., p. 43; Boyd, "The Introduction of Infectious Diseases among the Indians of the Pacific Northwest, 1774-1874."

40. Jerry O'Callaghan, *The Disposition of the Public Domain in Oregon* (Washington, D.C.: U.S. Government Printing Office, 1960), pp. 21-27.

41. Meany, "The History of the Lumber Industry in the Pacific Northwest to 1917," pp. 168-75; Ficken, *The Forested Land*, p. 43.

42. Meany, "The History of the Lumber Industry in the Pacific Northwest to 1917," p. 172.

43. Frederick J. Yonce, "Lumbering and the Public Timberlands in Washington: The Era of Disposal," *Journal of Forest History* 21 (1978): 9.

44. Ficken, *The Forested Land*, pp. 44-47.

45. Cox, *Mills and Markets*, p. 254.

46. Ibid., pp. 122-26, 280-81; Coman and Gibbs, *Time, Tide and Timber*, pp. 111-12; Meany, "The History of the Lumber Industry in the Pacific Northwest to 1917," pp. 175-76.

47. O'Callaghan, *The Disposition of the Public Domain in Oregon*, p. 74.

48. Coman and Gibbs, *Time, Tide and Timber*, p. 113; Meany, "The History of the Lumber Industry in the Pacific Northwest to 1917," pp. 194-205.

49. Ibid., p. 201.

50. O'Callaghan, *The Disposition of the Public Domain in Oregon*, pp. 75-78.

51. Yonce, "Lumbering and the Public Timberlands in Washington," p. 15.

52. Ficken, *The Forested Land*, p. 52.

53. Meany, "History of the Lumber Industry in the Pacific Northwest to 1917," pp. 206-8.

54. O'Callaghan, *The Disposition of the Public Domain in Oregon*, pp. 61-66.

55. Meany, "History of the Lumber Industry in the Pacific Northwest to 1917," pp. 209-11.

56. Tattersall, "The Economic Development of the Pacific Northwest to 1920," p. 149.

57. Meany, "The History of the Lumber Industry in the Pacific Northwest to 1917," pp. 212-14.

58. O'Callaghan, *The Disposition of the Public Domain in Oregon*, p. 81.

59. Bureau of Corporations, *The Lumber Industry, Part I*, pp. 99-100; Meany, "The History of the Lumber Industry in the Pacific Northwest to 1917," p. 314.

60. Ibid., pp. 215-18.

61. O'Callaghan, *The Disposition of the Public Domain in Oregon*, pp. 78-81.

62. Eugene A. Brady, "The Role of Land Policy in Shaping the Development of the Lumber Industry in the State of Washington," MA thesis, University of Washington, 1954, pp. 65-68.

63. Meany, "The History of the Lumber Industry in the Pacific Northwest to 1917," p. 221.

64. Ibid.; Brady, "The Role of Land Policy in Shaping the Development of the Lumber Industry," p. 226.

65. Meany, "The History of the Lumber Industry in the Pacific Northwest to 1917," p. 226.

66. Cox, *Mills and Markets*, pp. 46-47. This section relies heavily on Cox. The purpose here is to summarize historical actions that demonstrate value commitments to utilize timber for the purpose of economic gain, not to do historical research as such.

67. Ibid., pp. 10-12.

68. Ibid., pp. 13-20.

69. Ibid., pp. 21-33.

70. Ibid., pp. 48-63.

71. Ibid., pp. 71-99.

72. Ibid., p. 101.

73. Ibid., pp. 114, 129.

74. Ibid., pp. 199-205.

75. Ibid.

76. Ibid., pp. 206, 214-25.

77. Ibid., pp. 206-7.

78. Ibid., pp. 261-64, 284.

79. Ibid., pp. 284-95.

80. Tattersall, "Economic Development of the Pacific Northwest to 1920," pp. 185-207.

81. Andrews and Cowlin, *Forest Resources of the Douglas-Fir Region.*

5

Economic and Natural History:
Timber Harvesting and the
Decline of Old-Growth Forests

The historical development and growth of the forest products industry
has shifted the direction of natural history in the forests of the Pacific
Northwest. As a result of its timber harvesting and forest management
practices, the industry has truncated the normal successional pattern of
Pacific Northwest forests and in the process significantly reduced the
amount of land in stands of old-growth timber. Akin to modern agriculturalists, timberland owners have favored the ecologically simple but
highly productive early seres of the successional process over the more
complex later seres with their relatively lower net productivity.

Old-growth forests have been viewed by some as simply decaying
timber that should be salvaged and cleared away to make room for new
growth. Implicit in this view is the notion that old-growth ecological
characteristics differ little from those of younger forests. If this were the
case, the claim that old growth in a preserved state has noninstrumental
value or value in its own right would be difficult to make.

The chapter ahead presents and discusses estimates of the amount of
old growth that has been lost as a result of logging and outlines the
ecological consequences of that loss. The first step is to present and briefly
discuss an estimate of the land area in old growth lost as a result of
postsettlement timber harvesting. The details of the estimation procedure appear in the appendix to this chapter. The second step is to discuss
the unique ecological features of old-growth forests that are lost as a
result of their decline.

The Amount of Old Growth
Lost from Logging

In the very early days of logging in the Pacific Northwest, "highgrading," the cutting of only the largest and most valuable trees in a stand, was the common practice. Once the steam donkey replaced oxen as the principal means of moving logs through the woods, the practice of clearcutting with its more devastating ecological effects became widespread.[1] Clearcutting eased the task of moving trees from the harvesting site to yarding areas by removing anything in the way. Because Douglas fir is a shade-intolerant species and Douglas fir saplings were consequently thought to do best in the open sun, clearcutting was reinforced as the harvesting method of choice once forest landowners became interested in reforestation with the decline in availability of old-growth timber. The modern management method most commonly employed for Douglas fir is to undertake clearcut harvesting, burn the slash and remaining brush to suppress competitor species and reduce the potential for a forest fire, plant Douglas fir seedlings, and harvest the new growth when trees reach anywhere from 40 to 100 years of age.[2] The result is a truncation of the age of forests at approximately 100 years for commercial forestlands.

From 1860 to 1980 approximately 838 billion board feet of timber were taken out of forests of western Oregon and Washington (Table 5-1). The shear magnitude of this amount suggests by itself that the impact of harvesting on forest ecology must have been substantial.

Table 5-1
Timber Harvest Statistics for Western Washington
and Oregon, 1871-1980 (Millions of Board Feet)

Years	Western Washington		Western Oregon	
	Average	Cumulative	Average	Cumulative
1871-1880	126.7	1,266.5	106.9	1,067.8
1881-1890	510.1	6,367.0	256.4	3,632.4
1891-1900	1,127.9	16,646.1	484.5	8,477.2
1901-1910	2,876.1	46,406.7	1,193.4	20,410.8
1911-1920	4,133.0	87,736.9	1,880.0	39,210.6
1921-1930	6,453.2	152,268.9	3,122.0	70,430.4
1931-1940	4,352.3	195,791.7	2,982.0	100,250.0
1941-1950	4,507.6	240,867.2	7,053.0	179,779.9
1951-1960	4,481.8	285,684.8	8,773.6	258,515.6
1961-1970	6,057.1	346,256.1	8,301.6	341,531.1
1971-1980	6,774.0	413,996.3	8,269.0	424,221.1

Sources: See Table 4-4.

A clearer picture of the old-growth loss can be obtained from a comparison of estimates of prelogging old growth and contemporary old growth. Because of disturbances from fire and other natural events, prelogging forests contained stands of differing ages and were therefore not entirely old growth. The methodology for estimating prelogging old growth is presented in Appendix 5A along with the sources for contemporary estimates of old growth. Prelogging old growth in western Oregon covered some 10.4 million acres, or about 54 percent of a total area of 19.3 million acres. (See Tables 5A-1, 5A-3.) Prelogging old growth in western Washington amounted to approximately 9.1 million acres, or around 58 percent of a total area of 15.8 million acres.

Contemporary old growth in western Oregon amounts to approximately 1.8 million acres, while the figure for western Washington is 1.7 million acres (Table 5A-4). In western Oregon, 16.6 percent of the original old growth remains, and in western Washington 18.2 percent of the original is left. For both states together by the early 1980s approximately 82.5 percent of the original old-growth had disappeared. Of the old growth remaining, approximately one-third was reserved from cutting in wilderness areas and national parks in the mid-1980s (Tables 5A-4, 5A-5). With so little left, the intensity of the debate over preserving the rest is not surprising.

The Decline of Old-Growth Forests and Ecological Change

What exactly does the loss of 83 percent of the original prelogging old-growth forests mean? If the characteristics of old-growth forests differed little from young forests up to 100 years of age, then it would be difficult to argue that such a loss matters much. Recent research has demonstrated, however, that as succession proceeds in Pacific Northwest forests, significant changes in their ecological structure take place.[3] The truncation of the age structure at 100 years indeed matters. An 83 percent loss of old-growth forests will thus mean an 83 percent loss of an ecological system with certain unique structural elements. The loss of these structural elements will in turn negatively affect populations of certain plant and animal species. For some that are highly dependent on old-growth habitat, the decline is likely to be proportionate to the loss of habitat or even more than proportionate where timber harvesting patterns have resulted in the fragmentation of old growth into small habitat islands insufficient in size to support certain species. For some species that utilize old growth but are capable of surviving at a reduced level in younger forests, the decline may be less than proportionate. Two questions thus need answers: (1) What unique physical or structural characteristics emerge in Pacific Northwest forests as the successional process proceeds, and what are the effects of those characteristics on the functioning of the old-growth forest as an ecological system in terms of photosynthetic production, nutrient cycling, hydrological processes, and habitat provision? and (2) What is the likely relative impact of the loss of such characteristics on species of plants and animals that utilize old-growth forests?

Old-Growth Characteristics

After a major disturbance, such as wildfire or clearcut logging, a Pacific Northwest forest will go through several successional stages including the grass-forb (0-5 years), shrub (5-15 years), open pole-sapling (15-30 years), closed sapling-pole-sawtimber (30-80 years), large sawtimber (80-200 years), and old growth (200+ years).[4] As redevelopment of the forest proceeds through these different seral stages, the physical structure of the forest undergoes significant changes. Young forests contain dense stands dominated by pioneer species, such as Douglas fir, and support limited vegetation on the heavily shaded forest floor. As the forest ages, a natural thinning process occurs, the forest floor becomes more open, a multilayer canopy forms, and stand composition shifts from being almost entirely Douglas fir to a mixture of old-growth Douglas fir, western hemlock, western red cedar, and other species. An old-growth forest is characterized by a patchy herb-shrub layer, large living trees, large dead snags, and an abundance of organic litter on the forest floor, including large logs in various stages of decay. These are the key physical or structural characteristics that distinguish an old-growth forest from other seral stages. Young and mature forests lack large trees, large snags, and large downed logs, except where they have been carried over from the predisturbance forest. Young and mature forests also have a relatively uniform single-layered canopy and limited penetration of sunlight to the forest floor.[5]

The most apparent feature of an old-growth forest is its large coniferous trees. In the Pacific Northwest, conifers are able to dominate over deciduous trees because of their ready ability to adapt to the moderate wet winters and warm, dry summers characteristic of the area (see Chapter 2).[6] Deciduous trees are at a relative disadvantage because of their high rates of water loss in the droughty summer months and their inability to undertake photosynthesis in the wet, mild winter months. Unlike many ecological systems where the primary production of biomass is quickly cropped by heterotrophic consumers, biomass accumulates to unparalleled magnitudes per unit of land area in Pacific Northwest old-growth forests.[7] Except in a very old forest, Douglas fir is likely to be the dominant species among the large trees. Douglas fir is the typical pioneer species in disturbed areas, but it persists in relatively old stands because it is long-lived.[8] As a result of the periodicity of disturbance, a climax condition in which Douglas fir has completely disappeared is seldom reached in the Pacific Northwest.

Large trees, a key structural element in old-growth forests, first and foremost have their origins at the functional level as the dominant primary producers, transforming atmospheric carbon into organic material through photosynthesis. While this function does not differ conceptually from that of small trees in earlier successional stages, it differs quantitatively in the sense that production in old-growth forest stands is heavily concentrated in a comparatively few large individual trees per unit area. These stands have high rates of gross productivity, but because of high rates of respiration and tree mortality, there is typically little if any net increment to living tree biomass. By contrast, young stands have high rates of net productivity and biomass accumulation, but relatively small amounts accumulated in individual trees. The large trees in old-growth stands with their massive accumulations of organic material ultimately become the source of energy that drives the entire forest ecosystem, particularly when they are transformed through tree death into standing snags or fallen logs on the forest floor.[9]

As structures, large living trees have an important role to play in the functioning of the ecological system. The upper branches of large trees are prime habitat for nitrogen fixing lichens, which draw their nutrients from rainwater and convert atmospheric nitrogen into a form useful to plants. Since nitrogen fixing lichens, such as *Lobaria* sp., are uncommon in young forests, apparently because of the absence of adequate thermal buffering in young stands, the amount of nitrogen fixation is greater per unit area in old-growth forests.[10] Because of its large capacity to store water from rainfall and to consequently buffer temperatures, the canopy of old-growth forests provides an ideal microclimate for *Lobaria*. Old-growth forests also make a significant contribution to hydrologic budget relative to young forests through the interception of fog and mist by the branch and needle system of large trees, particularly in coastal areas where fog and mist is common.[11] The irregularity of the crown of large trees and their relatively distant spacing from one another contribute to the availability of light on the forest floor and the patchiness of the understory.[12] In densely packed young stands, the understory may be entirely absent or composed of a relatively few species adapted to low light conditions.

Large old-growth trees, with their tall, large-diameter trunks, heterogeneous crowns and branch systems, and microclimatic gradients beginning with the cool damp forest floor and ending at the exposed weather conditions at the top of the crown, provide a wide variety of habitat niches for a range of vertebrate and invertebrate animal species as well as a variety of mosses and lichens.[13] The cavities and irregularities of the crown are attractive nesting habitats for the rare spotted owl, and large protruding branches near the treetop serve as perches for the bald eagle along waterways. An abundance of insects are found around, on, and within the bark of large, old-growth trees and serve as a food source for a variety of birds and mammals, including bats that feed on flying insects above the crown. Birds and mammals also feed on the abundant foliage. As many as 1,500 species of invertebrates can be found in, on, and around a large old-growth Douglas fir.[14]

The unique role of large trees in old-growth ecological functioning by no means ends with tree death.[15] Dead trees become standing snags, downed logs on land, or downed logs in streams, and in these capacities continue to play a major ecological role for many years. Douglas fir snags last 50 to 75 years, while western red cedar snags can last 75 to 125 years.[16] The life span of downed logs on land is even longer, ranging up to 480 to 580 years for a 30 inch diameter Douglas fir log.[17] The volume of snags and downed logs in old-growth Douglas fir forests is among the highest reported for temperate forests.[18]

Snags are common in forests of all ages, but only old-growth forests and recent burns contain large snags. Large snags with their large accumulations of biomass become the feeding ground for a variety of bacteria, fungi, and insects. The unique function of snags, however, is as nesting sites for cavity-excavating birds, such as the pileated woodpecker. Hole-nesting birds are normally confined to snags over 24 inches in diameter at breast height. Cavities in snags are used by mammals as well as birds, and the species use of snags shifts as the state of snag decay changes. Cavities are often created by primary excavators in hard snags and are then used by other hole-nesting birds and mammals.[19]

In addition to the creation of snags, tree death can lead to an abundance of downed large logs on land in old-growth forests, logs that perform important nutrient and hydrologic cycling functions. They are principal energy sources for a variety of decomposer organisms that recycle phosphorus and nitrogen for use by primary producers. Downed logs are also an important habitat for nitrogen fixing bacteria, which convert atmospheric nitrogen into a form useable by primary producing plants. Both nitrogen and phosphorus concentrations in downed logs increase as decay progresses. The volume of water in downed logs also increases with decay, making them more attractive as habitat for both plants and animals.[20]

Downed logs perform a variety of habitat functions for a wide range of organisms, including mycorrhizal fungi, moisture-loving amphibians and reptiles, mammals, and birds. The logs are used as food sources, rearing and food storage sites, perches and lookouts, and paths for travel. They play an important role in the recolonization of fire-disturbed sites by providing a store of nutrients protected from fire by a high moisture content and by providing a pathway for small mammals from the surrounding forest into the burned-over area. Mycorrhizal fungi form a symbiotic relationship with tree roots, absorbing sugars produced by the tree and supplying nutrients to the tree roots from the surrounding soil. In a burned-over area, mycorrhizal fungi disappear completely and must be reintroduced for successful tree growth. Downed logs play a role in reintroduction by providing a pathway into bare areas for small animals that eat mycorrhizal fungi and spread the spores to new areas through defecation.[21] Certain mycorrhizae, such as truffles, fruit in rotten wood close to the tunnels of California red-backed voles found beneath downed Douglas fir logs. The voles in turn disperse the spores of the truffles, assuring the reproduction and genetic diversity of mycorrhizae. Mycorrhizae have been found to play and important role in biomass release as well as nutrient cycling in the Douglas-fir ecosystem. In addition to red-backed voles, flying squirrels feed heavily on fruiting fungi, dispersing their spores.

Fallen logs are also an important habitat for tree seedlings for such species as western hemlock, Sitka spruce, and Pacific silver fir. Seedlings are generally more numerous on nurse logs than the adjacent forest floor, particularly in the damper coastal forests. Tree seedlings seem to encounter difficulty competing for space with the mosses and herbs of the forest floor and, consequently, are more successful rooting in recently fallen logs, where competition is less intense.[22]

Downed logs also play a major ecological role in forest streams. Large logs in streams not only affect the carbon and nutrients available to aquatic organisms but also significantly influence the physical profile of small and medium sized-streams. In small streams, logs act like dams, creating a stepped profile of pools and riffles. In the process, the energy of the flowing water is dissipated and the potential for stream bank erosion is reduced. In intermediate-sized streams where logs can be redistributed by the flowing water, dams are less common, but clumps of logs nonetheless alter flow patterns and create habitat variety. In larger streams, logs become highly dispersed and have a minor impact on stream profile. While large logs may persist in streams through the development of second growth forests after major disturbances, in managed stands converted to a short rotation, logs will eventually disappear as major structural elements.[23]

In small streams, downed logs as well as litter fall from the surrounding forest provide a major source of organic carbon and nutrients for aquatic organisms. Because of canopy shading, primary production in streams is limited, and most of the energy used by aquatic organisms is imported from the surrounding forest. The pools and riffles are ideal habitats for a variety of invertebrate and vertebrate organisms, including a number of salmonids. The imported, or allochthonous, organic debris is first attacked by bacteria and fungi. These organisms increase the palatability of organic debris for invertebrate shredders, which in turn further reduce it to a form that is usable by collectors. The shredders and collectors are food for invertebrate and vertebrate predators, the latter of which can include salamanders and cutthroat trout.[24]

The relative impact of the surrounding forest on a stream depends on the size or order of the stream. A small, first-order stream is one that has no other streams flowing into it. A second-order stream results from the confluence of two first-order streams. Similarly, a third-order stream results from the confluence of two second-order streams. As the order increases, the width of the stream enlarges and the canopy opens permitting light energy to radiate directly on the stream's surface, shifting the energy base relatively in the direction of primary production by attached algae (periphyton) and plants (macrophytes). Not only does the forest become less important as a determinant of the physical profile of a stream but the energy base also shifts from imported organic debris to instream primary production. This causes a shift in the food web toward grazer organisms that feed on periphyton and macrophytes and away from shredders. Stream productivity also tends to increase as the canopy opens.[25]

A number of studies have shown that opening the canopy over streams through timber harvesting initially increases the productivity of higher predators, such as juvenile coho salmon and cutthroat trout. Timber harvesting negatively affects the emergence of fry from coho salmon eggs through sedimentation, but the impact of this on salmonid populations is apparently offset by earlier fry emergence due to warmer waters and higher levels of instream primary productivity and feeding opportunities for juvenile salmonids in unshaded clearcuts. For a time, the original pool-and-riffle stream profile may be preserved after timber harvesting, but without further inputs of large woody debris, the stepped profile will be replaced by a channelized profile with its rapid water flow and absence of pools. Consequently, once the postharvest canopy closes, both the habitat favored by salmonids and the higher productivity of the open stream are lost. Thus, for most of the rotation in a managed forest, salmonid productivity will be reduced relative to the initial clearcut as well as the old-growth forest. The old-growth forest will likely be intermediate in total stream productivity because of its partially open canopy in comparison to the closed canopy of the young forest and the completely open canopy of the clearcut. After several rotations, the stepped profile of streams will likely disappear completely, and the increased productivity associated with subsequent clearcuts would as a result be reduced because of the loss of pool and riffle habitat. Although it has yet to be proven, old-growth forests may be necessary to sustain the productivity of salmonids at historic levels. The input of large organic debris to streams as a stabilizing element may be required to provide salmonids with adequate habitat for rearing and feeding.[26]

Recent research on old-growth forests suggests that they are not biological deserts of overmature timber as once thought. Rather, old-growth forests are unique biological structures with unusual physical characteristics that carry out key biotic functions in ways that are much different from forests in earlier successional stages. Initial research findings also suggest that old growth supports certain plant and animal species in greater abundance than forests in earlier successional stages. While research results are not yet sufficiently refined to determine with precision whether an 83 percent decline in old growth has resulted in a proportional, less than proportional, or more than proportional decline in associated plant and animal species, nonetheless, some preliminary conclusions are possible.

Impact of Decline of Old Growth on Plants

For plants in Pacific Northwest forests, species richness tends to be at its maximum immediately following a disturbance, declines as the canopy closes, and increases again as a forest develops old-growth characteristics. In the early grass-forb and shrub seres of the successional process, many of the original species of the herb-shrub layer of the old-growth forest are retained, while invading, sun-loving pioneers are added.[27] With closure of the canopy, the herb-shrub layer becomes pauperized, with only a few highly shade-tolerant species surviving. With partial opening of the canopy in the old-growth forest, species richness again increases.[28] Despite this U-shaped schedule of species richness along the age gradient, there are few species that occur predominantly in old growth and none that appear to require old growth for survival. Foliose lichens, which occur in the canopy and play a major role in nitrogen fixation, are found in much greater abundance in old growth than younger stands. In the shrub layer, the Pacific yew, a highly shade-tolerant species, appears to develop most fully in the understories of old growth. Saprophytic plants, which require rich organic debris, are commonly found on the floor of old-growth forests. Since saprophytes derive their energy from the decomposition of organic matter rather than photosynthesis, they are able to prosper in the shaded environment of the forest floor. The old-growth forest floor also supports bunchberry dogwood and false mitrewort in greater abundance than earlier successional stages. Since the plant species strongly associated with old growth (Table 5-2) also occur in other successional stages, the decline in populations of these plants has probably been less than proportionate to the decline of old growth.[29]

Impact of Decline of Old Growth on Dependent Species

Amphibians, mammals, and birds that do appear to be dependent on old growth and, at the minimum, would likely experience population declines in proportion to the decline of old-growth are listed in Table 5-3. Each species is adapted to one or more of the unique habitat characteristics of old-growth forests. The Olympic salamander is attracted to the cold waters of headwater seeps and small streams in old-growth forests

Table 5-2
Plants Associated with Old-Growth Forests

Common name	Scientific name
Foliose lichen	*Lobaria* spp.
Western yew	*Taxus brevifolia* Nutt.
Bunchberry dogwood	*Cornus canadensis*
False mitrewort	*Tiarella trifoliata* var. *unifoliata*
Saprophytes	
Phantom orchid	*Cephalanthena austinea*
Pinesap	*Monotropa hypopitys* L.
Woodland pinedrops	*Pterospora andromeda* Nutt.
Candystick	*Allotropa virgata*

Table 5-3
Vertebrate Species Dependent on Old-Growth Forests

Common name	Scientific name
Olympic salamander	*Rhyacotriton olympicus*
Oregon slender salamander	*Batrachoseps wrighti*
Bats (various species)	*Myotis* sp.
Vaux's swift	*Chaetura vauxi*
Spotted owl	*Strix occidentalis*

with ample open cobble interstices that provide refuges for the larvae. The Oregon slender salamander is attracted to the interior of large, well-decayed fallen trees. Bats are apparently attracted to the canopy of old growth for roost sites. The Vaux's swift forages over both old-growth forests and clearcuts, but uses large, hollow snags for nesting.[30]

While the spotted owl has in general been shown to depend on old-growth forests through studies of its habitat and relative abundance by seral stage, the explanation for this dependence is still a subject of some debate.[31] Spotted owls do not construct their own nests and commonly use natural cavities available in large old-growth trees or snags relatively high off the ground. They also use the nests of other species that are not necessarily confined to old growth, suggesting that nest site availability would not necessarily be the only factor attracting spotted owls to old growth. Nest sites are available outside of old growth in snags and nests of other species, but they are seldom used by spotted owls. The plumage of spotted owls may be adapted to withstand cold winter conditions, but old growth may be required in summer as a roost site to avoid heat stress. Old growth is still highly attractive to spotted owls even when heat is not a factor. Old-growth forests could also provide protection from harsh winter weather. Neither the nest site availability nor the thermoregulation hypothesis explains the large size of the home range of the spotted owl and the favoring of old growth within the home range. The spotted owl specializes on prey that are relatively abundant in old-growth forests, such as the flying squirrel. Some of its prey are available in the shrub and pole-sapling stages of succession, but the spotted owl may be unable to forage successfully there because of the density of the cover. The large home range of the spotted owl could be explained by the variability of prey availability and the need to forage widely to maintain a steady supply. Finally, the spotted owl may have adapted to old growth to avoid predation on juveniles by goshawks and great horned owls, although juvenile spotted owls do not seem to avoid open areas. The spotted owl may also have adapted to old growth to avoid competition from the larger and more aggressive great horned owl.

Impact of Decline of Old Growth on Nondependent Species

With the historic decline in Pacific Northwest old-growth forests, populations of species dependent on old growth (Table 5-3) would probably decline at least in proportion to the reduced land area in old growth. Numerous other species use old growth, many of which use it more intensively than other seral stages of forest development, suggesting that old growth is a superior habitat for these species in comparison to younger forests. While these species can survive in young forests, old growth supports greater population densities, and populations of these species have likely experienced decline as old growth has diminished, although by less than a proportionate amount. Some of these species are listed in Table 5-4, each of which is attracted to certain habitat features of old-growth forests.

Forest Floor-dwelling Species

Beginning with forest floor-dwelling species, the tailed frog, like the Olympic salamander, is attracted to the cold, clear waters of small headwater streams. These stream-dwelling amphibians, including the Pacific giant salamander, also benefit from an absence of sediments that fill in crevices where larval forms find refuge. The Pacific giant salamander

Table 5-4
Vertebrate Species Associated with Old-Growth Forests

Common name	Scientific name
Tailed frog	*Ascaphus truei*
Pacific giant salamander	*Dicamptodon ensatus*
Dunn's salamander	*Plethodon dunni*
Northwestern salamander	*Ambystoma gracile*
Clouded salamander	*Aneides ferreus*
California red-backed vole	*Clethrionomys californicus*
Red tree vole	*Arborimus longicaudus*
Northern flying squirrel	*Glaucomys sabrinus*
Cavity-nesting birds	
Northern pygmy owl	*Glaucidium gnoma*
Western screech owl	*Otus kennicotlii*
Northern saw-whet owl	*Aegolius acadicus*
Northern flicker	*Colaptes ciuratus*
Pileated woodpecker	*Dryocopus pileatus*
Red-breasted sapsucker	*Sphyrapicus ruber*
Downy woodpecker	*Picoides pubescens*
Hairy woodpecker	*Picoides villosus*
Chestnut-backed chickadee	*Parus rufescens*
Red-breasted nuthatch	*Sitka canadensis*
Brown creeper	*Certhia americana*
Violet-green swallow	*Tachycinta thalassina*
Red crossbill	*Loxia curvirostra*
Pine siskin	*Carduelis pinus*

occupies somewhat larger streams than the Olympic, and preys on the eggs and larvae of the Olympic salamander. Possibly, the Olympic is adapted to the smaller headwater seeps to avoid predation of the larger salamander. Along with the Olympic and Pacific giant, Dunn's salamander has been found to be more heavily concentrated in the streams of old-growth forests than earlier seral stages. The higher incidence of the northwestern salamander, a terrestrial amphibian, in old growth may be related to the persistence of pools of water that provide breeding habitat. The clouded salamander is commonly found beneath the bark of decaying fallen trees, although it utilizes logging slash as well.[32]

Analyzing the dependence of forest floor-dwelling small mammals on old growth is problematic because of their heavy use of downed logs and the carryover of downed logs into naturally regenerated young forests. Although California red-backed voles are found in western Oregon forests of varying ages, their presence may be ultimately tied to the availability of large woody debris generated by old-growth forests. They use large logs in open areas and young forests as pathways for travel and for protection and feed on the mycorrhizal fungi that fruit in woody debris. Because it can take up to 500 years for a large log to decompose, and because such large logs are relatively immune to fire and other disturbances, a forest regenerated after a major disturbance, such as a fire, will contain large decomposing logs for many years. If all forests are converted to managed stands, large downed logs would eventually disappear, eliminating a key habitat element for certain forest floor mammals. Consequently, the decline of old growth, historically, may have reduced the populations of California red-backed voles even though they can be found in young as well as old-growth forests.[33]

Canopy-dwelling Species

One small canopy-dwelling mammal, the flying squirrel, seems to have a relatively strong attraction to old growth. The flying squirrel nests in naturally formed cavities more commonly found in old growth than young forests, and mycorrhizal fungi found in association with tree roots as well as downed logs forms a significant portion of its diet. The flying squirrel descends to the forest floor at night to dig for fungi. The flying squirrel also utilizes the epiphytic lichen, an organism that is heavily concentrated in the canopy of old-growth forests, as a food source.

Another canopy-dwelling mammal, the red tree vole, uses needles and twigs of the Douglas fir for nest construction and feeds almost exclusively on Douglas fir needles. Having little reason to leave the canopy, the red tree vole often spends its entire life without touching the ground.

Only to escape a predator will a tree vole free-fall to the forest floor, usually landing without apparent harm and scurrying back up to the canopy when it is safe again. Although red tree voles live in both young and old-growth forests, they are more heavily concentrated in the latter for reasons that are not entirely clear. One reason could be that the vole is a weak disperser, colonizing only those new stands that are adjacent to old growth.[34]

Bird Species

Cavity-nesting bird abundance apparently is strongly related to the abundance of relatively large, partially decayed snags, but not necessarily to old growth forests, at least in a direct sense. Only where snag abundance is higher in old growth than other age categories is the population of cavity-nesting birds found to be relatively larger in old growth than younger stands. However, because cavity nesters tend to prefer relatively large snags, there is a clear indirect connection with old growth. The decline of old growth under standard, even aged forest management practices results in a decline of the supply of relatively large snags. A decline of such snags reduces the amount of cavity-nesting habitat and consequently the populations of cavity-nesting species.[35]

Avian winter residents, such as the seedeating red crossbill and pine siskin, are strongly attracted to old growth. Because the abundance of seeds produced by the Douglas fir varies from year to year, old growth, with its greater variety of tree species relative to younger stands, may provide a more stable supply of seeds than the younger seral stages. The decline of old growth thus has probably resulted in a decline in winter resident birds.[36] Winter avian abundance was found by David Manuwal and Mark Huff to be at least twice as large in old-growth Douglas fir forests than in young and mature forests, suggesting that the structural characteristics and food sources in old growth provide special winter advantages. The list of species that have likely experienced less than proportionate declines as the land area in old-growth forests has diminished is preliminary and incomplete (Table 5-4). Other species should probably be added to it, such as the bald eagle, northern goshawk, and marbled murrelet. The bald eagle often uses large snags and old-growth trees near riparian zones as perches and nesting sites as does the northern goshawk.[37] The marbled murrelet, a marine bird, is thought to use old-growth trees as nest sites in coastal regions.[38] While lists of species whose populations are affected by the amount of land area in old-growth forests are subject to adjustments, it does seem clear that a variety of amphibian, mammal, and bird species has adapted to one degree or another to the unique habitat characteristics of old-growth forests.

Fragmentation of Old Growth

Could the decline in old-growth forests have resulted in a more than proportionate decline in the populations of some species? The answer to this question relates to the effects of old-growth forest fragmentation on the populations of certain species. In the national forests, harvesting of old-growth timber has often been undertaken in patches over an area rather than in a continuous cut. The effect of this has been to chop up the remaining old growth into discontinuous fragments or islands. The theory of island biogeography predicts that islands will tend to have fewer species of plants and animals than mainlands.[39] Given that intervening clearcuts and short rotation forests isolate remaining patches of mature and old-growth forests by serving as a barrier to migration of species between patches, the rate of species immigration to a patch will be reduced, and for a given species extinction rate, the number of species will decline. Also, the number of species will decline as the average patch size for mature and old-growth forests diminishes because minimum home-range size requirements will be met for fewer and fewer species that find primary habitat in mature and old-growth forests. Forest fragmentation can also reduce in-species genetic diversity by isolating populations and reducing the genetic flow between populations and by reducing the size of breeding populations. The net result can be reduced genetic variability within breeding populations and reduced fitness in the face of environmental change.

There is general evidence supporting island biogeography theory for terrestrial settings. The number of species of mammals in Mount Rainier National Park has decreased over time as the park has become increasingly isolated by timber harvesting and land development activities from surrounding forest habitats. The number of large mammals in western national parks has been shown to be correlated to the size of the park.[40] Because the fragmentation of forests in western Washington and Oregon is a recent phenomenon, its effects cannot yet be evaluated on a large scale. Time must past before the consequences of fragmentation can be felt. Some species are likely to be more vulnerable than others. According to Larry D. Harris, 118 vertebrate species find primary habitat in mature and old-growth forests, of which 40 cannot find such habitat in other seral stages. Some vertebrates are unlikely to enter the early seral stages, and as a result these stages will in effect be a migratory barrier. For birds, a clearcut is not likely to present a migratory barrier, whereas for a red-backed vole, a flying squirrel, or a moisture-loving salamander it could. In general, birds are least affected by habitat isolation, while amphibians are the most affected and mammals experience effects intermediate between birds and amphibians.[41] While it is too soon after patch-cut timber harvesting to fully evaluate the effects of habitat fragmentation on wildlife, in a study of northern California Douglas fir forest fragmentation, several species were found to be sensitive to fragmentation, including the fisher, gray fox, spotted owl, and pileated woodpecker.[42]

The Potential for Preserving Mature and Old-Growth Forests

Many wildlife habitat-use studies suggest that both mature and old-growth forests are often primary habitat for species not found in young forests (less than 100 years old).[43] Also, in the absence of disturbance from fire or timber harvesting, old-growth Douglas fir forests will ultimately be transformed into old-growth western hemlock or Pacific silver fir forests and will lose some of the old-growth characteristics that are associated with large, old Douglas fir trees. Because of modern fire suppression practices, preserved old-growth forests would not be subjected to disturbance from fire to the same extent as prehistoric old growth. Thus new old-growth Douglas fir forests will have to be created.[44] This suggests that mature natural forests (100-200 years old) should be preserved to create old-growth in the future as well as to provide primary habitat for some species not found in young forests.

The prospects for preserving mature forests along with old growth are somewhat better than preserving old growth alone (see Table 5-5). For forests of approximately 125 years and older, 21 percent of the original land area remains in Oregon and 20 percent in Washington. If existing mixed-age forests of 100 years and older are added to the data, the percentages increase to 34 percent for Oregon and 27 percent for Washington.[45] If mature forests preserved today have the potential to become old-growth forests in the future, then the long-term prospects for preserving old growth are somewhat better than the short-term prospects.

Table 5-5
Prelogging and Modern Mature and Old-Growth
Forest Land Area (Acres > 125 years)

	Oregon	Washington
Prelogging mature and old growth	12,530,977	10,741,824
Modern mature and old growth	2,626,000	2,156,000
Modern mature and old growth including uneven aged forests	4,308,000	2,860,000

Note: The prelogging figure was estimated using the methodology described in Appendix 5A. The modern estimates are taken from Richard W. Haynes, *Inventory and Value of Old-Growth in the Douglas-Fir Region* (Portland, Ore.: USDA Forest Service, GTR PNW-118, 1986). The estimates of old growth in wilderness areas are added to Haynes's figures. These estimates are from Peter H. Morrison, "Old Growth in the Pacific Northwest: A Status Report" (Washington, D.C.: Wilderness Society, 1988).

Appendix 5A

Prelogging and Modern Estimates of Old Growth

Nineteenth-century land survey data cannot be used for direct estimates of old growth because most forestland in the Pacific Northwest was not surveyed before timber harvesting began. The only solid information on prelogging forests available is in the first timber surveys conducted by the U.S. Forest Service in the 1933.[46] By this time extensive timber harvesting had been undertaken. Nonetheless, using a methodology developed originally by Van Wagner[47] and applied to the forests of western Washington by Fahnestock and Agee for the purpose of estimating prehistoric smoke production, it is possible to reconstruct the original age structure of forests in the Douglas fir region from the 1933 timber survey.[48] This methodology assumes that catastrophic fires are located randomly, are equally distributed in time, burn a roughly equal area, and are the principal disturbing element in the determination of forest age structure. This section will use this methodology to estimate the amount of western Oregon and Washington land in old-growth forests prior to the commencement of logging. An informed debate over the preservation of old growth requires that the existing indirect estimate of prelogging old growth by Franklin and Spies,[49] based on an extrapolation of the age structure of the forests in the Olympic and Mount Rainier national parks to all western Oregon and Washington forests, be checked for accuracy against one estimated from forest survey data. Once this is accomplished, then modern and prelogging estimates of old growth can be more fruitfully compared.

The First Forest Survey and Prelogging Forest Age Classes

The estimating procedure used here requires three steps. First, the prelogging area distribution between two age classes from the 1933 survey for five commercial forest types is estimated; second, the resulting age-class distributions and the negative exponential age-distribution function suggested by Van Wagner[50] are used to estimate the annual stand fire probability for each commercial forest type; and finally, the resulting fire probabilities and exponential age distribution functions are used to estimate the proportion of each forest type with prelogging stands greater than 200 years old, which are defined here to be old growth.

The 1933 forest survey can be adjusted and projected back in time to establish forest age classes prior to the beginning of timber harvesting. The survey identified and collected data on major commercial forest types, including Douglas fir, western hemlock, true fir-mountain hemlock, cedar (western red cedar and Port Orford white cedar), and Sitka spruce.[51] In the survey, land area was allocated to each type based on species dominance by volume, and the amount of land for each species was further subdivided according to tree diameter at breast height. Given these subdivisions, large and small size classes can be established for each commercial type, which in turn can be used as a basis for determining two separate age classes.

To accurately estimate land areas in the prelogging large category, cutover lands in the survey were reallocated to the large categories for the five different commercial types. Presumably, harvesting was confined to forests in the large size category prior to 1933 because of the large volumes of timber they yielded. Although there most likely was a trade-off between tree size and distance from the mill, with smaller trees nearer the mill being cut to avoid the cost of transporting the larger, more distant trees, mill machinery was probably designed to handle the larger size classes thus limiting the cutting of stands in the smaller size classes. Land areas in the survey categories "recent cutover" and "nonstocked old cutover" were, therefore, allocated to the large category of the different commercial types in accordance with relative harvest volumes estimated from log and lumber production reports.[52] Since approximately one-half of the area in the Douglas fir seedlings category was on lands that had been recently cut, according to the survey authors, one-half of the survey land area in seedlings was reallocated from the small to the large category for Douglas fir and proportionately divided between Washington and Oregon according to the amount harvested up to 1933 in each state.[53]

Deforested burned areas accounted for in the survey were partly the result of wildfire and partly the result of human intervention. Many fires occurred prior to the survey as the result of logging activity, usually on areas that had been recently logged. Since approximately 30 percent of burned areas was estimated by the survey authors to have been previously logged, this amount was reallocated to the large category of the five commercial types in proportion to their respective total harvest percentages.[54] The remainder was reallocated to the small category for the five commercial types in proportion to their percentages of total land area in each state.

The 1933 survey included species other than the five commercial types, rocky and subalpine areas, urban areas, and agricultural lands. Rocky and subalpine areas were excluded from the forestland base in this analysis, as was the Willamette valley because at the time of white settlement it was a prairie that was maintained as the result of aboriginal fire.[55] The remaining land area not already allocated to the five commercial types was assigned to an "all other" category, and the amount assigned to a large size class within the "all other" category was determined by taking an area-weighted mean of the proportions of land area assigned to the large size class for the five commercial types.

The final results of these adjustments to the 1933 survey data are presented in Table 5A-1 and constitute a prelogging estimate of the distribution of western Oregon and Washington forests between two size classes by commercial type prior to logging.

Fire Probabilities and Forest Age Classes

Before estimating the annual stand fire probabilities for each commercial type needed to establish the full age-class distributions, the size classes in Table 5A-1 must be converted to age classes. The relationship between the diameter of a tree and its age is dependent on site quality and stocking. Given a site quality, the age-size relationship can be found using a normal yield table. Such tables are available for Douglas fir, western hemlock, and Sitka spruce.[56] Site quality indices vary from lows of 80 to highs of 210 for Douglas fir and are measures of the productivity of different sites for growing timber. Although Fahnestock and Agee did not report their site quality assumptions, they apparently used an average site quality figure of 145 for Douglas fir and 140 for western hemlock and Sitka spruce in deriving the age from the yield tables for the minimum tree size in the large category for each of the three species.[57] The ages they used in their Table 1 are as follows: Douglas fir, 120 years; western hemlock, 118 years; Sitka spruce, 153 years; mountain hemlock-true fir, 120 years; and western red cedar, 153 years. The Douglas fir age was applied to mountain hemlock-true fir, and the Sitka spruce age was applied to red cedar because yield tables were not available for these species.

Since the distribution of forest area by site quality class is reported

Table 5A-1
Estimated Prelogging Forestland Area by Species and Size
Class: Western Oregon and Washington (Acres)

Species and size class	Oregon	Washington
Douglas fir		
Large (>20" d.b.h.)[1]	8,478,767	4,864,030
Small	3,366,037	2,300,168
Western hemlock		
Large (>20" d.b.h.)	398,268	2,024,380
Small	164,433	512,194
Mountain hemlock-true fir		
Large (>16" d.b.h.)	624,147	1,001,694
Small	149,339	164,934
Cedar		
Large (>24" d.b.h.)	83,466	525,786
Small	8,497	20,192
Sitka spruce		
Large (>24" d.b.h.)	161,364	180,527
Small	55,177	16,593
All other		
Large	2,602,246	2,077,949
Small	996,996	737,201
Willamette valley	1,905,630	
Rocky-subalpine	273,688	1,392,937
Total	19,268,055	15,818,585

Source: See the text for an explanation of sources and calculation of estimates.
[1]The term d.b.h. is short for diameter at breast height.

in the 1933 survey, an area-weighted average site quality class can be calculated separately for western Oregon and Washington.[58] The weighted mean site quality for western Oregon is 139, while the same figure for western Washington is 143. Using these site quality figures and yield tables, the age for the minimum tree diameter in the large categories can be determined. The ages for western Oregon are as follows: Douglas fir, 131 years; western hemlock, 120 years; and Sitka spruce, 155 years. The comparable figures for western Washington are: Douglas fir, 124 years; western hemlock, 113 years; and Sitka spruce, 147 years. In both states, the Douglas fir minimum age was used for the mountain hemlock-true fir commercial type, and the Sitka spruce minimum age was used for cedar. Because western hemlock is shade tolerant and can exist for many years in a suppressed state, the minimum age for its large category may underestimate the actual minimum age. If this is the case, then the amount of old growth would be underestimated for western hemlock forests.

Given the relative distribution of forests between large and small categories in Table 5A-1 and the above age estimates for the smallest diameter trees in the large categories for each commercial type, it is possible to estimate the annual stand fire probability for each commercial type using the equation for the cumulative proportion of stands up to a given age x suggested by Van Wagner, $\Lambda f(x) = 1 - e^{-px}$, where $\Sigma f(x)$ is the cumulative frequency of all age classes up to and including class x, e is the base of the natural system of logarithms, and p is the annual probability of burning.[59] With $1 - \Sigma f(x)$, the percentage of a stand above an age class, known from Table 5A-1 and the above diameter-age estimates, p can be calculated as well as the fire cycle, that is, the average number of years between fires, in Table 5A-2.

With the exception of Douglas fir, the fire cycles for western Washington are fairly close to those found by Fahnestock and Agee.[60] The difference for Douglas fir fire cycles arises from the greater allocation of land to the large category here because of refinements to the procedure used by Fahnestock and Agee.

For each species except Douglas fir, the fire cycle for Oregon was shorter than for Washington, a result that seems reasonable given western Oregon's somewhat drier habitats and hotter summers. The fire cycle for Washington Douglas fir could well be underestimated because much more of it had been harvested than in Oregon at the time of the 1933 survey, creating a greater possibility for error in estimating the large category for Washington. On the other hand, old-growth Douglas fir forests may be more persistent in Oregon than in Washington because of the former's greater frequency of low-intensity burns and lower frequency of severe fires.[61]

Old Growth Estimates

The annual stand fire probabilities in Table 5A-2 and the age distribution equation described above can be used to estimate the proportion of prelogging forestland in old growth (over 200 years old); then the amount of land in prelogging old growth can be calculated using the data on land area by commercial forest type in Table 5A-1. Although some old-growth characteristics can develop in forests with stands as young as 175 years, a more conservative cutoff point of 200 years seems reasonable as a definition of old growth.[62] Most modern studies of old growth also use a 200-year cutoff, although some use characteristics in addition to age in defining old growth, such as the presence of a multilayered canopy and a minimum number of snags and tonnage of logs per acre.[63] The

Table 5A-2
Estimated Prelogging Annual Stand
Fire Probabilities and Fire Cycles

Forest type	Western Oregon			Western Washington		
	1 − Σf(x)	Probability	Years	1 −Σf(x)	Probability	Years
Douglas fir	.716	.00255	392	.697	.00291	344
Western hemlock	.709	.00287	348	.798	.00199	501
Mountain hemlock-fir	.807	.00164	611	.859	.00123	816
Cedar	.908	.00062	1,606	.963	.00026	3,891
Sitka spruce	.746	.00189	529	.916	.00060	1,675
Other	.723	.00248	404	.740	.00245	409

Source: See the text for an explanation of sources and calculation of estimates.

Table 5A-3
Estimated Prelogging Old Growth (Acres over 200 years old)

Forest type	Western Oregon	Western Washington
Douglas fir	7,106,924	4,004,779
Western hemlock	318,171	1,702,010
Mountain hemlock-fir	557,674	913,431
Cedar	81,167	518,690
Sitka spruce	148,541	174,829
All other	2,191,913	1,740,794
Total	10,404,390	9,054,533

Source: See the text for an explanation of sources and calculation of estimates.

estimates of prelogging forestland in old growth are presented in Table 5A-3.

The calculations show that approximately 62 percent of the prehistoric forests were old growth, an amount that is within the 60-70 percent range suggested by Franklin and Spies.[64] However, because the forestland base assumed by Franklin and Spies was approximately 25 million acres as opposed to the 32 million acres derived from the 1933 forest survey and used here, the 19.5 million acres of prelogging old growth estimated here is somewhat greater than the 15-17 million acres estimated by Franklin and Spies.

The estimation procedure allows several possibilities for error. Assuming that the negative exponential distribution is an accurate description of forest age structure, using a single point in the age distribution to estimate the distribution as a whole carries the potential for bias. The estimates could also be erroneous if the forest age distribution does not fit the negative exponential equation very accurately. Hemstrom found that the age-class distribution for small watersheds at Mount Rainier National Park was bell-shaped, and, therefore, the negative exponential model could not be applied. For the park as a whole, however, a negative exponential model was used with some success.[65]

Prelogging and Contemporary Estimates of Old Growth

Given a prelogging estimate of old growth, the magnitude of decline in old-growth forests that has occurred as the result of postsettlement timber harvesting can now be established. To do so requires a modern estimate of remaining old-growth forests. While the results are subject to debate, the most comprehensive study of remaining old growth available currently (to 1991) is one undertaken by Richard W. Haynes for the U.S. Forest Service.[66] Haynes uses forest surveys from the late 1970s for Oregon and the early 1980s for Washington and other data sources to estimate the area and volume of timber by stand age. With Haynes's data in Table 5A-4 and the prelogging old-growth estimates (Table 5A-3), the loss of old growth can now be determined. By the early 1980s, approximately 82.5 percent of the original old growth in western Oregon and western Washington had disappeared. Most of the remaining old growth (17.5 percent of the original) is located in the national forests, the national parks, and on Bureau of Land Management lands in Oregon; very little is left on private and other public lands.

Table 5A-4
Contemporary Old Growth (Acres over 200 years old)

Landownership class	Western Oregon	Western Washington
Private	311,875	77,968
Nonfederal public	2,998	43,983
Bureau of Land Management	432,826	
National forests	1,005,594	869,648
National parks		659,732
Total	1,753,293	1,651,331
% prelogging	16.9	18.2

Source: Richard W. Haynes, *Inventory and Value of Old-Growth in the Douglas-Fir Region* (Portland, Ore.: USDA Forest Service, GTR PNW-118, 1986).

Haynes qualified his estimates, recognizing that the timber surveys he used were dated and that the use of stand age alone to define old growth may be inadequate from an ecological perspective. Peter Morrison of the Wilderness Society conducted his own analysis of six of the national forests using a broader definition of old growth and a more recent time period.[67] He also included old growth in designated wilderness areas, something that Haynes could not do because modern forest surveys exclude wilderness. In Morrison's study, old growth included forest stands with at least eight trees per acre exceeding 200 years in age or 32 inches in diameter. These stands also had to meet certain other old-growth criteria, such as the presence of a deep, multilayered canopy, a certain density of conifer snags, and the presence of two or more tree species. As can be seen in Table 5A-5, Morrison found somewhat less old growth than Haynes in the national forests.

Because the prelogging figures in Table 5A-3 are based strictly on age, they are comparable to Haynes's estimates but not to Morrison's as a consequence of the latter's more restrictive definition of old growth. A stricter definition of old growth would undoubtedly result in a lower prelogging estimate, but there is no way of determining by how much. A definition of old growth based solely on age is probably adequate for determining the relative decline in the amount of land in old-growth forests. Spies and Franklin suggest that perhaps 25 percent of the old growth estimated by Haynes has been cut since the last inventory data were collected.[68] If this were true, then the amount of old growth remaining would be approximately 13.1 percent of the prelogging level instead of 17.5 percent. At least 82 to 87 percent of the original old growth is gone, and only 5 percent or so of the original is permanently reserved in national parks and wilderness areas.

Table 5A-5
Comparison of Old-Growth Estimates
for Six National Forests (Acres)

State	Haynes	Morrison
Oregon	726,706	617,749
Wilderness		167,930
Washington	869,559	521,790
Wilderness		142,941
Total	1,596,265	1,139,529
Wilderness		310,871

Sources: Richard W. Haynes, *Inventory and Value of Old-Growth in the Douglas-Fir Region* (Portland, Ore.: USDA Forest Service, GTR PNW-118, 1986).

Peter H. Morrison, "Old Growth in the Pacific Northwest: A Status Report" (Washington, D.C.: Wilderness Society, 1988).
Note: The national forests included are Mount Baker-Snoqualmie, Olympic, Gifford Pinchot, Mount Hood, Willamette, and Siskiyou.

Notes

1. Elliott A. Norse, *Ancient Forests of the Pacific Northwest* (Washington, D.C.: Wilderness Society and Island Press, 1990), p. 30; White, *Land Use, Environment, and Social Change*, pp. 77-122.

2. E. Reade Brown, ed., *Management of Wildlife and Fish Habitats in Forests of Western Oregon and Washington* (Portland, Ore.: USDA Forest Service, Pacific Northwest Region, 1985), pp. 5-6.

3. The path-breaking work on the ecology of old-growth forests is J. F. Franklin, K. Cromack Jr., W. Denison, A. McKee, C. Maser, J. Sedell, F. Swanson, and G. Juday, *Ecological Characteristics of Old-Growth Douglas-Fir Forests* (Portland, Ore.: USDA Forest Service, General Technical Report, PNW-118, 1981).

4. Brown, *Management of Wildlife and Fish Habitats in Forests*, p. 26. The ranges are approximate and vary according to site quality.

5. Ibid., pp. 26-30; Franklin et al., *Ecological Characteristics of Old-Growth Douglas-Fir Forests*, pp. 3-4, 15.

6. R. H. Waring and J. F. Franklin, "Evergreen Coniferous Forests of the Pacific Northwest," *Science* 204 (1979): 1380-85.

7. Ibid.

8. Franklin et al., *Ecological Characteristics of Old-Growth Douglas-Fir Forests*, p. 1.

9. Ibid., pp. 6-8; Waring and Franklin, "Evergreen Coniferous Forests of the Pacific Northwest," pp. 1382-83.

10. Franklin et al., *Ecological Characteristics of Old-Growth Douglas-Fir Forests*, pp. 24-25. For estimates of epiphyte biomass on old-growth Douglas-fir trees, see Lawrence H. Pike, Robert A. Rydell, and William C. Denison, "A 400-Year-Old Douglas Fir Tree and Its Epiphytes: Biomass, Surface Area, and Their Distributions," *Canadian Journal of Forest Research* 7 (1977): 680-99.

11. Thomas A. Spies and Jerry F. Franklin, "Old Growth and Forest Dynamics in the Douglas-Fir Region of Western Oregon and Washington," *Natural Areas Journal* 8 (1988): 190-201.

12. Franklin et al., *Ecological Characteristics of Old-Growth Douglas-Fir Forests*, pp. 4, 20.

13. Spies and Franklin, "Old-Growth and Forest Dynamics," pp. 194-95.

14. Franklin et al., *Ecological Characteristics of Old-Growth Douglas-Fir Forests*, p. 25.

15. Jerry F. Franklin, H. H. Shugart, and Mark E. Harmon, "Tree Death as an Ecological Process: The Causes, Consequences, and Variability of Tree Mortality," *BioScience* 37 (1987): 550-56.

16. Ibid., p. 28.

17. Ibid., p. 84. For a detailed study of the volume of coarse woody debris (snags and downed logs and branches) and how it changes over succession, see Thomas A. Spies and Jerry F. Franklin, "Coarse Woody Debris in Douglas-Fir Forests of Western Oregon and Washington," *Ecology* 69 (1988): 1689-1702. In naturally regenerated forests, the volume of coarse woody debris tends to follow a U-shaped pattern over succession. Forests in early successional stages inherit coarse woody debris from the previous forest destroyed by some form of disturbance, such as fire. As succession proceeds, inherited coarse woody debris declines in volume, and as the forest ages, new coarse woody debris is produced.

18. Ibid., 1690.

19. Franklin et al., *Ecological Characteristics of Old-Growth Douglas-Fir Forests*, pp. 27-29; R. William Mannan, E. Charles Meslow, and Howard M. Wight, "Use of Snags by Birds in Douglas-Fir Forests, Western Oregon," *Journal of Wildlife Management* 44 (1980): 787-97.

20. Franklin et al., *Ecological Characteristics of Old-Growth Douglas-Fir Forests*, pp. 31-36. For a detailed analysis of the nitrogen cycle in logs and old growth in general, see P. Solins, C. C. Grier, F. M. McCorison, K. Cromack Jr., and R. Fogel, "The Internal Element Cycles of an Old-Growth Douglas-Fir Ecosystem in Western Oregon," *Ecological Monographs* 50 (1980): 261-85. Also see Chris Maser and James M. Trappe (eds.), *The Seen and Unseen World of the Fallen Tree* (Portland, Ore.: USDA Forest Service, Pacific Northwest Forest and Range and Experiment Station, GTR PNW-164, 1984).

21. Franklin et al., *Ecological Characteristics of Old-Growth Douglas-Fir Forests*, pp. 34-36; Maser and Trappe, *The Seen and Unseen World of the Fallen Tree*, p. 31; Chris Maser, James M. Trappe, and Ronald A. Nussbaum, "Fungal-Small Mammal Interrelationships with Emphasis on Oregon Coniferous Forests," *Ecology* 59 (1978): 799-809; Chris Maser, Zane Maser, Joseph W. Witt, and Gary Hunt, "The Northern Flying Squirrel: A Mycophagist in Southwestern Oregon," *Canadian Journal of Zoology* 64 (1986): 2086-89; Robert Fogel, "Mycorrhizae and Nutrient Cycling in Natural Forest Ecosystems," *New Phytologist* 86 (1980): 199-212.

22. Mark E. Harmon and Jerry F. Franklin, "Tree Seedlings on Logs in Picea-Tsuga Forests of Oregon and Washington," *Ecology* 70 (1989): 45-59.

23. Franklin et al., *Ecological Characteristics of Old-Growth Douglas-Fir Forests*, pp. 8-15.

24. Ibid.

25. Ibid; Michael L. Murphy and James D. Hall, "Varied Effects of Clearcut Logging on Predators and Their Habitat in Small Streams of the Cascade Mountains, Oregon," *Canadian Journal of Fisheries and Aquatic Science* 38 (1981): 137-45.

26. Ibid.; L. Blair Holtby, "Effects of Logging on Stream Temperatures in Carnation Creek, British Columbia, and Associated Impacts on the Coho Salmon (*Oncorhynchus kisutch*), *Canadian Journal of Fisheries and Aquatic Science* 45 (1988): 502-15; J. C. Scrivener and M. J. Brownlee, "Effects of Forest Harvesting on Spawning Gravel and Incubation Survival of Chum (*Oncorhynchus keta*)

and Coho Salmon (*O. kisutch*) in Carnation Creek, British Columbia," *Journal of Fisheries and Aquatic Science* 46 (1989): 681-96; John F. Thedinga, Michael L. Murphy, Jonathan Heifietz, K. V. Koski, and Scott W. Johnson, "Effects of Logging on Size and Age Composition of Juvenile Coho Salmon (*Oncorhynchus kisutch*) and Density of Presmolts in Southeast Alaska Stream," *Canadian Journal of Fisheries and Aquatic Science* 46 (1989): 1383-391.

27. Charles B. Halpern, "Early Successional Pathways and the Resistance and Resilience of Forest Communities," *Ecology* 69 (1988): 1703-15; Franklin and Dyrness, *Natural Vegetation of Oregon and Washington*, pp. 82-88.

28. Ibid.

29. Franklin et al., *Ecological Characteristics of Old-Growth Douglas-Fir Forests*, pp. 4-5; USDA Forest Service, *Wildlife and Vegetation of Unmanaged Douglas-Fir Forests* (Portland, Ore.: General Technical Report, PNW-GTR-285, 1991), pp. 111-21.

30. Andrew B. Carey, "Wildlife Associated with Old-Growth Forests in the Pacific Northwest," *Natural Areas Journal* 9 (1989): 151-62; Paul Stephen Corn and R. Bruce Bury, "Logging in Western Oregon: Responses of Headwater Habitats and Stream Amphibians," *Forest Ecology and Management* 29 (1989): 39-57; J. Mark Perkins and Stephen P. Cross, "Differential Use of Some Coniferous Forest Habitats by Hoary and Silver-Haired Bats in Oregon," *Murrelet* 69 (1988): 21-24; Donald W. Thomas, "The Distribution of Bats in Different Ages of Douglas-Fir Forests," *Journal of Wildlife Management* 52 (1988): 619-26; David A. Manuwal and Mark H. Huff, "Spring and Winter Bird Populations in a Douglas-Fir Forest Sere," *Journal of Wildlife Management* 51 (1987): 586-95.

31. Eric D. Forsman, E. Charles Meslow, and Howard M. Wight, "Distribution and Biology of the Spotted Owl in Oregon," *Wildlife Monographs* 87 (1984): 1-64; R. J. Gutierrez, "An Overview of Recent Research on the Spotted Owl," in Ralph J. Gutierrez and Andrew B. Carey, eds., *Ecology and Management of the Spotted Owl in the Pacific Northwest* (Portland, Ore.: USDA Forest Service, Pacific Northwest Range and Experiment Station, GTR, PNW-185, 1985), pp. 39-49.

32. Carey, "Wildlife Associated with Old-Growth Forests," pp. 153-54; Corn and Bury, "Logging in Western Oregon." Also, see USDA Forest Service, *Wildlife and Vegetation of Unmanaged Douglas-Fir Forests*, pp. 305-62.

33. Carey, "Wildlife Associated with Old-Growth Forests," p. 156; Maser and Trappe, *The Seen and Unseen World of the Fallen Tree*, p. 31; Maser, Trappe, and Nussbaum, "Fungal-Small Mammal Interrelationships with Emphasis on Oregon Coniferous Forests," pp. 799-809.

34. Carey, "Wildlife Associated with Old-Growth Forests," pp. 156-57; Maser, Maser, Witt, and Hunt, "The Northern Flying Squirrel," pp. 2086-89; Paul Stephen Corn and R. Bruce Bury, "Habitat Use and Terrestrial Activity by Red Tree Voles (*Arborimus longicaudus*) in Oregon," *Journal of Mammalogy* 67 (1986): 404-6. Also, see USDA Forest Service, *Wildlife and Vegetation of Unmanaged Douglas-Fir Forests*, pp. 241-302.

35. Carey, "Wildlife Associated with Old-Growth Forests," pp. 155-56; Mannan, Meslow, and Wight, "Use of Snags by Birds in Douglas-Fir Forests,

Western Oregon," pp. 787-97; Jill E. Zarnowitz and David A. Manuwal, "The Effects of Forest Management on Cavity-Nesting Birds in Northwestern Washington," *Journal of Wildlife Management* 49 (1985): 255-63. Also, see USDA Forest Service, *Wildlife and Vegetation of Unmanaged Douglas-Fir Forests*, pp. 123-74, 221-40.

36. Carey, "Wildlife Associated with Old-Growth Forests," p. 156; Manuwal and Huff, "Spring and Winter Bird Populations," pp. 589-90, 592-94. Also, see USDA Forest Service, *Wildlife and Vegetation of Unmanaged Douglas-Fir Forests*, pp. 207-18.

37. Brown, *Management of Wildlife and Fish Habitats*, pp. 266, 269-87.

38. Harry R. Carter and Spencer G. Sealy, "Inland Records of Downy Young and Fledgling Marbled Murrelets in North America," *Murrelet* 68 (1987): 58-63.

39. Larry D. Harris, *The Fragmented Forest: Island Biogeography Theory and the Preservation of Biotic Diversity* (Chicago: University of Chicago Press, 1984), pp. 71-107.

40. Ibid., pp. 72-73.

41. Ibid., pp. 44-68, 80.

42. Kenneth V. Rosenberg and Martin G. Raphael, "Effects of Forest Fragmentation on Vertebrates in Douglas-fir Forests," in Jared Verner, Michael L. Morrison, and John C. Ralph, eds., *Wildlife 2000: Modeling Habitat Relationships of Terrestrial Vertebrates* (Madison: University of Wisconsin Press, 1986), pp. 263-72.

43. Brown, *Management of Wildlife and Fish Habitats*.

44. Jack W. Thomas, Leonard F. Ruggiero, R. William Mannan, John W. Schoen, and Richard A. Lancia, "Management and Conservation of Old-Growth Forests in the United States," *Wildlife Society Bulletin* 16 (1988): 252-62.

45. See Table 5-5.

46. H. J. Andrews and R. W. Cowlin, *Forest Resources of the Douglas-Fir Region: A Summary of the Forest Inventory of Western Oregon and Western Washington*, Portland, Ore.: USDA Forest Service Pacific Northwest Range and experiment Station Research Note 13, 1934); Andrews and Cowlin, *Forest Resources of the Douglas-Fir Region*, (1940).

47. C. E. Van Wagner, "Age-Class Distribution and the Forest Fire Cycle," *Canadian Journal of Forest Research* 8 (1978): 220-27.

48. George R. Fahnestock and James K. Agee, "Biomass Consumption and Smoke Production by Prehistoric and Modern Forest Fires in Western Washington," *Journal of Forestry* 81 (1983): 653-57. For my use of this procedure to estimate prelogging old growth, see Douglas E. Booth, "Estimating Prelogging Old-Growth in the Pacific Northwest," *Journal of Forestry* 89 (1991): 25-29. Portions of this article are reprinted here with permission of the editor.

49. Jerry F. Franklin and Thomas A. Spies, "Characteristics of Old-Growth Douglas-Fir Forests," in *New Forests for a Changing World* (Bethesda, Md.: Society of American Foresters, 1984), pp. 328-34.

50. Van Wagner, "Age-Class Distribution and the Forest Fire Cycle."

51. Andrews and Cowlin, *Forest Resources of the Douglas-Fir Region, 1934 and 1940.*

52. F. L. Moravets, *Production of Lumber in Oregon and Washington: 1869-1948* (Portland, Ore.: Pacific Northwest Forest and Range Experiment Station, Forest Survey Report No. 100, December 1949); Brian R. Wall, *Log Production in Washington and Oregon: An Historical Perspective* (Portland, Ore.: USDA Forest Service, Resource Bulletin, PNW-42, 1972).

53. Andrews and Cowlin, *Forest Resources of the Douglas-Fir Region* (1940), p. 24.

54. Ibid., p. 51.

55. Habeck, "The Original Vegetation of the Mid-Willamette Valley, Oregon, " pp. 65-77; Johannessen et al., "The Vegetation of the Willamette Valley," pp. 286-302.

56. Reginald D. Forbes, *Forestry Handbook* (New York: Ronald Press, 1955).

57. Fahnstock and Agee, "Biomass Consumption and Smoke Production."

58. Andrews and Cowlin, *Forest Resources of the Douglas-Fir Region, 1934.*

59. Van Wagner, "Age-Class Distribution and the Forest Fire Cycle."

60. Fahnestock and Agee, "Biomass Consumption and Smoke Production."

61. P. H. Morrison and F. J. Swanson, "Fire History and Pattern in a Cascade Range Landscape" (Portland, Ore.: USDA Forest Service, General Technical Report, PNW-254, 1990).

62. Franklin et al., *Ecological Characteristics of Old-Growth Douglas-Fir Forests.*

63. Peter H. Morrison, "Old Growth in the Pacific Northwest: A Status Report" (Washington, D.C.: Wilderness Society, 1988).

64. Franklin and Spies, *"Characteristics of Old-Growth Douglas-Fir Forests."*

65. Miles A. Hemstrom, "A Recent Disturbance History of Forest Ecosystems at Mount Rainier National Park," Ph.D. diss., Oregon State University, 1979.

66. Richard W. Haynes, *Inventory and Value of Old-Growth in the Douglas-Fir Region* (Portland Ore.: USDA Forest Service, General Technical Report, PNW-118, 1986).

67. Morrison, "Old Growth in the Pacific Northwest."

68. Spies and Franklin, "Old Growth and Forest Dynamics in the Douglas-Fir Region of Western Oregon and Washington," pp. 190-201.

6

Timber Dependency and the Preservation of Old-Growth Forests

What is the relationship between the degree of economic dependence on an exploited natural resource and the extent of political support for the preservation of that resource in its natural state? Does a decline in economic dependency increase the likelihood that whatever remains of an exploitable resource will be preserved? While on the surface the answer to this question may seem obvious, in fact it is not. Entrenched economic interests often continue to exercise substantial political influence even after their relative economic importance has begun to shrink. The power of agriculture in the U.S. Congress is a standard example. The recent history of old-growth and wilderness preservation activities in the Pacific Northwest provides an interesting opportunity to investigate whether or not the relative shrinkage of the timber industry has opened up opportunities for wilderness preservationists to influence political decisions affecting old-growth forests.

As shown in Chapter 5, only 13 percent of the original old-growth forests in western Oregon and Washington remains, and by virtue of their large, old, majestic trees and various other characteristics, old-growth forests contain unique ecological systems having little in common with what is replacing them, young plantation forests where trees are grown and harvested on a 40-to-100-year cycle. In response to the disappearance of old growth, advocates of forest preservation have become increasingly vocal in recent years on the question of preserving the little that is left. This has occurred at the same time that the forest products industry has lost its position of dominance in the Pacific Northwest economy, especially in Washington State.

Has a decline in economic dependency on forest products in western

Oregon and Washington over the past several decades resulted in an increase in the amount of old-growth forestland preserved? An affirmative answer to this question implies that a decline in timber dependency makes possible a change in attitudes towards forests. With a shift in economic dependence toward industries unrelated to forest products, an attitude toward forests that is narrowly economic is no longer necessary to assure material prosperity. People of the Northwest can now form attitudes that are in opposition to timber interests without feeling they are biting the hand that feeds them. Moreover, with the emergence of new attitudes, the relative distribution of political influence over national forest, land-use decisions made by the U.S. Forest Service and the Congress is more likely to shift away from those who want to exploit forests for wood fiber toward those who want to preserve forests. The extent of this shift will depend, in part, on the degree to which the timber industry is able to maintain its relative political strength in the face of economic decline.

The first step in addressing the effect of timber dependency on forest preservation is to briefly trace the relative decline of the importance of the forest products industry in the Pacific Northwest economy. The relative decline of forest products in the regional economy is hypothesized here to have been caused in part by the growth of urban centers, which served as a base for the development of new industries unrelated to forest products. Forest products as a "pioneer industry" ironically helped to set the stage for its own relative decline by stimulating the development of these urban centers. Urban centers emerged historically as central places dependent on the larger timber economy, but once they attained a certain scale, they were able to take on an independent economic life of their own, liberating the Pacific Northwest economy from dependency on timber. Because timber is a renewable resource, absolute decline in harvesting need not and, thus far, has not occurred in the Pacific Northwest. (See Table 5-1.) Thus, absolute output decline is not an explanation for relative decline.

The difference in economic dependency on timber between Oregon and Washington makes possible an evaluation of the extent to which timber dependency influences the decisions to preserve wilderness and old-growth forests. Consequently, the second step will be to consider whether timber dependency has a deterrent effect on old-growth preservation and whether a decline of timber dependency is a possible explanation for recent increases in the extent of old-growth preservation in wilderness areas. This will be accomplished by (1) engaging in a comparative analysis of the history of wilderness and forest preservation in western Oregon and western Washington, and by (2) undertaking a detailed analysis of recent wilderness area recommendations by the U.S. Forest Service and the resulting wilderness preservation decisions by Congress.

The Relative Growth and Decline of the Forest Products Industry

In absolute terms, the output of the forest products industry in western Washington and western Oregon continued to exhibit considerable strength up to the 1980s. Timber harvesting grew rapidly up through the 1920s in western Washington and through the 1950s in western Oregon before reaching a plateau (Table 4-4). Timber harvests in Washington recovered in the 1960s and 1970s from a slump because of increased cutting of old-growth from public lands and increased cutting of maturing second growth timber on private lands. In the two states together, timber production has continued to grow, but the rate of growth is clearly trending downward and production appears to be leveling off.[1]

While timber harvests have not yet declined, the forest products industry as an economic force in the Pacific Northwest has diminished both absolutely and relatively. Forest products employment as well as forest products employment as a percent of manufacturing employment peaked in Washington in 1929 and in Oregon in 1951 (Table 6-1). In both states there has been a relatively slow decline in the level of forest products employment since 1951, but there has been a precipitous decline in the percentage of manufacturing and total employment in forest products. In other words, the once dominant position of forest products in the economies of Washington and Oregon has rapidly eroded in recent years. While the amount of wood fiber output in forest products has not declined, increasing labor productivity has reduced forest products employment, and other industries have emerged that as a group now overshadow the forest products industry, especially in Washington. Slowly declining forest products employment and the rapid growth of other industries together have resulted in the rapid relative decline of forest products.

What is the underlying explanation for the relative shrinkage of the forest products industry? First, forest products as a pioneer industry set the stage for the growth of other industries that eventually grew to a position of dominance in the local economy. While the forest products industry is "resource oriented" with processing facilities normally located close to the raw material source to reduce transportation costs, it needs large urban centers to provide transshipment services to distant markets, regional wholesale distribution services, specialized manufacturing, financing and other business services, higher education, regional government, and specialized medical care.[2] In the language of location theory,

Table 6-1
Forest Products Employment in Oregon and Washington

Year	1879	1889	1899	1909	1919	1929	1939
Washington							
Forest products[1]	625	10,979	21,400	46,800	61,500	71,316	56,918
% change		1,656.6	98.2	118.7	31.4	16.0	−20.2
Forest products as % manufacturing	58.8	63.2	66.0	64.4	45.4	55.4	52.3
Seattle							
Forest products	59	1,109	1,214	3,337	3,123	3,413	
Forest products as % manufacturing	33.9	27.4	11.8	23.8	6.6	12.1	
Oregon							
Forest products	843	5,034	6,300	16,000	26,500	40,512	42,467
% change		497.2	25.1	154.0	65.6	52.9	4.8
Forest products as % manufacturing	26.8	38.4	42.6	60.0	43.7	54.8	57.0
Portland							
Forest products	231	669	1,398	3,914	4,445	4,589	
Forest products as % manufacturing	20.9	6.9	13.2	26.3	13.8	17.6	

Year	1951	1959	1970	1980	1986
Washington					
Forest products	69,222	53,738	57,048	61,063	48,686
% change	21.6	−22.4	6.2	7.0	−20.3
Forest products as % manufacturing	38.6	24.7	23.3	19.4	17.0
Forest products as % total employment	13.4	9.0	6.9	4.8	3.5
Oregon					
Forest products	82,687	72,331	70,361	78,886	67,861
% change	94.7	−12.5	−2.7	12.1	−14.0
Forest products as % manufacturing	62.4	58.5	43.2	36.2	35.4
Forest products as % total employment	23.9	20.1	13.1	9.3	8.0

Sources: U.S. Bureau of the Census, *Tenth-Sixteenth Census of the United States, Manufactures, Vol. III* (Washington, D.C.: U.S. Government Printing Office, 1883, 1893, 1903, 1913, 1923, 1933, 1943); U.S. Bureau of the Census, *County Business Patterns, 1951, 1959, 1970, 1980, 1986* (Washington, D.C.: U.S. Government Printing Office, 1953, 1961, 1972, 1982, 1988). ¹Forest products includes lumber and allied products and pulp and allied products.

these cities function as "central places" for the larger regional economy.[3] Once created, these urban centers can provide the inputs needed for the development of new export oriented industries that can further stimulate local economic growth and eventually overshadow the pioneering resource oriented industry in terms of relative importance in the regional economy.[4]

Table 6-2
Urban Population Growth in Western Oregon
and Washington (Thousands)

	1880	1890	1900	1910	1920	1930	1940	1950	1960	1970	1980
Oregon											
Urban	72	148	194	365	437	546	615	873	1,038	1,279	1,575
Counties											
% change		105.6	31.1	88.1	19.7	24.9	12.6	41.9	18.9	23.2	23.1
Washington											
Urban	11	124	189	464	601	707	776	1,121	1,429	1,836	2,094
Counties											
% change		1027.3	52.4	145.5	29.5	17.6	9.8	44.5	27.5	28.5	14.1

Note: The urban counties in Oregon include Multnomah, Marion, Lane, Clackamas, Washington, and Polk. The urban counties in Washington include Snohomish, King, and Pierce. The sources are U.S. Bureau of the Census, *Twelfth-Fourteenth Census of the United States, Population Vol. III* (Washington, D.C.: U.S. Government Printing Office, 1903, 1913, 1923), and U.S. Bureau of the Census, *1980 Census of Population*, Vol. 1, Chapter A, Parts 39 and 49 (Washington, D.C.: U.S. Government Printing Office, 1983).

The development of the forest products industry helped to stimulate the creation of major urban centers in both western Washington and Oregon (Tables 6-1 and 6-2). Both forest products employment and urban population grew rapidly from 1890 to 1930 in Washington, with the growth rate for forest products employment generally exceeding that for urban population. From 1930 on, however, the growth rates diverge, with urban population growth continuing to be comparatively rapid and forest products employment beginning a downward trend. Prior to 1930, urban population growth appeared to be connected to growth of forest products, at least to the extent that the two had roughly parallel patterns of growth. The hypothesis that the two were likely connected is supported further by the fact that the Washington economy at this time was very heavily dependent on the forest products industry as indicated by the relatively high ratio of forest products to manufacturing employment. Since 1930, urban population growth and forest products growth have clearly become uncoupled. Forest products employment has declined while urban population growth has continued at a relatively rapid rate, suggesting that the urban economy has taken on an economic life of its own based on new categories of economic activity.

The data for Oregon follow a similar pattern, except that urban growth and forest products employment growth do not become uncoupled until after 1950. In Oregon, timber dependency continued to grow until the 1950s. In both Oregon and Washington, urban growth and forest products employment growth become uncoupled at the point where relative timber dependency begins to diminish.

A closer look at the economies of Seattle and Portland, the two major cities in the Pacific Northwest region, provides further evidence that the early economic development of these large urban centers was based indirectly rather than directly on the forest products industry. The data on manufacturing employment for Seattle and Portland and the states of Washington and Oregon in Table 6-2 indicate that the relative importance of the forest products industry in terms of lumber milling and processing in the two cities was much less than for the state as a whole between 1880 and 1930. The lumber industry was not nearly so dominant in the two cities as it was in the two states. However, the growth of both wholesale trade and manufacturing in the early history of the two cities can be traced indirectly to the growth of the lumber industry.

Both Seattle and Portland became major wholesale distribution centers for their respective local regions in the early twentieth century. Because of its central location on Puget Sound, Seattle became the home port for a "mosquito fleet" of small boats that served shoreline communities. The mosquito fleet was complemented by a growing network of local rail lines by the 1890s.[5] By virtue of its location at the confluence of the Columbia and Willamette rivers, Portland was also at the hub of a regional water transportation system as well as a network of local railroad lines. Portland also became the terminus of the first transcontinental railroad to enter the Pacific Northwest.[6] Seattle gained eastern railroad connections, but at a later date than Portland.[7] Their respective positions at the hubs of regional transportation systems assured Seattle and Portland a monopoly on wholesale distribution activity. However, since the local regions to which they distributed wholesale goods were heavily timber dependent, so was such wholesaling activity.

Being regional transportation hubs, both Seattle and Portland also became important job shop manufacturing centers, serving the regional timber industry.[8] Even though the manufacturing sectors in the two cities were not dominated by wood processing in the early twentieth century, the growth of manufacturing in Seattle and Portland did depend very much on the expansion of the forest products industry through its growing need for specialized machinery. The early twentieth-century economies of both cities by no means depended solely on the forest products industry. Portland was a major shipping center for agricultural products from eastern Oregon and Washington, and Seattle became the jumping-off point for Alaska-bound gold prospectors at the turn of the century and ultimately the principal transshipment point for the Alaska trade. During World War I, shipbuilding became an important industry in Seattle. Nonetheless, a significant portion of the early twentieth-century growth of Seattle and Portland can be traced indirectly to the expansion of the forest products industry, the mainstay of the Pacific Northwest economy.

With the uncoupling of urban growth from timber industry growth after 1930 in Washington and 1951 in Oregon, new forms of economic activity emerged that stimulated urban development and reduced regional dependency on forest products. The new categories of economic activity that played a central role in fueling economic growth in urban areas after 1930 in Washington included machinery, electronics, transportation equipment, instruments, and business services. The high-growth industry categories after 1951 in Oregon urban areas included machinery, electronics, instruments, and business services. In Washington, the transportation equipment category of employment was dominated by aircraft produced by the Boeing Company. In both Washington and Oregon, machinery employment included some employment in the production of computers, and electronics and electrical goods employment included some employment in electronic components, each of which was a relatively new, rapidly growing sector of the national economy. All these industries have a strong urban orientation (Table 6-3). To the extent that the forest products industry played a role in the creation of urban economies in Washington and Oregon, it aided in the creation of these urban-based industries that as a group are now replacing forest products as a dominant force in the regional economy.

Old-Growth Preservation and Timber Dependency

Has a decline in timber dependency over time in western Oregon and western Washington resulted in an increase in the preservation of forest-

Table 6-3
Employment in Rapid-Growth Urban-
Based Industries in Oregon and Washington

	1951	1986	% change	Urban Counties[1]	
				1986	% Total 1986
Oregon					
Nonelectrical machinery	4,227	14,891	252.2	11,603	77.9
Computers, office equipment		5,031			
Electrical machinery	968	12,656	1,207.4	9,419	74.4
Electronic components		6,779			
Instruments	440	13,396	2,944.5	10,837	80.9
Business services	3,850	35,452	820.8	28,756	81.1
Washington					
Nonelectrical machinery	5,380	17,509	225.5	9,090	51.9
Computers, office equipment		5,400			
Electrical machinery	1,015	14,035	1,282.3	9,470	67.5
Electronic components		7,012			
Transportation equipment	32,324	72,160	126.3	68,555	95.0
Instruments	248	7,982	3,118.5	7,002	87.7
Business services	5,561	63,156	1,035.7	43,290	68.5

Sources: U.S. Bureau of the Census, *County Business Patterns, 1951, 1986* (Washington, D.C.: U.S. Government Printing Office, 1953, 1988). [1]The urban counties figure is an estimate based on the midpoint of the employment ranges given. Because of disclosure problems, only ranges of employment are given at the county-level nonelectrical and electrical machinery and instruments in Oregon and electrical machinery and instruments in Washington. In case of instruments employment in Washington County, Oregon, the bottom of the range given was used because the midpoint would have resulted in a total that exceeded the figure for the state as a whole.

land substantially untouched by human hands? The major episodes of national park and wilderness preservation involving the locking up of forestland are listed in Table 6-4 along with the amount of land preserved. There appears to be a rough relationship between the amount of land preserved and the extent of timber dependency (see Table 6-1). In both states, the amount of land preserved has increased in recent decades as the degree of timber dependency has declined. Moreover, the amount of land preserved has been significantly greater in western Washington, which is relatively less timber dependent than western Oregon. This

Table 6-4
Land Area Preserved in National Parks and Wilderness Areas:
Western Washington and Oregon

Park or wilderness area	Date	Acres
Western Washington		
Mount Rainier National Park	1899	241,800
Olympic National Park	1938	898,292
1964 Wilderness Act wilderness areas	1964	322,359
North Cascades National Park	1967	508,000
Alpine Lakes Wilderness Area	1976	145,360
1984 Wilderness Act wilderness areas	1984	519,354
Total		2,635,165
Western Oregon		
1964 Wilderness Act wilderness areas	1964	300,040
Mount Jefferson Wilderness Area	1967	64,374
1978 Wilderness Act wilderness areas	1978	170,308
1984 Wilderness Act wilderness areas	1984	396,376
Total		931,098

Note: Land areas for wilderness areas were obtained by letter from each of the national forests in western Washington and Oregon. The data include only those portions of wilderness areas in western Washington and western Oregon. Other sources are North Cascades Study Team, *The North Cascades: A Report to the Secretary of the Interior and the Secretary of Agriculture* (Washington, D.C.: U.S. Government Printing Office, 1965, p. 23); Elmo R. Richardson, "Olympic National Park: 20 Years of Controversy," *Journal of Forest History* 12 (1968): p. 12; Allan R. Sommarstrom, "Wild Land Preservation Crisis: The North Cascades Controversy," Ph. D. diss., University of Washington, 1970, pp. 127, 133.

disparity between western Washington and western Oregon apparently carries over into the extent of old-growth forest preservation as well. While wilderness areas in three national forests in western Oregon contain approximately 168,000 acres of old growth, a figure that is somewhat greater than the 142,000 acres contained in western Washington wilderness areas, the amount of old growth preserved in western Oregon is overpowered by the approximately 660,000 acres of old growth found in western Washington national parks.[9]

While it is clear that the preservation of natural areas has been more extensive in western Washington than western Oregon, this does not prove by itself that declining timber dependency is the driving force behind preservation. To get a clearer picture of the role of timber dependency, a comparative analysis of the history of forestland preservation is needed for western Oregon and western Washington.

Forest preservation in the Pacific Northwest has its historical roots in the turn-of-the-century conservation movement whose primary emphasis was on the wise use of natural resources. The passage of the Forest Reserve Act in 1891 permitted the president of the United States to withdraw forestland from entry under the public land laws and place it in permanent reserves. While the reasons for the passage of this law continue to be a matter of scholarly debate, the law was supported by conservationists and a few noted preservationists. By adopting the strategy of attaching a measure to a conference committee bill up for consideration in the closing days of a congressional session, a small group of preservations and conservationists was successful in obtaining general forest reserve legislation. The legislation was also supported by western irrigation interests. The measure was introduced by Secretary of the Interior Noble under the influence of two conservationists, Bernard Fernow and Edward A. Bowers. There is also some evidence that Noble was influenced by John Muir and Robert Underwood Johnson, two preservationists. While the conservationists advocated wise use of resources and would find sustained-yield timber production acceptable, the preservationists, including the likes of John Muir and Robert Underwood Johnson who together had fought for the creation of the Yosemite National Park, were more interested in permanently preserving areas of natural beauty.[10]

A mixture of conservationist and preservationist motives underlay the creation of the early forest reserves in Oregon and Washington, reserves that were later transformed into national forests, national parks, and wilderness areas. Petitions for reserve status in Oregon were initiated on the one hand by municipalities interested in preserving key watersheds for their water supply and on the other by individuals interested in preserving the natural beauty of certain mountainous areas. The Oregon Alpine Club played a key role in the creation of forest reserves, and included among its membership important Portland businesspeople, bankers, and city officials. Municipal leaders in the city of Ashland, Oregon, were instrumental in the creation of the Ashland reserve in 1893. Local politicians in Portland along with the Oregon Alpine Club successfully supported the creation of the Bull Run Timberland Reserve in 1892 for the purpose of protecting the city's watershed. Preservationists in Oregon also supported the creation of reserves in the Mount Hood and Crater Lake areas as well as a Cascade reserve, including lands 12 miles on either side of the Cascade crest running the length of Oregon and covering an area of 4,492,800 acres. In addition to the Alpine Club and other preservationists, land speculators supported creation of the Cascade reserve because they could purchase state school lands in the reserve for $1.25 an acre and then exchange them for valuable timberland elsewhere in the public domain worth $2.50 an acre. The petition for the Cascade reserve put together by the Alpine Club leadership had a long list of endorsers that included the state's key political and business figures. Once the founder of the Alpine Club, William Gladstone Steel, became aware of the likelihood of land fraud as a result, he withdraw his support for the Cascade reserve and argued for the creation of just the Mount Hood and Crater Lake reserves. Nonetheless, the Cascade Reserve was created in 1893 in the face of opposition from Steel and homesteaders in the area.[11]

In marked contrast to Oregon, there was no substantial organized preservationist movement in Washington State during the 1890s. Even so, the Pacific Forest reserve around Mount Rainier was created. While there is no record of who filed the initial petition, the Land Office in its investigation justified the reserve on the grounds that timber was abundant elsewhere, privately owned timber would increase in value as a consequence of withdrawal, flooding and soil erosion from logging would be prevented, and that the scenic beauty of the setting surrounding the mountain would be protected. Letters supporting withdrawal came from a number of civic and political leaders in the state, and the reserve was created in 1895 with no apparent opposition.[12] The absence of an organized preservation movement in Washington did not seem to make much difference since forest reserves were created anyway. Opposition was absent because, at this point in history, the reserves were largely inaccessible and worthless for purposes of timber exploitation.

Preserving Mount Rainier

Soon after creation of the Pacific Forest reserve, a small group of presevationists, including the first individual known to have climbed Mount Rainier, a Northern Pacific Railroad geologist, and a tourism promoter who had written a guide to the mountain for tourists, began promoting the idea of a Mount Rainier National Park. Organized trips to the Mount Rainier, or Mount Tacoma as it was called by local residents, were already available to tourists from Tacoma in the 1890s. National support for the park was forthcoming from the National Geographic Society, the Geological Society, the American Association for the Advancement of Science, and the Sierra and Appalachian mountain clubs. Support also came from leading figures in the national preservation and conservation movements, such as Gifford Pinchot, John Muir, and Robert Underwood Johnson, editor of *Century Magazine*. In sum, support came from those who wanted Mount Rainier preserved for its scenic value and scientific interest on the one hand, and as a vehicle for the development of tourism on the other. The only apparent opposition to the park came from mining and grazing interests, but their opposition abated as soon as they discovered that resources there were of little value. The Seattle Chamber of Commerce sent a petition to Congress in favor of the park, indicating that local business interests strongly supported the park idea.[13] A barrier to the creation of the park was landholdings within the park boundaries by the Northern Pacific Railroad. This problem was overcome by granting the railroad in lieu land rights for relinquishing its holdings, turning the park into a boon for the railroad, which could select timberlands elsewhere of much greater value.[14] At the time, timber harvesting was too costly in the area and there were abundant supplies of virgin timber that were more accessible.

The Mount Rainier area was worthless for commodity and exploitation, and the mountain itself was monumental in character, the two necessary conditions suggested by Alfred Runte for the creation of a national park. In 1899, a bill was passed by Congress and signed by the president establishing the Mount Rainier National Park. Mount Rainier and the surrounding old-growth forests were preserved not because of a local preservationist movement but because of a national desire to preserve an object of unusual scenic beauty, and because of a local desire to reap economic gain from increased tourism. The creation of a park was also immeasurably aided by the political efforts of James J. Hill and his Northern Pacific Railroad in behalf of the park to gain the benefits of in lieu land selection.[15]

Up to 1895, little opposition was expressed to the creation of forest reserves, and support for reserves came from a relatively elite group of preservationists, which often included local businesspeople and professionals interested in outdoor recreation and enjoying the beauties of nature. Local politicians supported reserves because they were interested in preserving municipal watersheds, and in the case of Mount Rainier, local businesspeople desired to see it preserved from exploitation for its potential as a tourist attraction.

With the unilateral creation of thirteen new reserves in 1897 encompassing a gross area of 21.3 million acres located throughout the western states, the opposition to reserves intensified.[16] The creation of these reserves grew out of recommendations by a forest commission of the National Academy of Sciences formed for the purpose of investigating the extent to which forest reserves should be utilized as well as other issues. The 1891 forest reserve legislation neither provided for protection of reserves nor established the extent to which their resources could be exploited. While the commission was slow in making recommendations on forest management, it did suggest to President Grover Cleveland in the last days of his administration that more reserves be created, a suggestion that Cleveland acted on promptly, being fearful that his successor, William McKinley, would reverse reservation policy.[17] In Washington State, three new reserves were created as a result of the president's action: the Washington reserve of 3,594,240 acres; the Olympic reserve of 2,188,800 acres; and the Mount Rainier reserve of 2,234,880, an enlargement of the Pacific reserve.[18]

The Struggle for Olympic National Park

It was out of the Olympic reserve that the Olympic National Park was carved in 1938, the second major episode of permanent forestland and alpine preservation in the Pacific Northwest. The setting for the park controversy was the Olympic peninsula bordered by the Pacific Ocean to the west, the Strait of Juan de Fuca to the north, and Puget Sound to the east. The peninsula is physically dominated by the Olympic Mountains, a cluster of steep and sometimes glaciated peaks and small ranges divided by deep canyons and narrow valleys running about 50 miles in length. The mountains are surrounded by forests of Douglas fir, western hemlock, Sitka spruce, western red cedar, and Pacific silver fir. Some of the river valleys to the west of the mountains are noted for their luxuriant, moss-covered rain forests supported by over 200 inches of rain per year. The mountains and surrounding forests provide rangeland for the rare Olympic elk.[19] Of the approximately 4 million acres on the peninsula, President Cleveland withdrew 2,188,800 as a forest reserve in 1897. The reserve was subsequently reduced in size to 1,466,880 acres by President McKinley under pressure from local settlers, county politicians concerned with losses of property tax revenues, and logging interests. President Theodore Roosevelt restored 127,680 acres to the reserve in 1907.[20] In 1909 President Roosevelt established the Mount Olympus National Monument encompassing 615,000 acres in the central part of the national forest. The national monument withdrawal was in response to local concern over poaching of the Olympic elk and a request by the U.S. Biological Survey to establish a reserve to protect the elk. The withdrawal was given strong support by the newly formed Mountaineers, a Seattle-based outdoor recreation organization.[21] To the dismay of preservationists, Gifford Pinchot wrote the proclamation for the withdrawal so as to exclude the richest stands of westside old-growth rain forests in the Hoh, Bogachiel, Queets, and Clearwater river valleys where significant elk populations resided. Pinchot also included a provision in the proclamation that appeared to permit timber harvesting within the monument.[22]

Almost immediately, campaigns began by local timber and mining interests on one hand to reduce the size of the monument and by preservationists on the other to turn the monument into a national park. Olympic National Forest administrators favored either elimination or reduction of size of the monument. Under pressure from timber interests, Chief Forester Henry S. Graves recommended the elimination of significant timber stands from the monument reducing it in size by one-half, a recommendation that was accepted by President Woodrow Wilson and adopted in 1915. Because of opposition from timber interests, bills to create a Mount Olympus National Park never got anywhere.[23]

While park bills were introduced in 1916 and again in 1926, the movement for a Mount Olympus National Park languished until the formation of the Emergency Conservation Committee (ECC) by Willard Van Name and Rosalie Edge in 1930. Van Name was a highly respected zoologist at the American Museum of Natural History and had been carrying out a campaign against the U.S. Forest Service and the Park Service for failing to protect forests from exploitation. Edge was a philanthropist and lover of wildlife who had become disenchanted with the Audubon Association for its gun company connections and predator trapping programs.[24] Van Name and Edge were joined by a writer and newspaperman, Irving Brant, in their conservation efforts, initially focused on reforming the Audubon Association. Although the Emergency Conservation Committee lacked a mass base of support and was nothing more than an organizational shell for the efforts of Edge, Van Name, and Brant, it played the dominant role in bringing the Olympic National Park into existence. While other conservation groups, such as the Mountaineers and the Wilderness Society, supported efforts to create a park, it was the Emergency Conservation Committee that was the driving force.[25]

Throughout the 1920s, the U.S. Forest Service planned for utilization of the timber in the Mount Olympus National Monument as if it had not existed, while the U.S. Park Service denied that the monument was of park quality and refused to spearhead a movement to create a national park out of the monument.[26] This all changed when Franklin Roosevelt virtually dumped the monument in the Park Service's lap, much to the surprise of both the Forest and Park Service. An aggressive Harold Ickes, secretary of interior, was only too happy to take the monument under his jurisdiction.[27] Once the monument was transferred to the Park Service, the campaign for a park began in earnest with the central goal of bringing the westside old-growth rain forests under protection within park boundaries.

Opposition to a national park came primarily from the U.S. Forest Service, the governor of Washington State, the state planning council, and local timber interests. The governor and the planning council were primarily concerned with the loss of timber that would result from the creation of a national park.[28] The Forest Service took a defensive position arguing that the highest use of peninsula forests was for timber and that recreation was generally compatible with utilization for timber. The Forest Service argued that access to timber was needed in order to maintain employment and economic stability in the region into the future. Much of the timber on private lands in the area had been cutover, and the Forest Service claimed that national forest sawtimber was needed to bridge the gap until second growth timber matured on private lands. In addition, the Forest Service sought to establish a pulp industry on the peninsula to better utilize the western hemlock that was readily available in the national forest. The credibility of Forest Service plans was questionable in light of depressed conditions in the pulp and paper market as well as the sawtimber market during the 1930s. Nonetheless, the Forest Service used its economic arguments to mobilize opposition to the park proposal and suggested that the park service proposal would take income from 19,400 people in the peninsula area.[29] The Forest Service did attempt to mollify preservationist interests by creating a primitive area adjacent to the national monument in 1929 and expanding it in 1936 and by developing the so-called Cleator Plan for recreation in the national forest.[30] The Forest Service never did deal effectively with the Olympic elk preservation issue and was constantly plagued with complaints about excessive elk kills during regulated hunts and habitat accessibility problems for the elk.[31]

The Emergency Conservation Committee was ultimately successful in its goal of creating an Olympic National Park that encompassed significant stands of old-growth forests by arousing public opinion through the publication of pamphlets on the park distributed with funds provided by Rosalie Edge and through the use of the close ties Irving Brant had to the Roosevelt administration. Brant exposed to Ickes how the Park Service had actually resisted the idea of a park, and, in particular, a park that encompassed the westside rain forests.[32] Irving Clark, president of the Mountaineers, was also recruited to the ECC's campaign for a park.[33] The ECC's proposal for a large park with Ickes's approval was introduced in 1935 by Congressman Monrad C. Wallgren, whose district included much of the Olympic peninsula area.

In the face of continuing resistance to a large park by the Park Service itself, the Forest Service, and local timber interests, a bill was eventually sheperded through Congress and signed by the president in 1938 for an Olympic National Park of 648,000 acres, which could be expanded by presidential proclamation to 898,292 acres. The initial acreage excluded much of the westside old-growth, but this was brought into the park by the president soon after creation of the park.[34] Much of the credit for creation of Olympic National Park goes to President Roosevelt and his secretary of the interior, Harold Ickes. Ickes saw the expansion of the national park system as one of his principle missions. On the suggestion of Ickes, Roosevelt visited the Olympic peninsula in 1937 and shortly after requested that the Forest Service desist from further opposition to a park.

To summarize, the Forest Service defended its control over Olympic National Forest by emphasizing and articulating its value commitment to timber primacy and sustained-yield forestry.[35] The Park Service ironically seemed to support the Forest Service's desire to keep old-growth forests out of the park. The Park Service apparently did not want to antagonize the Forest Service or local timber interests. The Park Service wanted to preserve its capacity to trade timber for alpine scenery with the Forest Service and timber for land with private landowners.[36] The Forest Service could have taken the views of recreationists and preservationists seriously and adopted a far-reaching preservation oriented program such as one suggested by Bob Marshall, but it refused to do so.[37] Although there was opposition to plans for a national park by timber interests and political figures in state and local government, there was a relatively large group that favored the creation of a park, some of whom were attracted by the increased tourism and economic activity that the park would provide. If the Forest Service had been able to appeal to recreationist and preservationist values, it probably could have retained jurisdiction over a much larger area. After all, many preservationists were suspicious of the Park Service's strong inclination toward road construction and the development of tourist facilities in untouched areas of significant natural beauty. Instead, the Forest Service maintained its basic value commitment while sacrificing its domain of responsibility. The real prime mover behind park legislation was a very small group of nonlocal citizen activists in the Emergency Conservation Committee.

The Olympic National Park controversy was unique for a couple of reasons. For the first time a national park was created over the objection of local commodity interests and despite the fact that the park included significant stands of marketable old-growth timber. Because of its inaccessibility and because of extensive alternative supplies of standing timber, commodity interests paid little attention to Mount Rainier National Park at the time of its creation. According to Alfred Runte, as already noted, national parks were created in the nineteenth century out of worthless lands, that is, lands not containing valuable commodities. With the creation of Olympic National Park, the worthless lands requirement no longer applied in the national park creation process. Moreover, by the time of the creation of the park, the abundance of timber on private lands was diminishing, and it was becoming clear that the national forests were to become a major supplier of large, old-growth timber in the near future. Up to this point, the U.S. Forest Service had played a largely custodial role in the management of the national forests, and the timber industry had no real objection to the reserving of timberlands because it reduced the supply of timber to the market and kept the price for timber higher than otherwise. The Olympic controversy, consequently, marked a turning point in Pacific Northwest wilderness politics in the direction of confrontation between preservationists on the one side and the U.S. Forest Service and commodity interests on the other.

In the 1930s when the Olympic National Park debate was underway, timber dependency in Washington State was still near its peak. Because the Olympic National Park issue largely involved national interests and was decided at the highest political levels in the national government, local timber dependency probably played a limited role in determining the final decision on the extent of forest preservation. However, from the 1960s on, this all began to change. In the 1960s, local preservationists began to play a more significant role in decisions to preserve wilderness and forestland, particularly after the passage of the Wilderness Act in 1964. The passage of this act was the culmination of the growth of a national wilderness movement.

Emergence of the Modern Wilderness Movement

The modern wilderness preservation movement did not really gain substantial momentum in this country until the 1950s. Growing public support for wilderness preservation can be traced in part to the growing popularity of outdoor recreation and in part to the growing threat of economic development or resource exploitation in areas of natural beauty.[38] One form of resource exploitation that threatened pristine areas was timber harvesting in the national forests. Since relatively little timber was harvested from the national forests before World War II, conflict between advocates of forest preservation and timber utilization seldom occurred.[39] With the growth of demand for timber after the war, and with the declining availability of timber on private lands, this situation underwent a significant change. Timber cutting in the national forests increased dramatically, and conflict between wilderness preservation advocates and those desiring increased timber harvests from the national forests accelerated.

World War II was a turning point for timber production from the national forests. In 1929, the national forests provided only 4 percent of the U.S.

timber supply, and timber production from the national forests remained at relatively low levels in the 1930s. National forest timber production quickly increased during World War II, was up to 13 percent of the U.S. timber supply by 1952, and reached 22 percent in 1962. Since then, harvests from the national forests have remained about at the same level.[40] Much of the growth in national forest timber production after World War II took place in western Washington and Oregon, an area denoted by the Forest Service as the Douglas fir region.

Log production in the Douglas fir region dropped sharply during the Great Depression and recovered during and after World War II, surpassing previous peak levels in the 1950s (Table 4-4). Production growth continued in the 1960s and began to level out in the 1970s. The public portion of the harvest, including timber from state-owned and Bureau of Land Management lands as well as the national forests, increased from 22 percent in 1949 to 40 percent in 1970. Log production from the national forests increased from 10 percent of the total harvest in 1949 to 24.6 percent in 1970. Over this period, the Forest Service as well as other public sector owners of timberland clearly played an increasingly important role as major timber suppliers.[41]

Debate continues over the motivation of the Forest Service. Is it a value-driven agency following principles of timber primacy, sustained yield, and local community stability or is it driven by the classic bureaucratic propensity to enlarge its budget and scope of activity? Either view would explain the expansion of timber sales from the national forests after World War II.[42] The expansion of timber sales from World War II on was compatible with the founding goals of the Forest Service as originally articulated by Gifford Pinchot since there was ample room for timber harvest growth without violating sustained-yield principles, and it has been shown that increasing timber sales result in increased Forest Service budgets.[43] While expanding timber sales from the national forests is compatible with either set of motives, the creation of wilderness areas is not. Wilderness areas are inherently incompatible with timber primacy values, and wilderness areas by their very nature do not result in budget increases, since they do not require substantial resources for their administration.

Although the Forest Service lacked a fundamental interest in wilderness preservation, it was forced in the 1930s to pay more attention to wilderness preservation and recreation because of increasing threats by an expansion-minded secretary of the interior, Harold Ickes, to enlarge the domain of the National Park Service at the expense of the Forest Service.[44] In order to forestall incursions into its territory, the Forest Service adopted the so-called U-regulations to replace the less precise L-series of regulations. The L-regulations adopted in 1929 urged regional foresters to set aside areas where primitive conditions would be maintained. The new U-regulations established in 1939 created three categories of roadless area: wilderness, wild, and recreation. Timber harvesting and other activities were excluded from the first two categories and would be permitted in the third category only under restrictions established by the chief forester. Wilderness areas were to be over 100,000 acres in size while wild areas were to be less than 100,000 acres. Wilderness areas were to be established by the secretary of agriculture and wild areas by the chief forester, and all primitive areas were to be studied for reclassification under the new program. A major advocate within the Forest Service for the creation of wilderness in the national forests had been the well-known founder of the Wilderness Society, Robert Marshall. With Marshall's untimely death, however, opponents of wilderness preservation in the Forest Service regained influence, and progress was very slow in reclassifying primitive areas under the U-regulations. Nonetheless, an external threat to the Forest Service resulted in the creation of a regulatory framework for wilderness preservation.[45]

After World War II, both the national parks and forests were inundated with hoards of outdoor recreationists. The outdoor recreation boom was fueled by an unprecedented prosperity, increased leisure, and improved mobility associated with the growth of automobile ownership and an expanding highway system. Most recreationists were not interested in undergoing the rigors necessary to experience wilderness on its own terms by hiking long distances but wanted, instead, motorized access and developed facilities. After a period of stringent budget restrictions and general neglect during the war, national park facilities were in dismal shape, and the Park Service responded with a substantial spending program directed at expanding tourist facilities, often to the consternation of wilderness advocates.[46]

Because of its larger size, the national forest system has always provided more recreation opportunities than the national parks and faced a dramatic increase of use in the 1950s despite an apparent Forest Service bias against it. Recreation programs in the national forests had always been of secondary importance because of the Forest Service's primary value commitment to timber production. Nonetheless, the Forest Service was wary of the Park Service's aggressive attitude towards acquisition of national forestland for inclusion in national parks and consequently undertook a recreation program of its own and increased budget allocations specifically designated for recreation. Wilderness preservationists generally perceived the Forest Service as favoring timber production over wilderness and therefore supported the Park Service in its land acquisition efforts despite reservations about the latter's emphasis on tourist facility development.[47] The Forest Service's expanded recreation budget did not find favor with the traditional national forest commodity users, who looked dimly on increasing competition for resources from recreationists and wilderness preservationists.

In the 1950s, the Forest Service was faced with growing demand not only for recreation in the national forests but for timber as well. The forests products industry after World War II shifted from a position of advocating restrictions on timber production in the national forests before the war in the face of declining demand for wood products to advocating expanding production after the war in the face of rapidly growing demand. Conflict between wilderness preservationists and timber interests in this situation was inevitable and emerged over the issue of reclassifying primitive areas established by the 1929 L-regulations as wilderness or wild areas under the 1938 U-regulations. Because of the controversy surrounding reclassification and the need to follow an elaborate procedure, forest supervisors were instructed to manage primitive areas as if they had already been reclassified until they could be studied. In the 1950s, many acres were removed from wilderness designation because they contained merchantable timber, although they were replaced with substitute acres. The result was opposition to elimination of timberland by wilderness groups and an increasing belief that wilderness designation should be removed from Forest Service hands.[48]

Even though it had increased the recreation component of its budget, the Forest Service was still under fire from the preservationists because of its emphasis on timber production at the expense of wilderness preservation, and it still feared incursions on the national forests by the Park Service. To strengthen its hand in defending its territory against the Park Service and in balancing off the demands of the various special interests concerned with resource use in the national forests, the Forest Service pressed for a new statement of its mission explicitly incorporating recreation along with the traditional national forest commodity uses. The statement took form as the Multiple Use Sustained Yield Act of 1960, and it defined the multiple uses to include outdoor recreation, range, timber, watershed, and wildlife and fish. The concept of multiple use was set out in the bill as follows:

Multiple use means the management of all the various renewable surface resources of the combination that will best meet the needs of the American people; making the most judicious use of the land for some or all of these resources or related services over areas large enough to provide sufficient latitude for periodic adjustments in use to conform to changing needs and conditions; that some land will be used for less than all of the resources; and harmonious and coordinated management of the various resources, each with the other, without impairment of the productivity of the land, with consideration being given to the relative values of the various resources, and not necessarily the combination of uses that will give the greatest dollar return.

The act obviously lacks clarity and failed to establish concrete standards for resource use. The act gave the Forest Service considerable leeway in its resource use decision making.[49]

The Multiple Use Sustained Yield Act can be interpreted in two possible ways. First, the Forest Service sought the Act to give it the autonomy it needed to mollify the demands of recreationists and preservationists with the least amount of resources possible while pursuing its primary interest in timber management. Alternatively, the Forest Service sought the act in order to embrace the demands of the recreationists and to balance those demands against commodity interests in such a way as to maximize its sphere of activity and its budget.[50] Preservationists were clearly suspicious of the Forest Service's motivations, and the Sierra Club did not support the act on the grounds that the Forest Service was excessively timber oriented and could not be trusted to make decisions on wilderness creation.[51] While recreationists appeared to be satisfied, preservationists apparently could not be bought off by the act. In the eyes of the Forest Service, wilderness additions would be more damaging to timber harvesting opportunities than outdoor recreation, such as hunting, fishing, and skiing, and it would not likely garner very large budget increases. Whether the Forest Service was using the Multiple Use Sustained Yield Act to expand its basic value orientation to include recreation and other goals, to simply increase the recreation component of its budget, or to gain political flexibility in sticking to its long-standing commitment to timber primacy, it was not serving wilderness preservation interests, at least in the eyes of the Sierra Club.[52] Although the timber industry was skeptical of multiple use at first, on the grounds that it would dilute the 1897 legislative commitment to timber production and watershed preservation, timber interests decided to support the act after being assured that multiple use would not supersede the 1897 legislation.[53]

Not trusting the Forest Service and other public agencies to adequately protect wilderness areas, preservationists began in the 1950s to lobby for a wilderness bill. The political prospects for such a bill improved as the consequence of increased public support for wilderness preservation groups traceable to the general growth in outdoor recreation and to the substantial controversy surrounding the Echo Park Dam.[54] This Bureau of Reclamation's proposed dam on the Green River would have inundated much of the Dinosaur National Monument, but a Sierra Club and Wilderness Society campaign against the project ultimately won a congressional halt order despite intense opposition from water and development interests.[55] (See discussion in Chapter 1.)

This victory set the stage for the introduction of the first wilderness bill in 1956. The bill proposed to designate as wilderness areas almost all of the primitive areas in the national forests and forty-eight national parks and monuments and nineteen wildlife refuges and game ranges. Additions could be made by the president or Congress and modifications could be made by the secretary of agriculture or interior. The Forest Service, the Park Service, and the national forest commodity users were strongly opposed to the measure. The Forest Service saw it infringing on its multiple use policy, the Park Service resented the implication that it was not already protecting wilderness, and commodity users opposed the locking up of valuable resources.[56] Nine years of deliberation and sixty-five different bills were introduced before the Wilderness Act was finally passed in 1964. The act was a substantially scaled down version of the 1956 bill. Only those lands already designated as wilderness or wild lands under the 1939 U-regulations were automatically included as wilderness, and only Congress had the authority to designate new wilderness areas. In addition, certain established uses of wilderness areas could continue, and prospecting and mineral exploration could continue until 1983 after which previously filed claims could be worked under restrictions to preserve wilderness values. Although the act did not expand the wilderness system beyond that already existing under Forest Service regulations nor was it any more restrictive as to permitted uses, it gave national recognition to the wilderness concept, made wilderness areas easier to defend as part of a national system, extended the wilderness concept to the national parks and wildlife refuges, and placed limits on mining activity.[57]

The passage of the Wilderness Act really marks the beginning of the use of grassroots pressure group politics by wilderness advocates in their preservation efforts. While nothing new was won in the way of preserved areas, Congress now had the authority to designate new wilderness areas, and Congress could be more readily subjected to political pressure than the U.S. Forest Service or the National Park Service. A transition from the type of politics that prevailed in the Olympic National Park controversy, involving small groups of political elites, to the more contemporary politics of conflict between membership-based preservationist organizations, such as the Sierra Club and Wilderness Society on one side and the commodity-oriented U.S. Forest Service and timber interests on the other, was provided by the dispute surrounding the creation of the North Cascades National Park in the 1960s.

The North Cascades Controversy

The north Cascades controversy, as in the case of the Olympic National Park struggle, involved a conflict of visions for use of the area between preservationists and the two government agencies involved, the Forest Service and the Park Service. Unlike the Olympic case, a collection of nonwilderness recreationists were arrayed against the preservationists alongside commodity interests. The area involved in the controversy includes what today is the North Cascades National Park, the Mount Baker Recreation Area (administered by the Forest Service), the Glacier Peak and Pasayten wilderness areas, and the Ross Lake and Lake Chelan national recreation areas. The dominant feature of the area is a series of glaciated peaks beginning with Glacier Peak on the south and running north to the Canadian border. Some argue that these are among the most spectacular and beautiful peaks to be found in the mainland United States, and they are often referred to as the American Alps. These peaks divide the area into separate climatic zones, to the east, one characterized by sparse rainfall, and to the west, a wet temperate zone. On the west side are found heavy stands of high-quality, old-growth Douglas fir, particularly in the valley bottoms.[58]

Although access to the area prior to the 1950s was limited, resource development had nonetheless taken place. Extensive mining operations have been undertaken in the area, and a number of hydroelectric facilities have been constructed on north Cascade rivers. Large-scale timber harvesting has begun in the region only since World War II.[59] Prior to the 1950s, hiking and other recreational activity in the areas was limited because of difficult access, a situation that quickly changed with logging road construction.

Before passage of the national park legislation in 1968, the north Cascades area was under the management of the U.S. Forest Service. The area was originally part of the Washington forest reserve created in 1896 in the last days of the Cleveland administration.[60] A bill for a national park in the Mount Baker area was introduced as early as 1916, and the Park Service was recommending the establishment of a park in the north Cascades in the 1930s.[61] To forestall pressure from recreationists and the Park Service, the Forest Service established the Mount Baker Park Division in 1926, an unusual designation not used elsewhere, and the North Cascades Primitive Area and the Glacier Peak Cascade Recreation Unit in the 1930s. In 1940, the Glacier Peak unit was expanded and renamed the Glacier Peak Limited Area. Because of strong opposition from commodity users and local communities, the Forest Service backed off from a proposal for a more extensive limited area south of Glacier Peak in the 1930s.[62]

With increased timber harvesting from the three national forests located in the north Cascades in the 1950s, preservationists increased pressure on the Forest Service to set aside more areas as wilderness. The central concern of preservationist groups was the increased harvesting of old-growth timber in valleys that provided access routes to the scenic high country. These valleys were an integral part of the wilderness in the eyes of the preservationists. The Forest Service responded in 1957 with a proposal for a 434,000-acre Glacier Peak Wilderness Area, a proposal that excluded too much timberland according to preservationists. In 1959, the Forest Service modified this proposal by further reducing the amount of forested land along stream corridors by 11,075 acres. Because of an outcry from preservationists, the secretary of agriculture overruled local Forest Service officials and added 35,175 acres to the Glacier Peak Wilderness Area in 1960, a move that may have been stimulated by increased talk of creating a national park in the area.[63]

Having demonstrated an apparent bias towards timber harvesting, the Forest Service was increasingly viewed as an unreliable custodian of wilderness areas by preservationist groups. Consequently, in 1963, the North Cascades Conservation Council, a Seattle-based group of wilderness advocates, published its proposal for a North Cascades National Park composed of 1,038,665 acres that included the Glacier Peak Wilderness Area (458,508 acres), the Eldorado Peaks to the north, and adjacent stream valley bottoms. The amount of acres outside of the Glacier Peak wilderness in the proposal was 849,681, and the inclusion of this area in a park was projected to reduce allowed annual harvests in the national forests by 35.93 million board feet. The Chelan National Mountain Recreation Area was also proposed for lands near Lake Chelan, and a North Cascades Wilderness Area was proposed to replace the North Cascades Primitive Area. The document outlined the frustrations experienced by preservationists in their dealings with the Forest Service and carefully enumerated the advantages of National Park Service management. The Sierra Club had supported the creation of a national park for several years, publishing park proposals in the Sierra Club Bulletin.[64]

Although the North Cascades Conservation Council proposal included measures that attempted to diminish the opposition of local communities and commodity users, the opposition to a North Cascades National Park was nonetheless intense, and the subsequent history of the controversy involved the shaping of park boundaries in such a way as to satisfy key interest groups. Local communities and timber companies were concerned about the timber that would be locked up in a national park; the state game department was concerned with its loss of jurisdiction over large portions of the area and hunters were concerned with restrictions on hunting; and the state wanted to maintain control of a cross-Cascades highway that was under construction. These interests as well as the jurisdictional concerns of the Forest Service and Park Service served to shape the final form the park was to take.

The first major step in the process toward creation of a park, after the issue was initially raised by preservationist groups, was the creation of a joint study team by the departments of agriculture and interior to make recommendations for management of the public lands in the Cascades from Mount Rainier National Park northward to the Canadian border. The study team ended up focusing its attention on the North Cascades area. Both the Park Service and Forest Service made separate recommendations to the study team. The Forest Service recommended the creation of some additional wilderness and the protection of scenic values in the Eldorado Peaks area as well as opening it up to mass recreation and nonwilderness travel, but it did not suggest fundamental change to the existing land management system.[65] The Forest Service continued to emphasize the importance of timber harvesting for the area's economy and attempted to reconcile continued commodity use with the preservation of scenic values. Little was conceded to the preservationist view in the Forest Service proposal.

Recommendations by the National Park Service did, however, suggest substantial changes in management and jurisdiction, but to the consternation of the preservationists did not go beyond the geographical bounds of areas that were already preserved and involved a high level of development oriented to mass recreation and nonwilderness travel. The Park Service proposed the creation of two national parks, one in the Mount Baker area and one in the Glacier Peak area. The Eldorado Peaks, an area that preservationists strongly desired to see remain as wilderness, was to be included in an Eldorado-Chelan National Recreation Area where development would be permitted. The Park Service thus appeared to be no more oriented to wilderness preservation than the Forest Service. The Park Service expected preservationist support regardless of what it did, and it wanted to limit opposition to a park by including only areas that were already designated as wilderness.[66] A key goal of the preservationists, to gain wilderness status for the Eldorado Peaks area, was not met in either the Forest Service or Park Service proposals. Nor was their desire to bring protection to the forested valleys surrounding the Glacier Peak wilderness.

When public hearings were held, Forest Service management was generally supported by chambers of commerce, sportsperson's groups, and units of local government while a national park was strongly supported by preservationists. After three years of investigation and deliberation, the study team came up with it own recommendation. It proposed the North Cascades National Park, which would include the Picket Range and the Eldorado Peaks, and an Okanagon Wilderness Area to the east of the park.[67] To the horror of the preservationists, the study team envisioned a high level of visitation to the park that would be encouraged through expanded access by "road, trail, water, and air," including tram and helicopter access.[68] The proposal was essentially a political compromise. The Mount Baker area was omitted from the park under pressure from the Forest Service, timber interests, and ski operators; active mines were also excluded; and most important, hunting areas were left out of the park. Members of the Forest Service, nonetheless, voiced displeasure with the increased emphasis on recreation at the expense of timber production and the transfer of jurisdiction to the Park Service.[69]

After President Lyndon Johnson indicated the need for a national park in the north Cascades in 1967, the secretary of interior sent a bill to Congress for a park with the approval of the secretary of agriculture. The bill (S. 1321) was introduced by Washington's two senators, Henry Jackson and Warren Magnuson. The bill altered the study team proposal by creating Ross Lake National Recreation Area along Ross Lake and the Skagit River, excluding a part of the route of the north cross-state highway from the park, and creating the Pasayten Wilderness Area to the east of Ross Lake. The area recommended to be in the national park by the Study Team was reduced in the Senate from 698,000 acres to 570,000 acres.[70] The bill also included a 10,000-acre addition to the Glacier Peak Wilderness Area along two river valleys. The only major modifications to the Senate bill after hearings were undertaken was to create Lake Chelan National Recreation Area of 62,000 acres, reducing the size of the proposed park to 508,000 acres, and to expand the Ross Lake National Recreation Area.

Preservationists were dissatisfied with the bill voted out of the Senate and introduced their own bill (H.R. 12129) in the House as well as amendments to the House version (H.R. 8970) of the Senate bill expanding protected areas and giving the park immediate wilderness classification under the terms of the Wilderness Act. Basically, wilderness advocates were unhappy because the proposed park in the administration bill preserved less land than they advocated in their North Cascades Conservation Council prospectus (508,000 acres vs. 850,000 acres) and protected very little of the forested lowland valleys surrounding the proposed park.

Local communities concerned with reductions in allowable timber harvests, hunters, ski area developers, and mining interests expressed intense opposition to the administration bill in both the Senate and House
hearings. After some political maneuvering, the administration bill (H.R.
8970) passed the House without modification and was signed into law.[71]

The creation of North Cascades National Park was the product of a
political compromise between commodity interests, mass recreationists,
preservationists, and two competing government agencies, the Park and
Forest services. While the amount of land protected from development
was substantially less than what preservationists wanted, they did get the
Eldorado Peaks included in the park and were able to get significant
restrictions on road building included in the legislation. Hunters and skiers
also were able to get key areas of interest to them excluded from either
park or wilderness status, and the wood products industry was able to
prevent significant amounts of merchantable timber from being included
in either the park or wilderness areas.[72] As in the Olympic National Park
controversy, the Forest Service emphasized the importance of timber,
made only limited concessions to preservationists, and consequently lost
its jurisdictional battle to the Park Service.

Although the preservationists failed to get everything they wanted,
they had been the prime movers in setting off the controversy in the first
place, and new areas were indeed brought under protection from development or commodity use. The amount of commercial forestland locked
up as a result of the legislation reduced the Forest Service's allowable
harvest in the area by approximately 6 million board feet per year.[73] For
the first time, local wilderness preservation groups were the prime movers
in initiating debate over the permanent preservation of a significant natural
area, one that included stands of old-growth forests.

Pacific Northwest Wilderness
Preservation: 1964-1984

The history of wilderness preservation in the national forests immediately after passage of the Wilderness Act in 1964 involved several
significant occurrences: (1) the evaluation of previously designated primitive areas by the U.S. Forest Service for inclusion in the wilderness
system, (2) an attempt by preservationists to outflank the Forest Service
in designating wilderness areas with the promotion and passage of the
Endangered Wilderness Act, and (3) the investigation of roadless areas
by the Forest Service for possible inclusion in the wilderness system.
The roadless area process culminated in the so-called RARE II study and
the subsequent passage of wilderness bills for Oregon and Washington in
1984.

One of the compromises resulting in passage of the Wilderness Act was the exclusion of all Forest Service primitive areas from the wilderness system until they could be subjected to further study. The act required that the Forest Service study these areas within a 10 year period.[74] While the Wilderness Act defines wilderness somewhat ambiguously, the Forest Service adopted a "purist" definition of wilderness in its analysis of areas for possible inclusion in the wilderness system. Wilderness areas, from the Forest Service perspective, could not show the imprint of humans. While preservationists wanted to see wilderness areas managed in such a way as to minimize human impact on the land, they also wanted to expand the wilderness system and did not want to see areas having significant wilderness values excluded because of the presence of a few old buildings or a firebreak. Preservationists argued that the Forest Service took a purist position in order to minimize the amount of land that could ultimately be designated as wilderness.[75]

Mount Jefferson Wilderness

An example of conflict over the purity doctrine was the recommendation by President Johnson in 1967 for Mount Jefferson Wilderness Area of 97,000 acres. The recommendation was based on the Forest Service study of the previously existing primitive area and excluded Marion Lake, which penetrated 3 miles into the proposed wilderness area and included primitive boating and recreation facilities.[76] The original bill introduced in the Senate was amended to include the 3,000 acre Marion Lake area with a provision that it be returned to its wilderness condition by removing boats and facilities. The Wilderness Society argued that another area, which had been partially logged purposely to keep it out of the wilderness area, should be included because it served as a buffer zone containing lowland old-growth forest types; but Congress did not go along with this request.[77]

The creation of the Mount Jefferson Wilderness Area also marked the entrance of Oregon wilderness groups into preservationist politics. As early as 1961, a coalition of local groups, including the Oregon Cascades Conservation Council, Pacific Northwest Chapter of the Sierra Club, and Oregon Wildlife Federation had submitted a recommendation to the U.S. Forest Service for a 117,000-acre Mount Jefferson Wilderness Area.[78] A number of these same local groups as well as others participated at the hearings for the Mount Jefferson Wilderness Area, focusing much of the attention on the purity doctrine and expanding the boundaries recommended by the U.S. Forest Service to include lowland forest areas.[79] While this was an important event for the Oregon wilderness movement, it was not nearly of the scope of the movement for the North Cascades National Park in western Washington.

The Alpine Lakes Wilderness

Following the creation of North Cascades National Park, the next major episode involving preservation of a major natural area including old-growth forests was the creation of the Alpine Lakes wilderness and recreation areas. The process by which the Alpine Lakes Wilderness Area was created in 1976 was somewhat unique and does not fit into the primitive area or roadless area evaluation process. The regional forester had designated 256,000 acres as the Alpine Lakes Limited Area in 1946, a designation that meant the area was to be reserved from timber harvesting while it was studied for its wilderness and scenic values as well as for other resource uses. In 1965, the North Cascades Study Team, along with making recommendations for North Cascades National Park, recommended the creation of the Alpine Lakes Wilderness Area of 162,549 acres and the Enchantment Lakes Wilderness Area of 32,142 acres. Conservation groups had proposed 334,000 acres for wilderness in 1963. Subsequent proposals followed from three groups—the Alpine Lakes Protection Society, formed in 1968, for a 364,800-acre wilderness, the Northwest Chapter of the Sierra Club for a 533,000-acre wilderness, and the North Cascades Conservation Council for a 580,000-acre wilderness.

In the U.S. Forest Service's draft environmental impact statement on the Alpine Lakes area, wilderness alternatives ranging from zero to 365,000 acres were presented, and in its report on a proposed Alpine Lakes Wilderness Area the total acres considered was 292,192. By 1975, the wilderness preservation groups had coalesced around a proposal under the banner of the Alpine Lakes Protection Society for a 575,000-acre Alpine Lakes Wilderness Area and a 1,016,000-acre National Recreation Area surrounding it.[80] In congressional hearings, the preservationist proposal was pitted against a timber industry proposal for a 216,000-acre wilderness that excluded much of the forested valleys leading to the upland areas, and a U.S. Forest Service proposal of 292,000 acres.[81] In the final legislation, 306,934 acres was set aside for wilderness and 86,426 for intended wilderness.[82]

Wilderness advocates were thus able to win a wilderness bill much closer to their own proposal than to industry's. This occurred even though the timber industry lobbied heavily to limit the loss of forested valleys from the U.S. Forest Service timber base.[83] Although the North Cascades Study Team had initially proposed a wilderness area designation for the Alpine Lakes, the central force that seems to have led to ultimate designation of the Alpine Lakes Wilderness Area was the lobbying efforts of local preservation groups, in particular the Alpine Lakes Protection Society. The central issue in determining the configuration and acreage of the wilderness area was whether the wilderness area was to reach down into the lower valleys and encompass significant amounts of merchantable timber. The preservationists had some success in bringing old-growth in the lower valleys under wilderness designation in the face of significant opposition from the forest products industry.

De Facto Wilderness and Roadless Areas

The Wilderness Act required that the Forest Service complete its review of primitive areas by 1974. The review process excluded roadless and undeveloped areas within the national forests that potentially qualified for addition to the wilderness system, and the Forest Service hoped to put off a review of these areas until after 1974. However, pressure soon began to build for the inclusion of areas in the wilderness system that were not part of the review process, areas referred to as de facto wilderness by preservationists. Because the Forest Service had essentially been a custodial agency for the national forests up to World War II, much of the national forests remained untouched by commodity users and thus had wilderness characteristics.[84] Under pressure from local interests and the Wilderness Society, the first de facto wilderness bill passed in 1972 establishing Scapegoat Wilderness Area in Montana.

Desiring to maintain control of the wilderness designation process, the Forest Service began its Roadless Area Review Studies in 1971. In 1971-72, the Forest Service reviewed 1,449 roadless areas containing 55.9 million acres, and concluded that 12.3 million acres were worthy of further study for possible wilderness designation.[85] Preservationists, however, objected to these conclusion on the grounds that 44 million acres were dropped from consideration for ill-defined reasons and that eastern national forests and grasslands were left out of the inventory.[86] The Forest Service had hoped that its Roadless Area Review Studies (RARE I) would qualify as environmental impact statements under the National Environmental Policy Act, but this turned out not to be the case. The Sierra Club brought suit against the Forest Service in 1972 arguing that it should be required to produce a satisfactory environmental impact statement before proceeding with development in de facto wilderness areas, a provision accepted voluntarily by the Forest Service.[87] This decision, in effect, removed 56 million acres from utilization by commodity interests until detailed studies were undertaken, and gave the preservationist movement increased leverage in the wilderness designation process. The Roadless Area Review Studies provided wilderness advocates with a wealth of information on de facto wilderness not previously available.

The Endangered American Wilderness Act in Western Oregon

Another strategy adopted by wilderness groups to attempt to wrest control of the wilderness designation process from the Forest Service was the proposing of the Endangered Wilderness Act in 1977 by Representative Morris K. Udall of Arizona.[88] This bill included areas in Oregon not recommended by the Forest Service in RARE I and was intended to give preservationists the upper hand over the Forest Service in wilderness designation. Also, these areas did not fit the Forest Service's purist definition of wilderness. With support from the new administration, the bill passed in 1978, adding the disputed French Pete area to the Three Sisters Wilderness Area, increasing the size of the Kalmiopsis and Mount Hood wilderness areas, and creating the Wild Rogue Wilderness Area. While the Endangered Wilderness Act passed successfully, the Forest Service regained a significant degree of control over wilderness designation in the RARE II process even though it went into it reluctantly.[89]

The French Pete dispute is interesting because it typifies the kind of conflict between the Forest Service and preservationist groups that seems to be so common in the modern wilderness designation process. It is also interesting because it marks the first major political victory by Oregon wilderness advocacy groups where a significant amount of old growth was reserved, and this victory occurred after relative timber dependency had begun to decline in Oregon. After instituting the U-regulations in 1939, the Forest Service undertook a reclassification program involving the study of primitive areas under the old L-regulations to determine whether they should be classified as wilderness under the U-regulations.

As primitive areas previously secure from timber cutting because of their remoteness became more accessible with new road construction in the 1950s, reclassification became a highly controversial issue. Commodity users and mass recreationists, such as ski resort developers and users, did not want to see areas locked up in wilderness classifications that placed significant restrictions on land use. Under pressure from these groups, the Forest Service proposed removal of many acres from wilderness classifications, including 53,000 acres of merchantable timber (the French Pete area) from the Three Sisters Primitive Area in Oregon in 1954. The remaining 200,000 acres was classified as wilderness under the Forest Service scheme and became a permanent part of the wilderness system under the 1964 Wilderness Act. Timber interests originally wanted 70,000 acres excluded while some recreation groups would have been satisfied with an exclusion limited to 40,000 acres. Preservation groups held out for retention of all acreage in wilderness.[90] The regional forester explained in 1954 that additional harvesting of timber in the area would prevent local mills from closing.[91]

By the late 1960s, the original size of the unroaded portion of French Pete had been reduced, and the Willamette Forest supervisor was announcing more timber sales in the area. With encouragement from the Sierra Club, a Save French Pete Committee was organized by local wilderness preservationists. After a protracted battle with the preservationists on one side and the Forest Service and timber industry on the other, the area was added to the Three Sisters Wilderness Area with the passage of the Endangered American Wilderness Act of 1978.[92]

The Endangered American Wilderness Act constituted the first real success experienced by Oregon wilderness activists in preserving lowland old-growth forests, and it occurred at a later point in time than the initial successes of wilderness preservation efforts in Washington State. The absence of earlier preservationist victories in Oregon is not for lack of organizational activity. The Oregon Omnibus Wilderness Act, which was later collapsed into the Endangered American Wilderness Act, was conceived as early as 1971, although it did not emerge in Congress as a bill until 1975.[93] By the mid-1970s, Oregon was considered by some to be the "best-organized state in the country for wilderness action."[94] The Oregon Wilderness Coalition made up of some twenty local groups had formed by 1974, and it contained individual groups, such as Sierra Club chapters and Friends of the Three Sisters, which had formed as early as 1954. In the early 1960s, the Sierra Club supported an Oregon Cascades National Park, and it opened its first Northwest conservation representative office in Eugene in 1961. Yet, it was not until 1978 that a major wilderness expansion took place in Oregon. Why? Prior to that the resistance to wilderness by a politically powerful timber industry could not be overcome.[95] It was not until the 1970s that the relative dependency of the Oregon economy began to shrink significantly, potentially undermining timber industry political strength.

RARE II

Ad hoc preservationist proposals, such as the Endangered American Wilderness Act, and the environmental impact statement requirements of the National Environmental Policy Act created uncertainty about future access to national forest timber for the timber industry. To eliminate this uncertainty, the industry wanted a final determination of the allocation of forestlands to wilderness and timber production. After a meeting with industry representatives in 1976, the newly appointed assistant secretary of agriculture for conservation, Rupert Cutler, a former assistant executive directory of the Wilderness Society, agreed that the wilderness planning process had to be speeded up. The result was a second roadless area study process referred to as RARE II involving a total of 65.7 million acres. At this point in time, 15.7 million acres were already in the wilderness system and 3.5 million acres of proposed wilderness were included in bills pending before Congress.[96] While the Wilderness Society felt that RARE II would tend to favor the timber industry, the Sierra Club initially supported it but later became disillusioned by a perceived bias in the process in favor of industry. Although initially suspicious of RARE II, the timber industry took advantage of it and did a good job in presenting its views in public hearings and letter writing campaigns.

The end result was a recommendation of 15 million acres for wilderness, 36 million for nonwilderness, and 11 million for further planning. Preservationists were not pleased with the outcome, desiring to see more land placed in the further planning category. Commodity interests expressed qualified approval of the proposal. The result was a great disappointment to Washington and Oregon preservationists where 4,240,613 acres were recommended for nonwilderness, 637,000 for wilderness, and only 618,913 for further study. For the Pacific Northwest, RARE II appears to have worked to the advantage of commodity users in the national forests rather than preservationists. However, this result was modified significantly in the passage of the 1984 Washington and Oregon wilderness acts, a topic to be given extensive treatment in the next section.

Wilderness Preservation to 1984: Summary

To summarize preservationists' efforts up to 1984, in the early history of the movement to reserve forestlands from timber harvesting, the advocates for preservation were a rather small, elite group. They were able to accomplish the creation of forest reserves and the Mount Rainier National Park even though there was no mass outpouring of public demand to do so. One reason they were successful is that the lands involved at the time were essentially worthless for commodity production purposes. Timber supplies were abundant elsewhere and reserved lands were relatively inaccessible. By the time of the Olympic National Park controversy, conflict between preservationists and the U.S. Forest Service with its timber industry constituency had intensified. At this point, preservationists still constituted a relatively small, elite group.

The passage of the Wilderness Act in 1964 marked the beginning of heavy involvement by membership-based organizations, such as the Sierra Club and the Wilderness Society, in political efforts to preserve wilderness areas. The 1964 Wilderness Act did not add to the lands already reserved under Forest Service regulations, but it did assure the continued preservation of these lands, and it provided a vehicle for seeking to bring additional lands under a permanent preservation umbrella. The first major successes experienced by membership-based wilderness advocacy groups in the Pacific Northwest occurred in western Washington with the creation of North Cascades National Park in 1968 and Alpine Lakes Wilderness Area in 1976. Both of these victories occurred after a substantial reduction in economic dependency on timber in Washington State. While the final boundaries of the Mount Jefferson Wilderness Area in Oregon reflected a victory for wilderness advocates fighting against the purity doctrine, it cannot really be compared in scope to the creation of North Cascades National Park. The creation of Mount Jefferson Wilderness Area in some form was preordained by the requirement to evaluate primitive areas for wilderness classification by the 1964 Wilderness Act.

The first real victory by organized wilderness advocacy groups came in western Oregon with the passage of the Endangered Wilderness Act in 1978, but this occurred only after relative dependency on timber in the Oregon economy had declined significantly. Wilderness preservation victories have been less extensive and have come later in western Oregon than western Washington, where more old-growth forestland has been locked up historically. Thus, it appears timber dependency indeed may have played a role historically in determining the extent of forestland preservation.

RARE II, Wilderness, Old-Growth
Preservation, and Timber Dependency

While the higher level of forestland and old-growth preservation in western Washington relative to western Oregon and the recent growth in the amount of forestland preserved in both states are consistent with the hypothesis that declining timber dependency increases the political feasibility of forestland preservation efforts, neither of these phenomena really prove the point. A more careful analysis of the 1984 Oregon and Washington wilderness act additions to preserved lands can, however, provide additional insight into the role of timber dependency in the preservation of forestlands. These acts were the culmination of a roadless area review process (RARE II) by the U.S. Forest Service that resulted in recommendations to Congress for the preservation of some roadless areas as wilderness and the opening up of other roadless areas for commodity production.[97]

The allocations of roadless areas recommended by the Forest Service in its RARE II study for western Oregon and western Washington are presented in Tables 6-5 and 6-6. The proportion of the total roadless area

Table 6-5
Roadless Area Data for Western Oregon:
Average Values by U.S. Forest Service RARE II Designation

Variable	Wilderness	Non-wilderness	Further planning	Total
Development Opportunity Rating System (DORS)	8.29	12.18	7.00	11.35
Programmed Harvest (PH)	2.86	3.76	1.40	3.53
Wilderness Attribute Rating System (WARS)	19.00	18.27	21.00	18.49
Total roadless areas	14	67	3	84
Acres	195,524	1,026,105	64,836	1,286,465
% total acres	15.2	79.8	5.0	100
Total Programmed Harvest	40.04	251.92	4.20	296.52

Note: DORS, PH, and WARS are average values for roadless areas. PH is measured in terms of millions of board feet per year, as is total programmed harvest. The source for this table is USDA Forest Service, *RARE II Final Environmental Statement* (Washington, D.C.: U.S. Government Printing Office, 1979).

Table 6-6
Roadless Area Data for Western Washington:
Average Values by U.S. Forest Service RARE II Designation

Variable	Wilderness	Non-wilderness	Further planning	Total
Development Opportunity Rating System (DORS)	7.50	11.90	9.90	10.80
Programmed Harvest (PH)	3.47	4.29	3.16	3.95
Wilderness Attribute Rating System (WARS)	24.40	20.56	22.82	21.62
Total roadless areas	10	39	11	60
Acres	209,950	802,854	200,090	1,212,894
% total acres	17.3	66.2	16.5	100
Total Programmed Harvest	34.70	167.31	34.76	236.77

Note: DORS, PH, and WARS are average values for roadless areas. PH is measured in terms of millions of board feet per year, as is total programmed harvest. The source for this table is USDA Forest Service, *RARE II Final Environmental Statement* (Washington, D.C.: U.S. Government Printing Office, 1979).

recommended for wilderness by the Forest Service in both states was roughly the same, 17 percent for western Washington and 15 percent for western Oregon. For each roadless area, the Forest Service estimated the amount of programmed harvest that would be undertaken on an annual basis if timber harvesting was permitted. In western Washington, the percentage of total possible programmed timber harvest from roadless areas lost as a consequence of wilderness recommendations by the Forest Service was 14.6 percent, while the comparable figure for western Oregon was 13.5 percent. For western Washington, the programmed harvest lost because of Forest Service wilderness recommendations was 0.51 percent of the average total annual harvest for the 1970s, while the comparable figure for western Oregon was 0.48 percent.

These data suggest that the Forest Service did not take into account differences in timber dependency in the two states. Rather, the Forest Service may have been attempting to preserve its ability to sell timber to the greatest extent possible in both states. While the Forest Service is required by law to manage forests for multiple use, those who have studied the behavior of the Forest Service suggest that timber production and sales are its real goals.[98]

Some go so far as to suggest that the Forest Service behaves so as to maximize its budget. More land devoted to timber production and sales would bring forth larger budgets in comparison to land devoted to wilderness because a portion of timber sales revenue is returned to the local national forest for use in reforestation under provisions of the Knudsen-Vandenberg Act.[99]

Consequently, timber production and sales are likely to generate bigger budgets than the administration of wilderness areas. If the national forest administrators were pursuing similar ends in both Oregon and Washington, such as maximizing their budget levels, then there is no reason to expect that relative timber dependency would play much of a role in either state in decisions to allocate roadless areas to a wilderness category. In both states, the Forest Service would attempt to minimize the amount of land devoted to wilderness and keep those lands with the largest timber sales potential in the nonwilderness category. Given the similarity of roadless area characteristics and national forest goals in the two states, one would expect similar relative results in terms of wilderness allocations.

The Forest Service would also most likely assign those roadless areas to wilderness that have a relatively low potential for timber sales. This view is supported by some of the other data in Tables 6-6 and 6-7. This data includes the average values of the Wilderness Attributes Rating System (WARS), the Development Opportunities Rating System (DORS),

Table 6-7
U.S. Forest Service RARE II and
Congressional Wilderness Selection

	Western Oregon	Western Washington
RARE II		
Wilderness Acres	195,524	209,950
WARS	19.00	24.40
DORS	8.29	7.50
Total programmed harvest	40.04	34.70
Congress		
Wilderness Acres	396,376	519,354
WARS	20.77	24.00
DORS	10.68	8.05
Total programmed harvest	97.90	85.60

Note: WARS and DORS are in terms of mean values for roadless areas selected as wilderness. Total programmed harvest is defined in terms of millions of board feet per year. The sources for this table are U.S.D.A. Forest Service, *RARE II Final Environmental Statement* (Washington, D.C.: U.S. Government Printing Office, 1979) and letters from each of the national forests in western Washington and western Oregon detailing the land area in each of the 1984 Wilderness Act wilderness areas. The roadless areas that were wholly or partly included in 1984 Wilderness Act wilderness areas were determined using roadless area and wilderness area maps. Wilderness area boundaries do not generally coincide with roadless area boundaries because of boundary adjustments made by Congress. Consequently, some wilderness areas are larger than their constituent roadless areas and some are smaller. Programmed harvest figures for wilderness areas were adjusted to reflect this using the ratio of the wilderness area acreage to the constituent roadless area acreage for each roadless area.

and the programmed timber harvest (PH) in millions of board feet per year. The WARS rating is an index of wilderness quality, ranging from a low of 4 to a high of 28, and is based on four factors, including naturalness, apparent naturalness, opportunity for solitude, and opportunity for a primitive recreation experience. The DORS rating is essentially an index of a benefit-cost ratio for renewable nonwilderness resources ranging from 0 to 15, with benefits set equal to costs at the number 5. For western Washington and Oregon, this ratio would be predominantly based on timber production since other renewable resources are relatively unimportant. The programmed harvest figure is the average amount the Forest Service would harvest per year if the roadless area were not selected for wilderness.[100] The DORS rating is probably a reasonable measure of the market value of timber in a given roadless area. If so, the Forest Service would desire to keep roadless areas out of wilderness classification that not only have a high programmed harvest (PH), but also a high development opportunities rating (DORS). Indeed, both the average value of PH and DORS are lower in the RARE II wilderness classification than in the nonwilderness category for both states (Tables 6-5 and 6-6).[101] Clearly, the Forest Service was attempting to keep those roadless areas with a high DORS and high PH in the nonwilderness category where resource exploitation would be legally permitted.

The RARE II study was undertaken to serve as an environmental impact statement that would satisfy provisions of the National Environmental Policy Act.[102] Once an acceptable impact statement was completed, lands in the nonwilderness category could have been released for the purpose of resource exploitation. A California court, however, found RARE II to be insufficient as an environmental impact statement.[103] As a result of this decision, the Forest Service refused to release roadless areas for timber sales. In response, a number of states, including Oregon and Washington, passed wilderness bills permanently designating certain roadless areas as wilderness and releasing others for commodity exploitation.

The actual assignment of roadless areas to wilderness in the Oregon and Washington wilderness acts of 1984 suggests that Congress paid much more attention than the Forest Service not only to wilderness advocacy interests but also to relative timber dependency in the states of Oregon and Washington. A comparison of the Forest Service RARE II wilderness allocation and the final allocation to wilderness by Congress in the 1984 wilderness acts is presented in Table 6-7. Congress clearly increased the actual acres added to the wilderness system relative to the recommendations of the Forest Service. The number of acres recommended by the Forest Service for wilderness was increased in Congress by approximately 200,000 acres in western Oregon and 300,000 acres in western Washington from a roughly equal base of approximately 200,000 acres each in the two states. In western Washington, the result was the creation of wilderness areas with a total land area equal to approximately 43 percent of the original roadless area acreage, while in western Oregon the comparable figure was 31 percent. In terms of total acreage added to wilderness, western Washington wilderness advocates clearly fared better than their counterparts in western Oregon, although wilderness advocates in both states gained more from Congress than they did from the Forest Service. In both states, the total programmed harvest (PH) for roadless areas included as wilderness was significantly increased in the congressional selection of wilderness in comparison to the RARE II results, suggesting a greater extent of forest preservation by Congress in comparison to the Forest Service. Given that roadless areas had never been previously harvested, this implies that Congress increased the preservation of old-growth forests relative to the Forest Service in the wilderness selection process. The average value of DORS and PH for the roadless areas selected by Congress as wilderness was greater than for the Forest Service's RARE II allocation, suggesting that Congress was less worried about sacrificing timber harvests to preserve wilderness than the Forest Service.

In marked contrast to the Forest Service, Congress thus treated western Washington and Oregon differently, choosing a relatively lower level of wilderness preservation and forest preservation in Oregon. As already noted, the percentage of RARE II roadless area preserved in wilderness was 43 percent in western Washington in comparison to 31 percent in western Oregon. Similarly, the percentage of RARE II programmed harvest locked up in wilderness by Congress was 36 percent for western Washington and 33 percent for western Oregon, and the respective figures for the percentage of the 1970s average total annual harvest locked up in wilderness were 1.3 percent and 1.2 percent. Why did Congress treat western Washington more favorably than western Oregon wilderness and forestland preservation advocates?

One answer to this question is that Oregon was more timber dependent than Washington and would thus experience a greater relative employment loss than Washington for an equal relative loss of timber production base and programmed harvest. In 1980, forest products employment in Oregon was 78,886 while the comparable figure in Washington was 61,063. In Oregon, the forest products industry constituted 36.2 percent of manufacturing employment and 9.4 percent of private sector employment in 1980, while the comparable figures for Washington were 19.4 percent and 4.8 percent.[104] These figures suggest that local senators and congressmembers would be relatively more sensitive to a given percentage loss of forest products employment in Oregon than Washington. Assuming that forest products employment bears the same relationship to programmed harvest in the two states, a given percentage reduction in programmed harvest would have a greater impact on the unemployment rate in Oregon than Washington.

To the extent that local members of Congress trade forest products industry votes at the polls in exchange for wilderness preservationist votes, the relative cost in terms of forest products industry votes given up would be greater in Oregon than Washington. In local wilderness selection decisions, local members of Congress would likely have a disproportionate influence because of their capacity to engage in logrolling and vote trading with nonlocal members. Also, senators from Oregon and Washington were members of the committee that held hearings on the Oregon and Washington wilderness acts and recommended the acts to the Senate for approval.[105] In other words, the local congressional delegation in each state likely played a dominant role in shaping the final wilderness bills that passed Congress, and delegation members were probably influenced by the impact of these bills on their own reelection prospects.

An alternative explanation for the higher level of preservation in Washington than Oregon is that demand for wilderness was relatively greater in the former because of a 57 percent larger 1980 population, and Congress took this into account in allocating roadless areas to wilderness in the two states.[106] Since the Forest Service assigned equal amounts of roadless area to wilderness in the two states, such demand considerations apparently did not enter into its decision making. Population, however, is probably not a very good indicator of demand for wilderness use, particularly because such a small percentage of the population uses wilderness. A somewhat better measure of relative demand for wilderness may be membership in wilderness advocacy organizations. In 1981, Sierra Club membership was approximately equal at 4,062 for Washington and 4,052 for Oregon. In 1985, Wilderness Society membership in Oregon was 5,226 for Washington and 3,427 for Oregon, while the Sierra Club figures for Washington had increased to 8,069 and for Oregon to 6,515.[107] These data suggest that during the RARE II process in the late 1970s, membership in each of the wilderness groups was probably roughly equal in the two states even though Washington's population was greater. By 1985, the combined membership of the two groups was 34 percent greater in Washington than Oregon. If membership can be roughly interpreted as a measure of demand, demand was roughly equal in the two states at the time of the RARE II process even though Washington had a larger population, and demand was shifting relatively toward Washington by the mid-1980s.

Looking at such measures of demand provides an incomplete picture without considering the supply of wilderness available in western Washington and Oregon. The additional wilderness demanded by the residents of the two states will depend on the amount of wilderness already available. If substantial wilderness is already available, the additional amount demanded would likely be less. The availability of national park lands and wilderness prior to the passage of the 1984 wilderness acts was 2,115,811 acres in western Washington and 534,722 acres in western Oregon.[108] The availability of reserved lands where wilderness recreation could be undertaken was much greater in Washington than Oregon, suggesting that unfulfilled demand for wilderness was relatively greater in

Oregon than Washington. While population was only 57 percent greater in Washington, the amount of reserved lands in western Washington was 296 percent greater than in western Oregon. In relative terms, then, demand for added wilderness should be greater in Oregon than Washington. If demand was the determining factor, then relatively more wilderness and old growth should have been preserved in western Oregon than western Washington in the 1984 wilderness acts, but the opposite occurred, suggesting that timber dependency played a part in the final wilderness selection decisions by Congress.

A possible objection to the unfulfilled demand argument is that the creation of wilderness breeds increased demand for wilderness. The presence of designated wilderness stimulates use and learning by doing, and that in turn generates a still greater demand for designated wilderness. What is needed is a measure of actual expression of demand for wilderness at the time the RARE II wilderness allocations were being made to measure the relative strength of demand for wilderness. Such a measure is available in the number of signatures on documents collected by the U.S. Forest Service in favor of wilderness selection in the RARE II process for the two states, a figure that was 147 percent greater in western Oregon than Washington.[109] This suggests that at the time of the RARE II study, the demand for wilderness by residents of Oregon was much greater than for Washington residents. The signatures of advocates for nonwilderness designations were disproportionately higher in Oregon than Washington, too, but this likely was a reaction to a higher level of wilderness advocacy in Oregon than Washington. Presumably, the signature response of timber interests would be roughly proportional to their numbers in the face of a roughly equal threat to their interests. Because forest products employment is only slightly higher in Oregon than Washington, Oregon timber interests must have perceived a greater threat from wilderness advocates than Washington timber interests since nonwilderness signatures were 191 percent greater in Oregon than Washington.[110] If the demand for wilderness was greater in Oregon than Washington, this would have translated politically into a greater likelihood that wilderness advocates would vote on the basis of their wilderness preferences in Oregon than Washington elections, and as a result, Oregon politicians stood to gain more than Washington politicians from advocating wilderness, timber dependency aside. In other words, if timber dependency did not matter, Oregon should have done relatively better than Washington in congressional wilderness decisions. In fact it did worse, suggesting that timber dependency must have mattered sufficiently to more than offset the higher level of demand for wilderness and forest preservation in Oregon.

Conclusion

The extent of old-growth forestland preservation has increased historically in the Pacific Northwest at the same time that economic dependency on forest products has diminished, and the degree of forestland
preservation has been higher in western Washington than western Oregon, reflecting a lesser degree of economic dependency on forest products in Washington. The arguments set forth above suggest that there is
indeed an inverse relationship between old-growth preservation and timber dependency. If this analysis can be extended to public lands in general, it implies that the preservation of natural areas will tend to increase
as relative economic dependency on natural resource commodity production declines, even if absolute employment decline is the result. And
in the case of the Pacific Northwest forest products industry, the industry
itself helped set the stage for its own relative decline by fostering the
development of urban centers that in turn served as incubators for the
creation of industries free of dependency on timber.

If it can be generalized to other resources, this analysis provides a ray
of hope for those who desire to see the preservation of remaining natural
areas. If it is true that resource-based industries set the stage for the
development of industries less dependent on resources, then a historically diminishing economic dependency on natural resources makes possible a shift of attitudes toward the natural world. Nature can now be valued
for the nonmaterial benefits it brings in a preserved state, and it can even
be valued for itself independent of any instrumental benefits it brings to
human beings.[111] Such attitudinal shifts can, in the political arena, im-
pinge upon the further exploitation of natural resources.[112] The great danger
is that such shifts will come too late after much of the natural world is
irreversibly altered as a consequence of natural resource exploitation.

Notes

1. See Table 6-1 and Wall, *Log Production in Washington and Oregon.*
From the decade of the 1950s to the decade of the 1970s, average annual timber
harvests increased by approximately 1,800 million board feet. This increase is
roughly equal to the increase of log exports from Oregon and Washington over
the same period. This means that the amount of timber available to the domestic
milling industry was roughly stable in the 1960s and 1970s. For log export data,
see USDA Forest Service, *Production, Prices, Employment, and Trade in Northwest Forest Industries, First Quarter 1976* (Portland, Ore.: USDA Forest Service, Resource Bulletin, PNW-130, 1976) and USDA Forest Service, *Production,
Prices, Employment and Trade in Northwest Forest Industries, Fourth Quarter
1985* (Portland, Ore: USDA Forest Service, Resource Bulletin, PNW-130, 1986).

2. The theory of urban economic development suggests that this will be the case. It also suggests that new industries will develop once certain population thresholds and other economic conditions are achieved. See Alfred J. Watkins, *The Practice of Urban Economics* (Beverley Hills: Sage, 1980), chs. 2-5.

3. See Watkins; Hugh O. Nourse, *Regional Economics* (New York: McGraw-Hill, 1968).

4. For a theoretical analysis of this process, see Watkins, *Practice of Urban Economics*, chs. 2-4.

5. Alexander N. McDonald, "Seattle's Economic Development, 1880-1910," Ph.D. diss., University of Washington, 1959, pp. 30-32, 110.

6. Edwin J. Cohn, Jr., *Industry in the Pacific Northwest and the Location Theory* (New York: Columbia University Press, 1954), p. 27; Abner Baker, "Economic Growth in Portland in the 1880s," *Oregon Historical Quarterly* 67 (1966): 105-23.

7. McDonald, "Seattle's Economic Development," p. 90.

8. Cohn, *Industry in the Pacific Northwest*, pp. 44-45, 85; McDonald, "Seattle's Economic Development," pp. 113-27.

9. The wilderness old-growth estimates are from Morrison, "Old Growth in the Pacific Northwest" and the national park old-growth estimate is from Haynes, *Inventory and Value of Old-Growth in the Douglas-Fir Region.* While some wilderness areas in western Oregon are not included, their total land area is substantially less than the amount of western Washington national park land in old growth.

10. Dana and Fairfax, *Forest and Range Policy*, pp. 56-58; John Ise, *The United States Forest Policy* (New Haven: Yale University Press, 1920), p. 114; Nash, *Wilderness and the American Mind*, pp. 133-34; Hayes, *Conservation and the Gospel of Efficiency*, pp. 36, 114-18; Harold K. Steen, *The U.S. Forest Service: A History*, p. 27. Steen suggests that the members of the Public Lands Committee were fully aware of the content of section 24 of the bill that permitted the creation of forest reserves and approved its inclusion in the bill, indicating that there was significant support in Congress for forest reserves.

11. Lawrence W. Rakestraw, "A History of Forest Conservation in the Pacific Northwest," Ph. D. dissertation, University of Washington, 1955, pp. 29-55.

12. Ibid., pp. 42-44.

13. Arthur D. Martinson, "Mountain in the Sky: A History of Mount Rainier National Park," Ph. D. diss., Washington State University, 1966, pp. 41-55; Arthur D. Martinson, *Wilderness Above the Sound: The Story of Mount Rainier National Park* (Flagstaff, Ariz.: Northland Press, 1986), pp. 16, 24, 29-34.

14. Runte, *National Parks*, pp. 66-67.

15. For a fascinating discussion of these political efforts, see Carsten Lien, *Olympic Battleground: The Power Politics of Timber Preservation* (San Francisco: Sierra Club Books, 1991), pp. 8-15. Lien's analysis makes it sound as if the lobbying efforts of the Northern Pacific were the only reason that Mount Rainier National Park came into existence. To legitimize this effort, however, it seems likely that the monumental scenery standard would have to be met, and that there would have to be local support for the park.

16. Dana and Fairfax, *Forest and Range Policy*, pp. 60-61.

17. Ibid.; Ise, *The United States Forest Policy*, pp. 128-29; Rakestraw, "A History of Forest Conservation in the Pacific Northwest," p. 66.

18. Ibid. pp. 66-68.

19. Ben W. Twight, *Organizational Values and Political Power: The Forest Service Versus the Olympic National Park* (University Park: Pennsylvania State University Press, 1983), p. 32; Elmo Richardson, "Olympic National Park: 20 Years of Controversy," *Journal of Forest History* 12 (1968): 6-15.

20. Twight, *Organizational Values and Political Power*, p. 33; Rakestraw, "A History of Forest Conservation in the Pacific Northwest," pp. 126-35.

21. Twight, *Organizational Values and Political Power*, pp. 33-34; Lien, *Olympic Battleground*, pp. 32-38.

22. Ibid., p. 38.

23. Ibid., pp. 39-52; Twight, *Organizational Values and Political Power*, pp. 34-37.

24. Fox, *The American Conservation Movement*, pp. 174-82; Lien, *Olympic Battleground*, pp. 95-111; Twight, *Organizational Values and Political Power*, pp. 38-57.

25. This point is most clearly made in Lien, *Olympic Battleground*, pp. 111-212.

26. Ibid., pp. 104-18.

27. Ibid., pp. 119-21.

28. Richardson, "Olympic National Park," p. 8.

29. Twight, *Organizational Values and Political Power*, pp. 64-73.

30. Ibid., pp. 45-48, 78-80.

31. Ibid., p. 87.

32. Ibid., pp. 119-43. Lien's interpretation of the role of the Park Service is at odds with Ben Twight's, and is in many ways more convincing. Twight suggests that the Park Service is a prime mover in bringing forth a park (*Organizational Values and Power Politics*, pp. 59-80). Lien suggests that the Park Service has no interest in forest preservation as such and is primarily interested in promoting commercial tourism. Lien also argues that the Park Service often adopted Forest Service positions for fear of antagonizing it. In fairness to Twight, his goal is to analyze Forest Service behavior in the whole affair and demonstrate its rigid commitment to timber values. At this task he does an excellent job.

33. Lien, *Olympic Battleground*, pp. 125-26.

34. Ibid., pp. 131-212; Richardson, "Olympic National Park," pp. 6-15. The details of the political battle are fascinating and are described in detail by Lien.

35. Twight, *Organizational Values and Political Power*, pp. 107-16.

36. Lien, *Olympic Battleground*, pp. 256-57.

37. Ibid., pp. 94-95.

38. Dana and Fairfax, *Forest and Range Policy*, pp. 180, 190-94, 197-98.

39. The Olympic National Park debate being a notable exception.

40. Robert H. Nelson, "Mythology Instead of Analysis: The Story of Public

Forest Management," in Robert T. Deacon and M. Bruce Johnson, eds., *Forestlands: Public and Private* (San Francisco: Pacific Institute, 1985), p. 49.

41. Wall, *Log Production*, pp. 1-15.

42. For the value-driven view, see Twight, *Organizational Values and Political Power*, pp. 15-28. For the budget maximization view see Ronald N. Johnson, "U.S. Forest Service Policy and its Budget," in Deacon and M. Bruce *Forestlands*, pp. 103-33 and Randal O'Toole, *Reforming the Forest Service* (Covelo, Calif.: Island Press, 1988), pp. 98-171.

43. O'Toole, *Reforming the Forest Service*, pp. 112-23.

44. Dana and Fairfax, *Forest and Range Policy*, pp. 151-57.

45. Ibid., pp. 133, 155-58.

46. Ibid., pp. 190-93.

47. Ibid., pp. 193-94.

48. Ibid., pp. 197-98, 199-200.

49. Ibid., pp. 197-204.

50. Johnson, "U.S. Forest Service Policy and its Budget," pp. 115-23.

51. Dana and Fairfax, *Forest and Range Policy*, p. 204.

52. Steen, *The U.S. Forest Service*, pp. 301-7.

53. Ibid., pp. 304-7.

54. Ibid., p. 303; Dana and Fairfax, *Forest and Range Policy*, p. 197.

55. Craig W. Allin, *The Politics of Wilderness Preservation* (Westport, Conn.: Greenwood Press, 1982), pp. 89-94; Nash, *Wilderness and the American Mind*, pp. 209-20.

56. Nash, *Wilderness and the American Mind*, pp. 222-23; Michael McCloskey, "Wilderness Movement at the Crossroads," *Pacific Historical Review* 41 (1972): 348-49; Allin, *The Politics of Wilderness Preservation*, pp. 133-36.

57. Dana and Fairfax, *Forest and Range Policy*, pp. 217-21.

58. North Cascades Study Team, *The North Cascades: A Report to the Secretary of the Interior and the Secretary of Agriculture* (Washington, D.C.: U.S. Government Printing Office, 1965), pp. 25-26.

59. Ibid., pp. 26-75.

60. Rakestraw, "A History of Conservation in the Pacific Northwest," pp. 66-68.

61. North Cascades Study Team, *The North Cascades*, p. 29; Alan R. Sommarstrom, "Wild Land Preservation Crisis: The North Cascades Controversy," Ph.D. diss., University of Washington, 1970, pp. 31-37.

62. Ibid., pp. 33-38.

63. Ibid., pp. 41-46.

64. Ibid., pp. 47-48; North Cascades Conservation Council, "Prospectus for a North Cascades," Seattle, October 1963.

65. Sommarstrom, "Wild Land Preservation Crisis," pp. 74-75; North Cascades Study Team, *North Cascades*, pp. 158-74.

66. Ibid., pp. 175-81; Sommarstrom, "Wild Lands Preservation Crisis," pp. 75-79.

67. North Cascades Study Team, *The North Cascades*, pp. 76-125.

68. Ibid., p. 107; Sommarstrom, "Wild Land Preservation Crisis," pp. 79-82.

69. Sommarstrom, "Wild Lands Preservation Crisis," pp. 89-94.

70. Ibid., p. 127.

71. Ibid., pp. 126-33; U.S. House of Representatives, *The North Cascades, Part I*, Hearing before the Subcommittee on National Parks and Recreation, Committee on Interior and Insular Affairs, 90th Congress, 2d Session, on H.R. 8970 and related bills, Seattle, Wash., April 19-20, 1968 (Washington, D.C.: U.S. Government Printing Office, 1968).

72. Ibid., pp. 143-54.

73. U.S. House, *The North Cascades, Part I*, p. 129.

74. Dennis M. Roth, *The Wilderness Movement and the National Forests: 1964-1980* (Washington, D.C.: USDA Forest Service, 1984), p. 11.

75. Ibid., pp. 1-10; Allin, *The Politics of Wilderness Preservation*, pp. 157-60.

76. U.S. Forest Service, *Mt. Jefferson Wilderness: A Proposal* (Portland, Ore.: U.S. Forest Service, Pacific Northwest Region, 1967).

77. Roth, *The Wilderness Movement*, pp. 14-15; David Brown, "Oregon Wilderness Handbook," BA thesis, Honors College, University of Oregon, 1977, pp. 27-28; U.S. Forest Service, *Mt. Jefferson Wilderness*, p. 16.

78. Obsidians, Inc., Chemeketans, The Mountaineers Conservation Division, Oregon Cascades Conservation Council, Pacific Northwest Chapter of the Sierra Club, and Oregon Wildlife Federation, "A Proposal for a Mt. Jefferson Wilderness Area," Eugene, Oregon, December 22, 1961.

79. U.S. Senate, *San Gabriel, Washakie, and Mount Jefferson Wilderness Areas*, Hearing before the Subcommittee on Public Lands, Committee on Interior and Insular Affairs, 90th Congress, 2d Session, on S. 2531, S. 2630, and S. 2751, February 19-20, 1968 (Washington, D.C.: U.S. Government Printing Office, 1968).

80. U.S. Forest Service, "Report on the Proposed Alpine Lakes Wilderness," Portland, Pacific Northwest Region, 1975; Allin, *The Politics of Wilderness Preservation*, p. 152; Richard Fiddler, "The Alpine Lakes . . . Seattle's Backyard Wilderness," *Sierra Club Bulletin* 61 (February 1976): 4-7.

81. U.S. House of Representatives, *Alpine Lakes Area Management Act*, Hearing before the Subcommittee on National Parks and Recreation, Committee on Interior and Insular Affairs, 94th Congress, 2d Session, Part I, on H.R. 3977, H.R. 3978, H.R. 7792, June 17, 1975 (Washington, D.C.: U.S. Government Printing Office, 1975).

82. USDA Forest Service, "Draft Environmental Statement on a Recommended Land Use Plan for the Alpine Lakes Area in the State of Washington," Portland, Pacific Northwest Region, 1973.

83. Fiddler, "The Alpine Lakes," p. 7.

84. Roth, *The Wilderness Movement*, pp. 24-34.

85. Ibid., p. 37; Allin, *The Politics of Wilderness*, pp. 160-61.

86. Dana and Fairfax, *Forest and Range Policy*, p. 300.

87. Roth, *The Wilderness Movement*, pp. 36-38; Allin, *The Politics of Wilderness*, pp. 160-61.

88. Brown, "The Oregon Wilderness Handbook," p. 39; Allin, *The Politics of Wilderness*, pp. 192-93.

89. Roth, *The Wilderness Movement*, pp. 49-61; Alan Tautges, "The Oregon Omnibus Wilderness Act of 1978 as a Component of the Endangered American Wilderness Act of 1978, Public Law 95-237," *Environmental Review* 13 (1989): 43-62.

90. Dana and Fairfax, *Forest and Range Policy*, pp. 197-98.

91. Roth, *The Wilderness Movement*, p. 49.

92. Ibid., pp. 49-51.

93. Tautges, "The Oregon Omnibus Wilderness Act," pp. 44-45.

94. Robert T. Wazeka, "Organizing for Wilderness: The Oregon Example," *Sierra Club Bulletin*, October 1976, p. 49.

95. Ibid., pp. 47-50.

96. Ibid., pp. 52-61; Dana and Fairfax, *Forest and Range Policy*, p. 301; Allin, *The Politics of Wilderness*, pp. 161-65.

97. USDA Forest Service, *RARE II Final Environmental Statement* (Washington, D.C.: U.S. Government Printing Office, 1979).

98. Twight, *Organizational Values and Political Power*, pp. 3-28.

99. O'Toole, *Reforming the Forest Service*, pp. 138-71.

100. USDA Forest Service, *RARE II*, pp. W-1 to W-5, 14-15, 21.

101. For a more detailed econometric analysis of the determinants of wilderness selection, see Douglas E. Booth, "Timber Dependency, and Wilderness Selection: The U.S. Forest Service, Congress, and the RARE II Decisions," *Natural Resources* 31 (1991): 715-39. In this study, DORS was found to be a positive statistically significant determinant of roadless area assignment to nonwilderness for western Oregon while PH was found to be a positive statistically significant determinant of nonwilderness assignment for western Washington. Portions of this article are reprinted here with permission of the editor.

102. Ibid.

103. *Sierra Club v. Butz*, 349 F. Supp. 934 (N.D. Cal. 1972).

104. See Table 6-2.

105. U.S. Senate, *Oregon Wilderness Act of 1983*, Hearing before the Subcommittee on Public Lands and Reserved Water, Committee on Energy and Natural Resources, 98th Congress, 1st Session, on H.R., 1149, Bend, Ore., July 21, 1983 (Washington, D.C.: U.S. Government Printing Office, 1983), p. 635; U. S. Senate, *Washington State Wilderness Act of 1983*, Hearings before the Subcommittee on Public Lands and Reserved Water, Committee on Energy and Natural Resources, 98th Congress, 1st Session, on S. 837, Spokane, Wash., June 2, 1983, Seattle Wash., June 3, 1983, Washington, D.C., September 30, 1983 (Washington, D.C.: U.S. Government Printing Office, 1983).

106. U.S. Bureau of the Census, *1980 Census of Population, Vol. 1, Chapter A,* Parts 39 and 49 (Washington, D.C.: U.S. Government Printing Office, 1980).

107. Membership data were obtained from the headquarters offices of the Sierra Club and Wilderness Society.

108. See Table 6-5.

109. USDA Forest Service, *RARE II,* pp. U-1 to U-40.

110. Ibid.

111. See Chapter 1 for a discussion of the idea of valuing nature for itself.

112. The methodology of this chapter in a general sense follows that described in Barbara Leibhardt, "Interpretation and Causal Analysis: Theories in Environmental History," *Environmental Review* 12 (Spring 1988): 23-26. This paper involves a dynamic analysis of ecology, human economic relations, and human cognition, with the emphasis on the latter two components.

7

Valuing Nature and the Preservation of Old-Growth Forests

A decline in timber dependency by itself cannot be the only explanation for an increase in the extent of old-growth forest preservation. For this to have happened, there must have been a group of individuals with political influence that valued old-growth forests in their preserved state. A decline of timber dependency simply removed a potentially significant economic restraint on the formation and expression of preservationist values. Why did advocates of preservation value old-growth forests? Did their reasons for valuing old growth in a preserved condition change and evolve over time? Because of the historical tendency in this country to give the highest priority to economic growth and growth in exploitation of natural resources, these questions are particularly important.

Preservation of old-growth forests in their natural state must be done for primarily nonmaterial reasons, but those reasons may still be instrumental and may still be based on the fulfillment of economic goals. People may want to preserve old growth because it provides a unique setting for various forms of outdoor recreation or the observation of natural beauty. They may also want to preserve it because it increases tourism or improves the productivity of the commercial salmon fishery by increasing the quality of spawning habitat.

These modes of valuation do not take us very far from the conventional economic view of natural resources as means for fulfilling instrumental ends. The mode of valuing, however, makes a quantum leap from the economic to the ethical realm when people begin to value old growth for itself independent of any instrumental ends. Since ethical values tend to be held with greater fervor than simple economic preferences, an ethical foundation for valuing old growth may well increase the intensity of

preservationist efforts in the political arena. Such intensity may be needed to offset this country's historical tendency to politically support resource extraction and the economic activity that goes with it.

The purpose of this chapter is to investigate the historical evolution
of attitudes toward old-growth forests and their associated natural habitat as expressed by advocates of forest and wilderness preservation.
Because of the limited role that preservationists played in the creation
of Mount Rainier National Park and the limited amount of information
available, the analysis will begin with the campaign for Olympic National Park. For the addition of Olympic and North Cascades national parks
and all subsequent wilderness areas in western Oregon and Washington,
attitudes expressed during the political decision-making process by preservationists will be garnered from congressional testimony and various
preservationist publications. In each case, the content of the testimony
by each advocate for preservation will be analyzed to determine the type
of values expressed. By coding the type of value arguments made by
each individual in congressional testimony, the shifting frequency of
different types of arguments favoring old growth or wilderness preservation can be analyzed. For example, has the frequency of instrumental
arguments decreased and ethical arguments increased over time? This is
important because a shift from an economic and instrumental mode of
valuation to an ethical mode significantly alters the way in which natural
resource preservation questions ought to be judged. If individuals look
on nature, specifically old-growth forests, in ethical terms, then, as will
be shown in Chapter 9, the standard benefits-cost approach to valuing
natural resources no longer applies.

Coding Arguments Made for Wilderness
and Old-Growth Preservation

The coding system used for analyzing the testimony of wilderness and
old-growth preservation advocates before Congress is presented in Table
7-1. For each person who testified, a determination was made as to
whether or not arguments were utilized as a justification for preserving
natural areas in either wilderness areas or national parks (Table 7-1).
These particular arguments were selected because they are mentioned
frequently in the literature on wilderness preservation[1] and they provide
a relatively comprehensive list of the types of arguments actually used
by individuals testifying before Congress. Not all testimony was devoted
to the use of these arguments. Some individuals simply indicated their
support for preservation without any justification. Some presented detailed descriptive information on particular natural areas or presented

critical evaluations of U.S. Forest Service policy on logging and wilderness preservation. The vast majority, however, did make use of arguments listed in Table 7-1.

The determination of whether a particular argument was used in individual testimony was relatively straightforward with one exception. To establish whether someone was arguing in favor of wilderness because it is a place where people can engage in recreation activities or experience natural beauty or because it is a habitat where wildlife, forests, or rare plants can be preserved was generally easy. The only real difficulty was establishing whether those testifying were arguing that wilderness, wildlife, or forests ought to be preserved because they are valuable in their own right. In general, I concluded that those testifying were doing so if they claimed that wilderness areas or their constituent organisms have intrinsic value or value in their own right, are sacred and deserving of reverence, have rights to exist, or are deserving of moral concern. Since making this judgment involved some interpretation on my part, I have included the key quotations for each case in Appendix 7A so readers can arrive at their own conclusions.

In Table 7-1, the arguments have been divided into general categories. While the categories and specific arguments are for the most part self-explanatory, further elaboration of the arguments is needed for a reasonable understanding of both their meaning and the coding procedure.

Preserving wilderness and forests was frequently justified in congressional testimony on aesthetic, spiritual, and psychological grounds (category A, Table 7-1). Wilderness, in the eyes of those testifying, serves needs that are at once intangible and instrumental. They are intangible because they do not involve the physical consumption of anything, but they are nonetheless instrumental because they fulfill a felt desire. The argument that wilderness ought to be preserved for its monumental scenery or its natural beauty is one of the earliest used in preservation history. As Alfred Runte argues, the necessary condition for preservation of the early national parks was the presence of monumental scenery.[2] Wilderness, according to those giving congressional testimony, can also serve as a place for spiritual reflection and for gaining an understanding of one's connection to the rest of the natural world. Finally, some giving testimony argued that wilderness and forests are needed as places where individuals can seek solitude and repair the psychological damage rendered by the problems and pace of a modern urban and industrial society.

Another common argument for the preservation of wilderness and forests in congressional testimony is that they are needed as a setting for outdoor recreation of various types (category B, Table 7-1). The recreation argument is not necessarily independent of other preservation ar-

Table 7-1
Coding System for Arguments Made by Wilderness
Advocates in Testimony before Congress

A   Fulfillment of aesthetic, spiritual, and psychological needs (intangible, instrumental)
1.   Natural beauty, monumental scenery
2.   Place for spiritual reflection, gaining a connection to nature
3.   Place for solitude, escape
4.   Preservation of wilderness as a cultural symbol, resource

B. Recreation (instrumental intangible)
5.   Outdoor recreation—hiking, camping, mountain climbing, fishing, hunting, wildlife observation, photography

C. Preservation of nature (tangible instrumental, intangible instrumental, non-instrumental)
6.   Preservation of ecosystems, biotic communities, biotic diversity
7.   Preservation of wildlife and plantlife
8.   Preservation of rare, threatened, and endangered species
9.   Preservation of watersheds
10.   Preservation of climatic stability, ecosystem services
11.   Preservation of old-growth forests, virgin forests, forested valleys

D. Preservation of nature for ethical reasons
12.   Ecosystems, species, plants, or animals are valued in themselves or for themselves; they have rights; they have intrinsic value; they are objects of human concern exclusive of any instrumental value; all life is sacred, an object of reverence (noninstrumental)
13.   Preservation of nature for the sake of future generations (instrumental)

E. Economic and other arguments
14.   Wilderness has little or no resource value; preservation results in little job loss; resources can be obtained elsewhere at equivalent or lower costs; land cannot be reforested (worthless lands argument; negative instrumental)
15.   Preservation of wilderness for research, scientific interest, education (intangible instrumental)
16.   Wilderness has economic value—tourism, outdoor goods industry, commercial fisheries habitat, source of genetic material (tangible instrumental)

---

guments. For example, to enjoy the natural beauty of a given wilderness may require participation in some form of outdoor recreation. Nonetheless, the two arguments, recreation and preservation of natural beauty, were often made separately in congressional testimony and were consequently coded separately here.

The arguments in categories A and B (Table 7-1) are basically instrumental. That is, the preservation of wilderness is justified on the grounds that it provides some benefit to human beings. It provides an opportunity to engage in recreation, enjoy natural beauty and solitude, or engage in spiritual reflection. For some of the arguments listed in category C (Table 7-1), the extent of their instrumentality is unclear. In many instances, individuals testifying simply argued that wilderness ought to be preserved because, as a result, ecosystems, plants, wildlife, endangered species, and old-growth forests will be preserved. This argument was made without any explicit justification being given for preservation. In other words, there is no way to tell from the testimony whether testifiers believed that natural beings ought to be preserved because they provide human benefits or because they are valuable in their own right independent of any benefits they provide to human beings. Some explicitly mentioned instrumental reasons for preserving wildlife, such as the improvement of hunting, but many did not. Those who did not either believed that the instrumental value of wildlife, plants, or ecosystems is understood and does not require explanation or believed that natural beings have noninstrumental value and that this does not require explanation. Another possibility is that they feared using noninstrumental reasons because of the alien position of noninstrumentalist thought in a world dominated by instrumentalist views.

Some who testified argued on ethical grounds for the preservation of wilderness and old-growth forests (category D, Table 7-1). The most popular ethical argument was that wilderness ought to be preserved for the sake of future generations. While for present generations this is a noninstrumental argument—they do not benefit from preservation—the preserved areas will provide instrumental benefits to future generations. Although this is an ethical argument, it is also ultimately an instrumental argument since the preserved areas will be of benefit to human beings. A somewhat less popular ethical argument, but one that was increasingly used over time in congressional testimony, is that wilderness or its constituent ecosystems or organisms are valuable for themselves. In other words, wilderness ought to be defended and preserved not just for the instrumental benefits it provides for human beings but for the sake of the ecosystems, plants, and animals that it contains.

Finally, economic arguments for wilderness preservation were also popular in congressional testimony along with scientific and educational arguments (category E, Table 7-1). Wilderness was often argued to be worthless in the sense that few marketable commodities or jobs would be lost as a result of preservation. In the case of forests, the argument was sometimes made in testimony that reforestation would be difficult if not impossible in high-elevation areas under consideration for inclusion in a national park or designated wilderness areas. As a result, it was argued, these areas would have little long-term value in commodity production and ought to be preserved from timber cutting. In addition, designated wilderness areas and national parks were seen by some of those testifying as means for fostering the tourist business and increasing local economic activity.

Before looking at the results of the argument coding analysis, focusing on the views of wilderness advocates testifying before Congress needs justification. Why consider the views of only those who testify before Congress as opposed to the views of the public in general? First and foremost, the views of those who testify before Congress in all probability carry more weight in the political process than the views of the silent, anonymous public. Some of those testifying got Congress's attention because they were representatives of key interest groups with the capacity to deliver votes at election time. However, in field hearings outside of Washington, D.C., many who testified were not connected with interest groups and were testifying because they felt strongly about wilderness and old-growth preservation issues. These individuals in the eyes of members of Congress probably represented the views of many other voters. Members of Congress lack precise information on public attitudes and will thus take the positions of those testifying as partially representative of voters at large. For a member of Congress, some information on public attitudes is better than none. The alternative to looking at testimony before Congress in evaluating public attitudes towards wilderness issues would be to employ public opinion surveys. Obviously, information from such surveys would be highly useful, particularly if the motivation for supporting particular positions were addressed, but in doing a historical study such as this one, a survey approach is impossible. Surveys are only useful for assessing public attitudes with respect to contemporaneous issues, not historical events.

Shifting Attitudes toward Wilderness and Forests in Testimony before Congress

The goal in analyzing testimony before Congress dealing with wilderness and national park preservation is to establish which arguments were used most frequently by preservationists and to discern if there is any change in the extent to which particular arguments were used over time. Field hearings held by congressional committees in the Pacific Northwest and hearings held in Washington, D.C., were analyzed.[3] Hearings on legislation leading to the creation of Olympic and North Cascades national parks were evaluated as well as hearings on the 1959 Wilderness Act, creation of the Mount Jefferson and the Alpine Lakes wilderness areas, the Oregon Omnibus Wilderness Act and the Endangered American Wilderness Act (the former was incorporated in the latter), and the 1984 Oregon and Washington State wilderness acts. In the case of the 1964 Wilderness Act, only local hearings held in the Pacific Northwest were evaluated. While the 1964 Wilderness Act did not increase the area under a wilderness designation by the U.S. Forest Service, it did render those designations more permanent. The results of the analysis are presented in Tables 7-2 through 7-5.

Table 7-2
Percentage of Advocates Making Wilderness
Preservation Arguments in Congressional
Testimony—Field Hearings

Argument	Percentage of advocates making argument[1]					
	(1) 1959 Wild. Act	(2) 1968 N. Casc.	(3) 1976 Alp. Lake	(4) 1976 Ore. Omn.	(5) 1984 Wash. Wild. Act	(6) 1984 Ore. Wild. Act
1. Natural beauty	20.0	60.3	28.8	37.3	39.4	24.0
2. Spiritual reflection	16.3	8.8	8.8	12.0	10.1	8.9
3. Solitude	13.8	8.3	8.8	13.3	13.1	10.3
4. Cultural resources	3.8	0.0	0.0	2.6	6.0	0.7
5. Outdoor recreation	78.8	61.4	41.3	29.3	55.6	43.2
6. Preserve ecosystems	1.3	5.5	5.0	17.3	18.2	24.0
7. Preserve wildlife, plantlife	8.8	6.9	10.6	34.7	43.4	65.8
8. Preserve endangered species	0.0	0.3	0.6	14.7	11.1	11.6
9. Preserve watersheds	11.3	1.1	1.2	17.3	21.2	21.9
10. Preserve ecosystem services	0.0	0.3	0.0	6.7	1.0	0.7
11. Preserve old-growth forests	8.8	11.6	10.6	8.0	16.2	21.2
12. Nature valued in its own right	0.0	1.4	5.6	6.7	5.0	5.5
13. Preserve for future generations	35.0	26.7	18.8	26.6	22.2	8.9
14. Worthless lands	16.3	5.5	11.3	24.0	27.2	24.0

15. Preserve for scientific purposes	35.0	7.4	4.3	10.6	16.2	13.0
16. Preserve for economic purposes	8.8	8.0	10.0	13.3	24.2	19.2
Diversity index (total)	258	214	165	274	330	313
% instrumental 6,7,8,11	58.3	45.3	41.4	62.9	52.0	52.9

¹The subject of the testimony for each column is as follows: (1) 1959 National Wilderness Preservation Act, (2) North Cascades National Park, (3) Alpine Lakes Wilderness Area, (4) Oregon Omnibus Wilderness Act, (5) 1984 Washington State Wilderness Act, (6) 1984 Oregon Wilderness Act.

Sources: U.S. Senate, *National Wilderness Preservation Act*, Hearings before the Committee on Interior and Insular Affairs, 85th Congress, 2d. Session, on S. 4028, Bend, Ore., November 7, 1958; U.S. Senate, *National Wilderness Preservation Act—1959*, Hearings before the Committee on Interior and Insular Affairs, 86th Congress, 1st Session, on S. 1123, Seattle, Wash., March 30-31, 1959; U.S. Senate, *The North Cascades*, Hearings before the Subcommittee on Parks and Recreation of the Committee on Interior and Insular Affairs, 90th Congress, 1st Session, on S. 1321, Washington, D.C., Seattle Wash., Mt. Vernon, Wash., and Wenatchee, Wash., April 24-25, May 25, 27, and 29, 1967; U.S. House of Representatives, *The North Cascades, Part I*, Hearings before the Subcommittee on Interior and Insular Affairs, 90th Congress, 2d. Session, on H.R. 8970 and related bills, Seattle, Wash., April 19-20, 1968; U.S. House of Representatives, *The North Cascades, Part II*, Hearings before the Subcommittee on Interior and Insular Affairs, 90th Congress, 2d. Session, on H.R. 8970 and related bills, Wenatchee, Wash., July 13, 1968; U.S. House of Representatives, *Alpine Lakes Area Management Act*, Hearing before the Subcommittee on National Parks and Recreation of the Committee on Interior and Insular Affairs, 94th Congress, 1st Session, on H.R. 3977, H.R. 3978, H.R. 7792, Seattle, Wash., June 28, 1975; U.S. House of Representatives, *Alpine Lakes Area Management Act*, Hearing before the Subcommittee on National Parks and Recreation of the Committee on Interior and Insular Affairs, 94th Congress, 1st Session, on H.R. 3977, H.R. 3978, H.R. 7792, Wenatchee, Wash., July 19, 1975; U.S. Senate, *Oregon Omnibus Wilderness Act*, Hearing before the Subcommittee on the Environment and Land Resources of the Committee on Interior and Insular Affairs, 94th Congress, 2d. Session, on S. 1384, Grants Pass, Ore., October 25, 1976; U.S. Senate, *Washington State Wilderness Act of 1983*, Hearings before the Subcommittee on Public Lands and Reserved Water of the Committee on Energy and Natural Resources, 98th Congress, 1st Session, on S. 837, Spokane, Wash., June 2, 1983, Seattle, Wash., June 3, 1983, Washington, D.C., September 30, 1983; U.S. Senate, *Oregon Wilderness Act of 1983*, Hearings before the Subcommittee on Public Lands and Reserved Water of the Committee on Energy and Natural Resources, 98th Congress, 1st Session, on H.R. 1149, Bend, Ore., July 21, 1983, Salem, Ore., August 25, 1983.

Table 7-3
Rank Order of Arguments Made by Advocates
of Wilderness Preservation in Congressional
Testimony—Field Hearings

Argument	Rank order of the argument[1]					
	(1)	(2)	(3)	(4)	(5)	(6)
	1959	1968	1976	1976	1984	1984
	Wild.	N.	Alp.	Ore.	Wash.	Ore.
	Act	Casc.	Lake	Omn.	Wild.	Wild.
					Act	Act
1. Natural beauty	4	2	2	1	3	3
2. Spiritual reflection	5	5	8	11	12	12
3. Solitude	7	6	8	9	11	11
4. Cultural resources	12	0	0	16	14	15
5. Outdoor recreation	1	1	1	3	1	2
6. Preserve ecosystems	13	10	11	6	8	3
7. Preserve wildlife, plantlife	9	9	5	2	2	1
8. Preserve endangered species	0	14	14	8	12	9
9. Preserve watersheds	8	13	13	6	7	6
10. Preserve ecosystem services	0	14	0	14	16	15
11. Preserve old-growth forests	9	4	5	13	9	5
12. Nature valued in its own right	0	12	10	14	15	14
13. Preserve for future generations	2	3	3	4	6	12
14. Worthless lands	5	10	4	5	4	3
15. Preserve for scientific purposes	2	8	12	12	9	8
16. Preserve for economic purposes	9	7	7	9	5	7

[1]The subject of the testimony for each column is as follows: (1) 1959 National Wilderness Preservation Act, (2) North Cascades National Park, (3) Alpine Lakes Wilderness Area, (4) Oregon Omnibus Wilderness Act, (5) 1984 Washington State Wilderness Act, (6) 1984 Oregon Wilderness Act.

Table 7-4
Percentage of Advocates Making Wilderness
Preservation Arguments in Congressional
Testimony—Washington D.C.

Argument	Percentage of advocates making argument[1]						
	(1) 1968 N. Casc.	(2) 1968 Mt. Jeff.	(3) 1976 Alp. Lake	(4) 1976 Ore. Omn.	(5) 1978 End. Wild. Act	(6) 1984 Wash. Wild. Act	(7) 1984 Ore. Wild. Act
1. Natural beauty	68.8	42.9	54.5	45.5	50.0	25.0	8.7
2. Spiritual reflection	0.0	0.0	9.1	5.0	0.0	0.0	8.7
3. Solitude	0.0	14.3	0.0	9.1	10.0	0.0	4.3
4. Cultural resources	0.0	0.0	0.0	0.0	12.5	34.8	0.0
5. Outdoor recreation	62.5	42.9	72.7	45.5	50.0	50.0	47.8
6. Preserve ecosystems	0.0	14.3	0.0	45.5	20.0	37.5	34.8
7. Preserve wildlife, plantlife	12.5	42.9	9.1	45.5	30.0	87.5	69.6
8. Preserve endangered species	0.0	0.0	0.0	18.2	0.0	12.5	13.0
9. Preserve watersheds	0.0	7.1	9.1	45.5	35.0	37.5	39.1
10. Preserve ecosystem services	0.0	0.0	0.0	0.0	0.0	0.0	0.0
11. Preserve old-growth forests	25.0	21.4	27.2	9.1	10.0	50.0	17.4
12. Nature valued in its own right	0.0	0.0	0.0	0.0	0.0	0.0	0.0
13. Preserve for future generations	12.5	14.3	0.0	18.2	20.0	12.5	8.7
14. Worthless lands	6.3	28.6	18.2	6.4	45.0	37.5	43.5
15. Preserve for scientific purposes	12.5	7.1	0.0	5.5	15.0	0.0	8.7
16. Preserve for economic purposes	6.3	14.3	0.0	3.6	0.0	50.0	47.8
Diversity index (total)	206	250	191	277	290	413	387
% instrumental 6,7,8,11	60.0	85.7	100.0	50.0	63.6	66.7	38.9

[1]The subject of the testimony for each column is as follows: (1) North Cascades National Park, (2) Mount Jefferson Wilderness Area, (3) Alpine Lakes Wilderness Area, (4) Oregon Omnibus Wilderness Act, (5) Endangered American Wilderness Act, (6) 1984 Washington State Wilderness Act, (7) 1984 Oregon Wilderness Act.

Sources: U.S. Senate, *The North Cascades*, Hearings before the Subcommittee on Parks and Recreation of the Committee on Interior and Insular Affairs, 90th Congress, 1st Session, throughout on S. 1321, Washington, D.C., Seattle, Wash., Mt. Vernon, Wash., and Wenatchee, Wash., April 24-25, May 25, 27, and 29, 1967; U.S. Senate, *San Gabriel, Washakie, and Mount Jefferson Wilderness Areas*, Hearings before the Subcommittee on Public Lands of the Committee on Interior and Insular Affairs, 90th Congress, 2d. Session on S. 2531, S. 2639, and S. 2751, Washington, D.C., February 19-20, 1968; U.S. Senate, *Alpine Lakes Management Act of 1976*, Hearing before the Committee on Interior and Insular Affairs, 94th Congress, 2d. Session on H.R. 7792, Washington, D.C., June 22, 1976; U.S. House of Representatives, *Alpine Lakes Management Act*, Hearing before the Subcommittee on National Parks and Recreation of the Committee on Interior and Insular Affairs, 94th Congress, 2d. Session on H.R. 3977, H.R. 3978, and H.R. 7792, Washington, D.C., June 17, 1975; U.S. Senate, *Oregon Omnibus Wildernss Act*, Hearing before the Subcommittee on Parks and Recreation of the Committee on Energy and Natural Resources, 95th Congress, 1st Session on S. 658, Washington, D.C., April 21, 1977; U.S. Senate, *Endangered American Wilderness Act of 1977*, Hearing before the Subcommittee on Parks and Recreation of the Committee on Energy and Natural Resources, 95th Congress, 1st Session on S. 1180, Washington, D.C., September 19-20, 1977; U.S. House of Representatives, *Endangered American Wilderness Act*, Hearings before the Subcommittee on Indian Affairs and Public Lands of the Committee on Interior and Insular Affairs, 95th Congress, 1st Session on H.R. 3454, Washington, D.C., February 28, March 1, May 2 and 6, 1977; U.S. Senate, *Washington State Wilderness Act of 1983*, Hearings before the Subcommittee on Public Lands and Reserved Water of the Committee on Energy and Natural Resources, 98th Congress, 1st Session on S. 837, Spokane, Wash., June 2, 1983, Seattle, Wash., June 3, 1983, Washington, D.C., September 30, 1983; U.S. House of Representatives, *Additions to the National Wilderness Preservation System*, Hearings before the Subcommittee on Public Lands and National Parks of the Committee on Interior and Insular Affairs, 98th Congress, 2d. Session on S. 837, Washington, D.C., June 7, 1984; U.S. House of Representatives, *Additions to the National Wilderness Preservation System*, Hearings before the Subcommittee on Public Lands and National Parks of the Committee on Interior and Insular Affairs, 97th Congress, 2d. Session on H.R. 7340, Washington, D.C., December 2 and 6, 1982; U.S. House of Representatives, *Additions to the National Wilderness Preservation System*, Hearings before the Subcommittee on Public Lands and National Parks of the Committee on Interior and Insular Affairs, 98th Congress, 1st Session on H.R. 1149, Washington, D.C., February 14, 1983; U.S. Senate, *Oregon Omnibus Wilderness Act of 1983*, Hearings before the Subcommittee on Public Lands and Reserved Water of the Committee on Energy and Natural Resources, 98th Congress, 1st Session on H.R. 1149, Washington, D.C., October 20, 1983.

Table 7-5
Rank Order of Arguments Made by Advocates of
Wilderness Preservation in Congressional
Testimony—Washington D.C.

Argument	Rank order of the argument[1]						
	(1)	(2)	(3)	(4)	(5)	(6)	(7)
	1968	1968	1976	1976	1978	1984	1984
	N.	Mt.	Alp.	Ore.	End.	Wash.	Ore.
	Casc.	Jeff.	Lake	Omn.	Wild.	Wild.	Wild
					Act	Act	Act
1. Natural beauty	1	1	2	1	1	8	10
2. Spiritual reflection	0	0	0	8	11	0	10
3. Solitude	0	6	0	8	9	0	4
4. Cultural resources	0	0	0	0	0	9	6
5. Outdoor recreation	2	1	1	1	1	2	2
6. Preserve ecosystems	0	6	0	1	6	5	6
7. Preserve wildlife, plantlife	4	1	5	1	5	1	1
8. Preserve endangered species	0	0	0	6	0	9	9
9. Preserve watersheds	0	10	5	1	4	5	5
10. Preserve ecosystem services	0	0	0	0	0	0	0
11. Preserve old-growth forests	3	5	3	8	9	2	8
12. Nature valued in its own right	0	0	0	0	0	0	0
13. Preserve for future generations	4	6	0	6	6	9	10
14. Worthless lands	7	4	4	11	3	5	4
15. Preserve for scientific purposes	4	10	0	12	8	0	10
16. Preserve for economic purposes	7	6	0	13	0	2	2

[1]The subject of the testimony for each column is as follows: (1) North Cascades National Park, (2) Mount Jefferson Wilderness Area, (3) Alpine Lakes Wilderness Area, (4) Oregon Omnibus Wilderness Act, (5) Endangered American Wilderness Act, (6) 1984 Washington State Wilderness Act, (7) 1984 Oregon Wilderness Act.

The Olympic National Park legislation is not considered in the tables because so few advocates for creation of the park testified. The testimony was lengthy but generally involved few individuals. The prime mover in lobbying for the Olympic National Park was the Emergency Conservation Committee with its three key operatives, Rosalie Edge, Willard Van Name, and Irving Brant (see Chapter 6). Edge and Van Name testified before Congress in Washington, D.C., and their arguments as well as those of other park advocates were generally instrumental and intangible. The main argument employed in testimony was that a park should be created to preserve not only the scenic high country but also the heavily timbered valleys with their rain forests and very large old trees. The primary reason given for preserving these forests was their natural beauty.[4] Some also argued that creation of a national park would benefit the local economy by attracting tourists to the area.

Willard Van Name argued that a primary reason for creating the park was to preserve the winter range of the Roosevelt elk and protect the elk from hunters. The elk used the lowland forests as winter habitat. While Van Name argued strenuously for preservation of the elk in an Emergency Conservation Committee pamphlet as well as before Congress, he never did really state why the elk should be preserved, except that it was an endangered species.[5] The purpose of elk preservation was not to increase hunting opportunities because national parks by law precluded hunting. Van Name argued as if no further justification was needed beyond stating that the elk was threatened with extinction.

The idea of establishing a park to preserve a species was apparently new. Up to this time, the central argument used to justify national parks was the preservation of monumental scenery, although this argument was often supplemented with the view that national parks increase tourism. As already noted, the key necessary condition for creation of a park, according to Alfred Runte, was that its lands be worthless for purposes of commodity production.[6] This was not the case for Olympic National Park with its stands of large old-growth forests, but at least two of those testifying in favor of the park pointed out that the number of jobs that could be sustained by logging instead of preserving the old growth would be relatively small.[7]

In contrast to the Olympic National Park hearings, the field hearings (held in various locations in the Pacific Northwest) for the legislation listed in Table 7-2 involved relatively large numbers of individuals testifying. The field hearings also involved a much larger number than Washington, D.C., hearings on the same legislative issues (Table 7-4). The field hearings and the Washington, D.C., hearings were distinctly different in character. The latter involved a small number of individuals who were generally representatives of interest groups giving lengthy testimony, much of it on technical details, while the former involved a larger number of individuals giving short, concise testimony. Because the field hearings with more individuals testifying are more broadly representative, the analysis of shifts in the frequency of use for particular arguments over time concentrates on the field hearings. The first step in the analysis is to consider trends in frequency of use for each of the arguments listed in Table 7-1. The data on frequency of use are presented in Table 7-2, while the rank order of frequency of use for individual arguments is presented in Table 7-3.

For the first three arguments (natural beauty, spiritual reflection, and solitude), there is no obvious trend over time in frequency of use. It is not surprising that the natural beauty argument was used most frequently by advocates of North Cascades National Park, given the dramatic quality of the landscape in the area. Preservation of wilderness as a cultural resource or symbol was seldom used as an argument. A few native Americans did testify that certain potential wilderness areas contained locations of cultural significance to them, and some argued that wilderness symbolizes frontier conditions faced historically by white settlers. By far the most popular argument was that wilderness ought to preserved for recreational purposes. While substantial, the frequency of use for this argument did diminish somewhat in the 1970s and 1980s as other arguments gained in popularity. For testimony on the Oregon Omnibus Wilderness Act and the 1984 Oregon Wilderness Act, this argument lost its number one rank order position to the natural beauty and wildlife preservation arguments, respectively.

The most dramatic changes in frequency of use occur for the ecosystem, plant and animal, endangered species, and watershed preservation arguments. Preservation of ecosystems or plants and animals was seldom mentioned as a reason for preserving wilderness in testimony on the 1964 Wilderness Act and the North Cascades National Park. The ecosystem preservation argument moved from a rank order of 13 for the 1959 Wilderness Act testimony to a rank order of 3 for the 1984 Oregon Wilderness Act testimony. The plant and wildlife argument moved over the same period from a rank order of 9 to a rank order of 1. Preservation of ecosystem services was not a popular argument, while the preservation of old-growth forests occupied the middle range of rank orders and was fairly stable over time in terms of frequency of use, supporting the notion that forest preservation was a significant goal of wilderness preservation for many who testified.

The preservation of ecosystems and organisms for their own sake was not mentioned by anyone in the 1959 Wilderness Act Pacific Northwest field hearings, but was mentioned by 5 of the 334 preservation advocates who testified in the North Cascades National Park field hearings. This argument was not explicitly made in the Dinosaur National Monument hearings in the 1950s, nor was it made in the Olympic National Park hearings in the 1930s (see Chapter 1). The north Cascades hearings occasioned its first usage. In the 1970s and 1980s, the frequency of use rose to 5-6 percent of preservationists testifying in field hearings. Preservation for future generations was a relatively popular argument in most of the hearings, although its popularity seemed to fall off in the 1984 Oregon Wilderness Act hearings. The worthless lands argument was also comparatively popular throughout the hearings, as was the preservation for economic purposes, the latter gaining some in popularity over time.

Finally, the preservation of wilderness for scientific and educational purposes was a relatively common argument made in congressional testimony. This argument was used with greatest frequency in field hearings on the 1959 Wilderness Act, possibly because it was one of the reasons mentioned in the act itself for preserving wilderness, along with preservation of natural beauty, recreational opportunities, and wildlife.[8]

Three major trends of special interest can be observed in the data reported in Table 7-2: (1) an increase in the diversity of arguments used over time, (2) an increase in the use of arguments that are open ended in the sense that they are neither explicitly instrumental or noninstrumental in character, and (3) the emergence of the use of the argument that wilderness is valuable in its own right independent of what it can do for human beings. Because the concern of this chapter is primarily with shifting attitudes toward wilderness and old-growth forests, each of these trends is important and requires further discussion.

In the more recent hearings on Pacific Northwest preservation issues, a wider variety of arguments were typically used by advocates of wilderness and forest preservation. The diversity of arguments used can be roughly measured by summing up the percentage using each argument for each preservation issue. If every individual made every argument for each preservation issue in Table 7-2, then the sum, the diversity score, would be 1,600 given 16 possible arguments. If each person used only the same three arguments, for example, the score would be 300. Hence, the summation of the percentage of wilderness advocates making each argument can serve as a rough measure of the diversity of arguments employed, and the diversity score, as can be seen in Table 7-2, does have an upward trend over time. The point is a simple one—the rhetoric used by wilderness preservation advocates appears to have gained in sophistication over time. Certainly, the arguments employed in justifying the 1984 Oregon and Washington wilderness acts were more diverse and complex than those employed by the advocates for Olympic National Park in the 1930s. The complexity and diversity of the rhetoric reflects the emergence of new kinds of arguments made for the preservation of wilderness and old growth.

Perhaps the most dramatic change over time in the testimony, one that contributed to the complexity of arguments favoring preservation, was the increase in the use of ecosystem, plant and animal, endangered species, and old-growth forest preservation as arguments for the justification of wilderness. The growing use of these arguments reflects an increasing concern with the preservation of ecosystems and their constituent organisms. And, again, whether this concern was rooted in instrumental or noninstrumental views of nature is not always clear in the testimony.

From 40 to 60 percent of those using ecosystem, plant and wildlife, endangered species, and old-growth forest preservation arguments implied that they were doing so for instrumental reasons, such as increasing the opportunities for hunting, fishing, or the observation of nature (see Table 7-2, % instrumental 6, 7, 8, 11). A few supported ecosystem preservation instrumentally for the ecosystem services they provide, such as clean air, clean water, and climatic stabilization (argument 6). On the other hand, 40 to 60 percent argued for ecosystem or flora and fauna preservation without explicitly stating any instrumental reason.

Some of these individuals could be making their arguments because they believe that ecosystems or their constituent organisms have value in their own right, but their beliefs are not known and are open to speculation. The fact that they leave their position unexplained could indicate that they hold a noninstrumentalist view and fear that it may not be readily understood or accepted. The idea of nonhuman organisms having value in their own right may not have much appeal to instrumentally oriented members of Congress, who are perhaps more inclined to look at what different interest groups gain or lose and the relative capacities of those groups to influence election results than the finer points of ethical justification for preserving the natural world. In all the testimony made by wilderness advocacy groups in Washington, D.C., hearings (Table 7-4), no one argued for wilderness on noninstrumental grounds, suggesting that such arguments would not have been received with much favor.

Nonetheless, some of those testifying in field hearings did make concrete noninstrumental arguments suggesting that nature is valuable in its own right and should be defended independent of any instrumental values it provides (Table 7-2, argument 12). (The comments of those making such arguments are provided in Appendix 7A.) Wilderness was assumed to be valued in its own right if the arguement was that wilderness or its component organisms have intrinsic value, have rights to exist, are sacred, are objects of reverence, are equivalent in value to human beings, or are morally considerable. A claim of intrinsic value usually means that the object has value in itself independent of instrumental benefits. Similarly, a claim that something has rights presumes that it has value in itself or value in its own right. To claim that something is sacred or deserving of reverence presumes that it has value in its own right or is a part of some larger being (i.e., God) that is of value noninstrumentally. Finally, to claim that something is deserving of moral concern is to imply that it is valuable in its own right. None of these statements presumes any particular philosophical foundation for the idea of value in its own right. Such value could be intrinsic in the sense that something having intrinsic value has a specific teleological goal it pursues. This would fit the objectivist view of value described in Chapter 1. Or such value could be conferred by valuing agents who value something independent of any instrumental benefits they receive from it. This would fit the subjectivist view also described in Chapter 1.

Those who used noninstrumental arguments in congressional testimony did not rely on them entirely and tended to intermingle them with instrumental arguments. In doing so, they seemed to believe that their position was buttressed with one type of argument lending support to the other. The general attitude seemed to be that wilderness and old-growth forests should be preserved because it is the right thing to do, and if those forests yield instrumental human benefits, this makes the justification for doing so all the easier.

Noninstrumental arguments, even when intermixed with instrumental arguments, may not find a favorable audience with those in positions of political power who are used to viewing things in instrumental terms. Therefore, the rather low pertages for those arguing that ecosystems or organisms are valued for themselves (Table 7-2, 12) may represent the tip of the iceberg insofar as real attitudes are concerned. Remember, John Muir suppressed his noninstrumental valuations of the natural world in his public arguments for the preservation of natural areas (see Chapter 1). Since people will often refrain from making arguments that they feel may be unacceptable to listeners they are trying to convince, the fact that some do make such arguments may reflect the depth of their feelings, or may indicate that such arguments are gaining in acceptability. One major public opinion survey conducted in the early 1980s did find that many accept the idea that nature is valuable in its own right.[9] The point is a simple one: the relatively small percentage of wilderness advocates explicitly making noninstrumental arguments for the preservation of wilderness and old-growth forests may not fully reflect the extent to which noninstrumental values are actually held by wilderness advocates.

Beyond the 5 percent or so who made noninstrumental arguments explicitly in the late 1970s and early 1980s, the actual proportion of wilderness advocates that would support the idea that wilderness and its constituent organisms have value in their own right cannot be determined from Pacific Northwest congressional testimony on wilderness issues. It is true, however, that the proportion making such arguments increased from zero in the 1950s to a positive figure in the 1970s and 1980s. In the next chapter, we will see whether or not focusing on the endangered species issue increases the extent of noninstrumental arguments made by preservationists. In the late 1980s and early 1990s did explicitly noninstrumental moral arguments for preserving nature come out of the closet?

Evolution, Holism, and Noninstrumental Values in the Wilderness Preservation Movement

To better understand the final stage of the old-growth preservation movement to be taken up in Chapter 8, certain emergent trends in preservationist thinking need to be elaborated more fully, trends that are apparent in articles in the *Sierra Club Bulletin* as well as in congressional testimony. Fundamental to preservationist thought from the 1950s on was a new view of the functioning of Darwinian evolution and Aldo Leopold's ecologically based land ethic. Together, the Darwinian and Leopoldian approaches to understanding nature led in the direction of a noninstrumental valuing of natural ecosystems.

In writing about the philosophical outlook of the Sierra Club in the 1960s, Susan Schrepfer convincingly argues that the club's leadership accepted the post-1950s Darwinian synthesis, which denied the idea that evolution was directed toward the goal of evolving ever more complex life forms (i.e., human beings).[10] Under directed evolution, the human species was seen as the culmination of the evolutionary process by virtue of its superior intellectual capacities and ability to develop a complex culture and technology. The notion of directed evolution dominated biological thinking in the first half of the century, according to Shrepfer, but was largely rejected by scientists in the 1940s. In its place was substituted the original Darwinian position that evolution is a consequence of chance variation in genetic material and opportunistic selection of genetic traits in response to changing environmental conditions. According to the Darwinian synthesis, the human species was the result of chance adaption to environmental change, not the final end of the evolutionary process. As Schrepfer points out, "club activists no longer saw man as the summit of directional evolution."[11] Rather, they saw all species as valuable because of their contributions to genetic diversity and began to question the virtues of technological and industrial advances that threatened genetic diversity and the survival of species. The club went so far as to ask the courts to give legal standing to wild areas and their plants and animals.[12] While it was unsuccessful in its attempt, this move at a philosophical level indicates acceptance of the idea that nonhuman natural beings have rights and are subjects of moral concern.

According to Aldo Leopold, "All ethics so far evolved rest upon a single premise: that the individual is a member of a community of inter-dependent parts," and that the "land ethic enlarges the boundary of the community to include soils, waters, plants, and animals, or collectively: the land."[13] This idea that human beings are part of a biotic community flows naturally from the Darwinian conclusion that humans are members of but one species among many, all of which originate from a common process. Rather than being at the culmination of the evolutionary process and thus legitimately dominating nature, in Leopold's view "a land ethic changes the role of *Homo sapiens* from conqueror of the land-community to plain member and citizen of it."[14] While Leopold never explicitly discusses the issue of whether land has value in its own right, the viewing of land in ethical terms and the placing of the human species on the same plane as other organisms, by implication suggests the acceptance by him of a noninstrumental view of land. Nonetheless, Leopold by no means rejects the instrumental values of land and wilderness. He sees wilderness specifically as an aesthetic, recreational, and scientific resource and as a place where the preservation of wildlife can be fostered.[15]

Leopold's life work can be seen, in a sense, as an attempt to integrate the scientific, aesthetic, and ethical dimensions of the land and wilderness. As both Max Oelschlaeger and Bryan Norton point out, Leopold's attitude toward nature evolves from a utilitarian view of the land as a producer of game animals for human use, to the view that land is a living organism that needs to be protected from the ravages of modern land use practices.[16] For Leopold, ecological understanding fosters an aesthetic appreciation of the forces of nature; this in turn fosters a love for nature; and love of nature is the necessary premise for a land ethic. Oelschlaeger sees Leopold's thinking as moving toward a postmodern ecocentric attitude toward nature, while Norton sees Leopold as seeking out a rationale for the preservation of nature that integrates instrumentalist and noninstrumentalist values.[17] For Norton, both the utilitarian aggregators who want to quantify the benefits of wilderness preservation and the moralists who see nature as valuable in its own right can find a common ground in the preservation of the ecological context, the fount of both instrumental and noninstrumental values. While Norton does not see Leopold ultimately accepting a position that nature is valuable apart from human use, it does seem clear that there is an evolution in Leopold's attitudes from the scientific and utilitarian, to the aesthetic, and finally to the ethical. To enjoy the beauty of nature is to receive an instrumental benefit, but it is also to identify with the creative potential of nature's evolutionary process and to realize that the process is something that should enter the ethical realm, not because it provides benefits to human beings, but because it is valuable in its own right as an order creating enterprise.

However one views Leopold philosophically, his conception of the land ethic has had a profound effect on the attitudes of activists in the wilderness and old-growth forest preservation movement. In a sense, activist thought as expressed in both congressional testimony and writings recapitulates the development of Leopold's thinking, moving from esthetics and ecological understanding toward ethics. In the 1960s wilderness advocates in the Pacific Northwest relied to a large extent on recreational, aesthetic, and scientific arguments to justify their position. In the 1970s and 1980s, wilderness legislation was increasingly supported on the grounds that ecological systems ought to be preserved. Some of those testifying made rather complex arguments about the human relation to nature, suggesting generally that human beings are a part of a larger whole, arguments that differ little in basic meaning from those made by Leopold (see Appendix 7B). In the 1967 Senate hearings on the north Cascades, one proponent of the park claimed that a land ethic has evolved to replace "the old self-centered theory that the earth was made for man alone." In the 1975 House hearings on the Alpine Lakes wilderness, one advocate talks about "development of an ecological conscience, something perhaps most completely formed from our first experience of ourselves as part of a larger, all-encompassing whole." In Senate hearings on the Oregon Wilderness Act in 1983, a wilderness proponent indicated that "from an essentially anthropomorphic view of wilderness— man in or near the center—I found myself swinging radically to the biocentric view which places man 'in the corner' (so to speak) as an equal with all the other forces that shape the land and make the ecological system work."

Whether these individuals were familiar with the works of Darwin or Leopold is not known, but certainly their views are consistent with the Darwinian synthesis and Leopold's conception of the land community. In congressional testimony, as already noted, there is a movement over time toward a more complex attitude toward nature, one that sees wilderness and forests in their natural state as not only a source of particular instrumental benefits, but as containing complex ecological systems deserving of preservation because they both deliver human benefits and are valued in their own right.

While a movement toward a holistic view of nature and the idea that nature is valuable in its own right constitutes a minor trend by comparison to the continued dominance of disconnected instrumental arguments for wilderness preservation presented in congressional testimony, the trend is rather stronger in articles by wilderness activists in the *Sierra Club Bulletin*. The need for a land ethic was expressed as early as 1952 in an article by Charles C. Bradley:

It is a fair bet that our ethical sense will evolve in the future as it has in the past and that it will be extended finally to the earth and all its inhabitants. . . . The preservation of wilderness is a good first step in a land ethic, for by it we concede the possibility that other forms of life have at least the right to live, and it gives us time to focus our intellect on the problem.[18]

In a 1956 article, A. Starker Leopold rejected the notion that we preserve wilderness for recreation, scientific study, and aesthetic appreciation alone and argued instead that "the only possible force that could be motivating the effort to preserve natural areas is the moral conviction that it is right—that we owe it to ourselves and to the good earth that supports us to curb our avarice to the extent of leaving a few spots untouched and unexploited."[19] In earlier articles, David Brower, the executive director of the Sierra Club, focused on the conventional arguments for wilderness,[20] but by 1962 he was arguing that wilderness produces "a wealth of organic forms of unpredictable value,"[21] and by 1964 he was suggesting that "wilderness will not be safe enough until there is a broader appreciation of it, until we learn to extend reverence for life to other life than our own."[22] Elaborating on a holistic vision in a 1967 article, Brower makes the following statements:

Wilderness is no longer extensive enough to protect itself. Man must now protect it from himself. He must supply the sense, the hearing, the taste, the smell, the touch, the seeing, making sure that he does not blindly oppose progress but that he never lets blind progress go unopposed. What progress seems to have achieved is so spectacular that it preempts our attention; it lets us forget the most important element of all—the life force, the unbroken link to the beginning of life on earth, that from the long-ago beginning on down to each of us has never failed to reproduce itself well and move on. That force, in two billion years, has also produced a miraculous complexity of living things, each more dependent upon the others than we know. It has produced organic wholeness, and Robinson Jeffers would have us "love that, not man apart from that."[23]

Here we have the clearest statement yet of Darwin and Leopold synthesized. It is the marvel of evolution that has created the land community with all its interdependencies, and we should love not only our own species but organic life as a whole.

A holistic and ethical vision of nature became the official position of the Sierra Club in its 1970 "Report of the Wilderness Classification Study Committee." The role of this committee was to organize studies of potential wilderness areas and to present testimony on them at public hearings. In this report, the need for wilderness was addressed, and the key conclusions were as follows:

> A new land ethic is essential for man's survival, one in which man must love, respect and admire the natural world, one under which he has an obligation to protect nature and the earth from his own activities. Man's law must adapt to this obligation, and he must adjust his way of life to live as a member of the land community, rather than as a conqueror. . . . The new land ethic must be based on the concept that a thing is right when it tends to preserve the integrity, stability and beauty of the biotic community.
>
> In the new land ethic, wilderness must be preserved for its inherent value. Portions of the planet must be protected from man's impact, for the primary value of wilderness is the natural environment preserved within it.
>
> Man should be welcome in any wilderness area only on the condition that he accepts it as wilderness and does not damage it, and only in such numbers as an individual area can withstand without noticeable impairment. Only recreational and scientific facilities compatible with preservation of an area should be allowed in any wilderness.[24]

The influence of Leopold in the report is obvious, as is the primacy of preserving wild nature for its own sake.

Conclusion

In the 1950s, wilderness preservationists relied heavily on disconnected instrumental arguments in testimony before Congress. They argued that wilderness should be preserved in order to increase recreation opportunities, preserve natural beauty for public enjoyment, and provide opportunities for scientific research. By the 1960s, a few of those giving testimony began to see the preservation of whole ecosystems as a goal of wilderness preservation and began to conceive of the human being as a part of, rather than as a conqueror of, nature. In the 1970s and 1980s, the number of those testifying that a central purpose of wilderness preservation was to preserve ecosystems increased significantly. Moreover, the number of those seeing nature as valuable in its own right increased from none in the 1950s to around 5 percent in the 1970s and 1980s. While this signifies a possible trend toward an ethical view of nature by wilderness advocates, instrumentalist arguments nonetheless continued to dominate wilderness advocacy testimony in the Pacific Northwest through 1984. Whether this changed significantly in the late 1980s and early 1990s with the emergence of the spotted owl issue is the subject of the next chapter. The largest of the wilderness advocacy organizations, the Sierra Club, had by 1970 clearly adopted a holist and ethical view of the natural world as the basis for justifying the preservation of wilderness.

Appendix 7A

Valuing Nature for Itself: Comments from Hearings, 1968-1983

House Hearings, North Cascades, Seattle, 1968:

It [North Cascades] has extremely high, in fact "priceless" intrinsic value as a splendid portion of our national heritage.[25]

Wilderness has intrinsic value that cannot be priced on today's market.[26]

. . . if we have any regard to mankind, we must have some reverence or regard for the planet which has nourished life as we know it and for the myriad related forms and species of life with which our human lives coexist.[27]

This proposed park has an immense intrinsic value of itself for ourselves to enjoy when we desire to go into it. The park plan prepares for an ever-increasing demand on the area, to protect it from exploitation and to preserve it for the greater value of the nature contained therein.[28]

House Hearings, Alpine Lakes, Seattle, 1975:

We do not base our testimony in support of the citizens bill on economics because we believe that other factors will and should determine the future of the Alpine Lakes. The lakes country must be evaluated for its intrinsic worth.[29]

Some persons have been raised to believe that all nature must be controlled by mankind and everything must be utilized. In their view use is good, nonuse is bad. Others hold that we humans must coexist with what else is on the Earth and that we have no exceptional rights to eliminate everything in our path.[30]

I look upon this great mountain province as my home and consider myself a citizen of it. Realizing that this area is my home, I would like to see it protected as anyone would like to have his home protected, but there are many other animal citizens to whom this country is more properly their home than mine or anyone's. Unfortunately we do not yet have these other citizens represented in our legislative process. People must represent them since only in our legislative process will their home become secure.[31]

I wish to bring to your attention three items on the rights of wild things, wild creatures and wild things and wild trees have a right to survive in the wilderness.[32]

Our lives here are closely tied to the forests, as living things of sanctity and beauty, not just crops and products.[33]

Schweitzer wrote: "The stronger the reverence for natural life, the stronger grows also that for Spiritual life." It is man's sympathy with all creatures that firm makes him truly a man. "To the man who is truly ethical all life is sacred, including that which from the human point of view seems lower in scale."[34]

The values of wilderness are intrinsic and are being destroyed throughout this country because they are not readily economical.[35]

House Hearings, Alpine Lakes, Wenatchee, 1975:

These mountains, meadows, valleys, and streams are more important than any single occupation, mine included. My friends, these wild lands were here long before us and they have a right to remain long after we are gone.[36]

I have been horrified by much of the testimony this morning in that wilderness is supposed to have only the value of the odd person who happens to wander through it. I believe wilderness has value in its own right and I am willing to support wilderness in other parts of the world where I have no access.[37]

Senate Hearings, Oregon Omnibus Wilderness Act, Grants Pass, 1976:

What is wilderness? It is a beautiful, wild, natural place where plants and animals have evolved over the centuries and have adapted and live in harmony. . . . Can we put a price tag on wilderness? I say only to say that it is priceless. Some can look on the trees in the forest and see only what could be made out of it in the way of dollars and cents. I look upon trees and plants as almost something sacred, related to us in a very intimate way.[38]

It is distressing that so few have yet come to really understand the intrinsic value of the land itself.[39]

As a carpenter I have a moral commitment to wilderness. I don't want the feeling that I'm using up the last timber from a once great forest.[40]

As we start to take seriously the goal of sharing the planet with other living things, rather than exploiting it for human purposes only, protection of wilderness becomes urgent.[41]

Man is an animal, and there are many other animals with whom we share this planet from whom much is yet to be learned. Each is entitled to his place. Just because ours is considered the higher intelligence does not give us the right to take over what little space is left for the wild creatures who cannot survive elsewhere.[42]

Senate Hearings, Washington State Wilderness Act, Spokane, 1983:

There is intrinsic value in mountains, trees and slopes which is in the eye of the beholder.[43]

I think it is important that we understand that those areas are valuable in and of themselves, even if not even one single backpacker was allowed into them.[44]

Forests and especially the big trees have as much a right to live as any other beings on this planet.[45]

Senate Hearings, Washington State Wilderness Act, Seattle, 1983:

Washington's wild heritage deserves protection "because it is there." It is the existing value of nature itself that calls for preservation.[46]

. . . because of the need to teach a reverence for all life, we have environmental education programs in this State that utilize wilderness areas as an educational tool.[47]

Senate Hearings, Oregon Wilderness Act, Bend, 1983:

God wanted to humble us into recognizing that nonhuman creation has value to Him totally apart from our self-seeking human designs on it.[48]

We are privileged here in Oregon to have these species still with us and owe this to our expanses of wilderness and roadless area. I feel that we have a moral responsibility to these animals and consider the acreage in the House Bill to be a minimum allocation for their protection.[49]

Very little has been written about the intrinsic value of the undisturbed, naturally evolving plant communities. . . [50]

All wilderness is biocentric. The land and the plant and animal life deserve protection on their own merits.[51]

Let us also assume that each of these wild areas are homeland for numerous life forms . . . let us assume that these forms are unique, as valuable and as much a part of creation as we humans. Can we not afford to set aside 4.5 million additional acres as homeland for non-humans?[52]

Senate Hearings, Oregon Wilderness Act, Salem, 1983:

Minimum morality, as well as practical considerations, dictates concern for other living things on this planet.[53]

This is a proposal that's a little different from anything you've probably seen before. It's not based solely on economics; it's based largely on emotion and respect, respect for nature. We feel it's time for people to admit that there are things more important or as important as human activities, and that there is value in things that don't directly bring us material profit. Wilderness should be wilderness for the sake of a forest, not as an issue of recreation or commerce.[54]

Appendix 7B

Ecological Holism and the
Human Connection to Nature:
Comments from Hearings, 1967-1983

Senate Hearings, North Cascades, Seattle, 1967:

> The old self-centered theory that the earth was made for man alone to exploit has long ago been disproved. In its place has evolved a new set of land ethics. . . . [55]
>
> . . . to have dominion over the earth must mean to have responsibility for the earth. Man cannot be an exploiter, but a partner with God in creation.[56]

House Hearings, North Cascades, Seattle, 1968:

> Many of these people are professionals in related fields of ecology. Their conviction comes from knowledgeable concern with the interrelatedness of the life of man and all forms of life.[57]
>
> I seriously question whether any human being can even come close to understanding himself and his life if he has no acquaintance with or comprehension of the ways of nature—that natural world from which and with which he has evolved on this planet over at least two-billion years, and with which his life is still intimately and inextricably entwined.[58]

House Hearings, Alpine Lakes, Seattle, 1975:

> It seems to me that what is called for now is the development of an eco-logical conscience, something perhaps most completely formed from our first experience of ourselves as part of a larger, all-encompassing whole. . . . I believe part of an alternative solution to our problems is to recognize the wisdom found in the homeostatic, self-balancing forces of nature; in short to develop an ecological conscience and to give nature a vote.[59]
>
> In a very real sense these great forests are my church. Here, in the green silence, there is peace and serenity and the sure knowledge that I am a part of all creation. . . . Yet all of us need this sense of place, the knowledge that each of us is truly a part of the whole.[60]

Senate Hearings, Oregon Omnibus Wilderness Act, Bend, 1977:

> I want my child to grow up with a better perspective of man's relationship and dependence on nature, and he can only get this if there are wilderness areas left for him to use.[61]

A visit to the wilderness is, for me, a spiritual experience. It makes me feel more a part of the world, and helps me to recognize man's interdependence with nature.[62]

Senate Hearings, Oregon Wilderness Act, Salem, 1983:

From an essentially anthropomorphic view of wilderness—Man in or near the center—I found myself swinging radically to the biocentric view which places man "in the corner" (so to speak) as an equal with all the other forces that shape the land and make the ecological system work.[63]

Notes

1. Holmes Rolston III, "Values in Nature, pp. 113-28; and "Valuing Wildlands," *Environmental Ethics* 7 (1985): 23-48.

2. Runte, *National Parks*, pp. 33-47.

3. In the published record of congressional hearings, a submitted written statement often follows the actual transcript of the testimony. Both the written statements and the actual testimony were coded, and arguments appearing in the written statement but not in the actual testimony were included in the analysis. The written statements were often more comprehensive and longer than the actual testimony. The apparent reason for not all arguments being presented in the actual testimony was the pressure of time limits that were frequently placed on all those testifying.

4. U.S. House of Representatives, *Mount Olympus National Park*, Hearing before the Committee on the Public Lands, 74th Congress, 2d. Session, on H.R. 7086, Washington, D.C., April 23-25, 27-30, May 1 and 5, 1936 (Washington, D.C.: U.S. Government Printing Office, 1939).

5. Ibid., pp. 96-104; Emergency Conservation Committee, "Protect the Roosevelt Elk," Publication no. 69 (New York: Emergency Conservation Committee, March, 1938).

6. Runte, *National Parks*, pp. 48-64.

7. U.S. House of Representatives, *Mount Olympus National Park*, pp. 97, 204.

8. Wilderness Act of 1964, *U.S. Code*, Public Law 88-577.

9. Lester W. Milbrath, *Environmentalists: Vanguard for a New Society* (Albany: State University of New York Press, 1984).

10. Susan R. Schrepfer, *The Fight to Save the Redwoods: A History of Environmental Reform: 1917-1978* (Madison: University of Wisconsin Press, 1983), pp. 79-102.

11. Ibid. p. 99.

12. Ibid.; *Sierra Club v. Morton et al.*, 405 U.S. 727 (1972).

13. Leopold, *A Sand County Almanac*, p. 239.

14. Ibid., p. 240.

15. Ibid., pp. 280-95.

16. Oelschlaeger, *The Idea of Wilderness,* pp. 205-42; Bryan G. Norton, *Toward Unity among Environmentalists* (New York: Oxford University Press, 1991), pp. 39-60.

17. Oelschlaeger, *The Idea of Wilderness,* pp. 238-42, 293; Norton, *Toward Unity among Environmentalists,* pp. 53-60.

18. Bradley, "Wilderness and Man," p. 65.

19. A. Starker Leopold, "Wilderness and Culture," *Sierra Club Bulletin* 42 (June 1957): 37.

20. David R. Brower, "Scenic Resources for the Future," *Sierra Club Bulletin* 41 (December 1956): 1-10; "Wilderness Conflict and Conscience," *Sierra Club Bulletin* 42 (June 1957): 1-12.

21. David Brower, "Definitions for Inner Space," *Sierra Club Bulletin* 47 (December 1962): 39.

22. David Brower, "The Irreplaceables, Foundations, and Conventional Heresy," *Sierra Club Bulletin* 49 (December 1964): 9.

23. David Brower, "Toward an Earth International Park," *Sierra Club Bulletin* 52 (October 1967): 20.

24. Francis Walcott et al., "Report of the Wilderness Classification Study Committee," *Sierra Club Bulletin* 55 (Nov.-Dec. 1970): 17-19.

25. U.S. House of Representatives, *The North Cascades, Part I,* p. 457.

26. Ibid., p. 524.

27. Ibid., p. 549.

28. Ibid., p. 557.

29. U.S. House of Representatives, *Alpine Lakes Area Management Act,* Hearing before the Subcommittee on National Parks and Recreation of the Committee on Interior and Insular Affairs, 94th Congress, 1st Session, on H.R. 3977, H.R. 3978, H.R. 7792, Seattle, Wash., June 28, 1975 (Washington, D.C.: U.S. Government Printing Office, 1975), p. 71.

30. Ibid., p. 145.

31. Ibid., p. 183.

32. Ibid., p. 190.

33. Ibid., p. 242.

34. Ibid., pp. 249-50.

35. Ibid., p. 259.

36. U.S. House of Representatives, *Alpine Lakes Area Management Act,* Hearing before the Subcommittee on National Parks and Recreation of the Committee on Interior and Insular Affairs, 94th Congress, 1st Session, on H.R. 3977, H.R. 3978, H.R. 7792, Wenatchee, Wash., July 19, 1975 (Washington, D.C.: U.S. Government Printing Office, 1975), p. 149.

37. Ibid., pp. 152-53.

38. U.S. Senate, *Oregon Omnibus Wilderness Act,* Hearing before the Subcommittee on the Environment and Land Resources of the Committee on Interior and Insular Affairs, 94th Congress, 2d. Session, on S. 1384, Grants Pass, Ore., October 25, 1976 (Washington, D.C.: U.S. Government Printing Office, 1976), p. 78.

39. Ibid., p. 165.

40. Ibid., p. 166.
41. Ibid., p. 250.
42. Ibid., p. 258.
43. U.S. Senate, *Washington State Wilderness Act of 1983*, p. 173.
44. Ibid., p. 361.
45. Ibid., p. 367.
46. Ibid., p. 410.
47. Ibid., p. 600.
48. U.S. Senate, *Oregon Wilderness Act of 1983*, p. 88.
49. Ibid., p. 145.
50. Ibid., p. 147.
51. Ibid., p. 179.
52. Ibid., p. 185.
53. Ibid., p. 569.
54. Ibid., p. 1005.
55. U.S. Senate, *The North Cascades*, Hearings before the Subcommittee on Parks and Recreation of the Committee on Interior and Insular Affairs, 90th Congress, 1st Session, on S. 1321, Washington, D.C., Seattle, Wash., Mt. Vernon, Wash., and Wenatchee, Wash., April 24-25, May 25, 27, and 29, 1967 (Washington, D.C.: U.S. Government Printing Office, 1967), p. 321.
56. Ibid., p. 322.
57. U.S. House, *The North Cascades, Part I*, p. 452.
58. Ibid., p. 457.
59. U.S. House, *Alpine Lakes Area Management Act*, pp. 224-25.
60. Ibid., p. 244.
61. U.S. Senate, *Oregon Omnibus Wilderness Act*, p. 58.
62. Ibid., p. 237.
63. U.S. Senate, *Oregon Wilderness Act of 1983*, p. 997.

8

Valuing Endangered Species
and Old-Growth Forests:
Toward Ethical Holism

By the end of the 1980s, the movement to preserve old-growth forests in the Pacific Northwest had entered a new and much more serious phase. As a consequence of successful court actions brought by preservationist groups, timber harvesting in most western Oregon and western Washington old-growth forests was brought to a halt in 1989 and again in 1991 and 1992. The success of these court actions can be traced to research findings suggesting that the northern spotted owl is dependent on old-growth forests and is threatened with extinction because of the decline of those forests. The economic consequences of halting timber harvesting in old growth far exceeds those of past preservation efforts, and the result has been a political polarization of preservationists, who advocate saving spotted owls and old growth, and workers in the timber industry, who see spotted owl preservation as threatening their own livelihood.

The purpose of this chapter is to first summarize events leading up to the stoppage of old-growth timber harvesting and then to explore further the value underpinnings of old-growth preservation. Our central concern will be to determine whether more that just instrumental values explain the intense interest in the preservation of old-growth forests.

Old-Growth Preservation
and the Spotted Owl

Up to and including the passage of the Oregon and Washington wilderness acts in 1984, the preservation of old-growth forests was the consequence of a larger movement for the creation of national parks and wilderness areas. While the preservation of old growth was one of the motives for creating national parks and wilderness areas, it was not always the central goal. In the 1980s, the movement to preserve Pacific Northwest old growth took on a life of its own independent of wilderness preservation issues.

Interest in preserving old-growth was stimulated by provocative research findings overturning the conventional wisdom that old-growth forests were wildlife wastelands devoid of biological interest.[1] Research by Jerry Franklin and his colleagues undertaken in the 1970s and 1980s suggested that old growth was a unique, biotically diverse ecosystem type. In addition, research by Eric Forsman and others found that at least one species, the spotted owl, was dependent on old growth and, as a consequence of old-growth habitat decline and fragmentation, was threatened with extinction.[2] These research results found a sympathetic audience among wilderness preservationists and environmentalists with their emerging holistic view of the natural world.

With the completion of the RARE II wilderness struggle in 1984, Pacific Northwest preservationists turned to the spotted owl and old-growth preservation issues. While groups such as the Wilderness Society continued to pursue expansion of the wilderness system, other means for preserving forests took on greater importance, for example, intervening in the national forest planning process. The National Forest Management Act, passed in 1976, was an attempt by Congress to spell out more carefully the meaning of multiple use and sustained yield, the guiding principles of national forest management. Under this act each national forest was to formulate a 50-year management plan, and, in response, the Wilderness Society established a Forest Management Program in 1981 to monitor planning on each national forest.

In 1984, this program was merged into the Resource Planning and Economics Department, whose principle function was to evaluate forest plans in order to root out timber sales generating revenues below costs and determine the impacts of such plans on roadless areas, wildlife, and ecosystems. At the local level, coalitions of individuals from a variety of conservation groups, including the Wilderness Society, Sierra Club, and local Audubon societies, would analyze forest plans as they were released, generate publicity, and supply comments to the Forest Service about negative impacts. When necessary these groups entered administrative appeals or went to court to attempt to modify the plans.[3] The Wilderness Society devoted substantial resources to monitoring the national forest planning process for the specific purpose of saving old-growth forests in the Pacific Northwest. In June of 1988, the society released its longest and most detailed report on any conservation subject ever, entitled "End of the Ancient Forests." This report addressed how the carrying out of national forest plans without modification in the Pacific Northwest would fragment and decimate remaining stands of old growth.[4] The society also devoted considerable resources to determining the amount of national forestland remaining in old growth.[5] These efforts were designed to support interventions in the national forest planning process.

Rather than seeking permanent preservation in a wilderness classification, the key strategy followed by preservationists in the 1980s was to undertake administrative appeals of both Forest Service and Bureau of Land Management (BLM) planning and operational procedures, and ultimately to undertake court suits when necessary. Appeals were frequently made on the grounds that environmental impact statements and environmental assessments under the National Environmental Policy Act were inadequate.

While in the early 1980s appeals of old-growth timber sales were generally made on the grounds that recreational or other nontimber uses would be lost, by the late 1980s, the most frequent basis for an appeal was the loss of spotted owl habitat.[6] The spotted owl was designated as a candidate for protection under the Endangered Species Act in 1973, and by 1977, the Forest Service and BLM had adopted spotted owl management plans. Although these and subsequent plans were viewed by many as inadequate, administrative appeals of them were denied by the Forest Service and BLM in the late 1970s and early 1980s. In 1985, the secretary of agricultural sustained one such appeal, and the Forest Service was required to write an environmental impact statement for spotted owl management. The release of the final environmental statement for spotted owl management led to a major court case in Seattle, *Seattle Audubon Society, et al. v. F. Dale Robertson, et al.* Shortly before this, another court case involving the spotted owl commenced in Portland, *Portland Audubon Society v. The Secretary of Interior, Donald Hodel*, against the BLM. Both cases tied up old-growth timber sales for significant periods of time.

The Portland case was brought against the BLM in October of 1987 on the grounds that it had not prepared a supplemental environmental impact statement taking into consideration new information on the possible extinction of the spotted owl. The BLM was planning to go ahead with timber sales on the assumption that Congress had exempted it from considering new information as normally required under the National Environmental Policy Act. In appropriations bills (Section 312 or 314, 1987-1990 Interior Appropriations Bills), Congress had stated that the BLM and Forest Service could continue management of their lands under existing resource management plans without considering new information that became available subsequent to the completion of those plans. The contention of the plaintiff in the Portland suit was eventually rejected by the district court in May of 1989, a decision that was sustained by the appeals court in September of the same year. The court agreed that the BLM indeed should consider new information under the National Environmental Policy Act, but the court argued it could not force the BLM do so because of the congressional exemption. In the meantime, sales of some 500 million board feet of old-growth were delayed.[7]

The Seattle case had an even wider ranging impact on old-growth harvests because it encompassed all the national forests in Washington and Oregon. In response to perceived inadequacies in the Forest Service spotted owl plan, the Seattle Audubon Society and other preservation groups brought suit against the Forest Service in March of 1989 under the National Forest Management Act (NFMA) and the Migratory Bird Act. As a result of this suit, a preliminary injunction was issued halting timber sales in national forest spotted owl habitat.[8]

In the meantime, the U.S. Fish and Wildlife Service, apparently bending to political pressure from timber interests, decided not to list the spotted owl as a threatened species under the 1973 Endangered Species Act. Doing so would have required both the BLM and the Forest Service to fully protect spotted owl habitat. The Fish and Wildlife Service was subsequently sued by environmental organizations and forced to reverse its decision. Effective July 23, 1990, the spotted owl was listed as a threatened species in Oregon, Washington, and California.[9] In response to the spotted owl listing, the Forest Service asked that the injunction against logging old growth be stayed while it conferred with the Fish and Wildlife Service over management of the spotted owl as required under the Endangered Species Act. But because the conferences dragged on beyond the time limit set in the court ruling, the injunction was reimposed in September of 1989.[10]

As a consequence of this litigation, Congress was coming under increasing pressure from the timber industry to do something to get timber sales underway again. Local politicians from areas economically dependent on timber harvesting in Washington and Oregon bitterly denounced the obstructionist legal tactics of old-growth preservationists.[11] In response, the so called Hatfield-Adams bill was passed and signed into law in October of 1989. This bill was the result of a summit between environmentalists, fish and wildlife managers, and forest industry interests organized by Governor Neal Goldschmidt, Senator Mark Hatfield, and Congressman Les AuCoin, all from Oregon. The intention of the summit, held in Salem, Oregon, was to work out a compromise between the various interests, although it was strictly advisory to the congressional delegations of Washington and Oregon. The final bill (Section 318, 1990 Interior Appropriations Bill) was worked out in Washington, D.C., with preservationists managing to reduce the mandated cut on Forest Service and BLM lands from 8.0 billion board feet to 7.3 billion board feet for fiscal year 1990 and to moderate provisions precluding preliminary injunctions against timber sales. Under the final bill, court suits involving timber sales could be brought so long as temporary injunctions lasted no longer than 45 days.[12]

A basic purpose of the bill was to limit the threat to timber sales from court action during the fiscal year 1990 while at the same time providing some protection to old-growth forests and the spotted owl until final plans could be worked out for protecting the spotted owl and complying with the Endangered Species Act. Key provisions of the bill, in addition to those mention above, included the lifting of court injunctions on 1.1 billion board feet of timber, the directing of the Forest Service to minimize the cutting and fragmentation of ecologically significant old growth and to review and revise its spotted owl management plan and increase the size of designated spotted owl management habitat by 25 percent, and the creation of citizen advisory boards to review and suggest modifications to timber sales.[13] As a result of the passage of this bill, the law suit by Seattle Audubon against the Forest Service was dismissed. However, on September 18, 1990 the Ninth Circuit Court of Appeals declared that the bill violated the separation of powers doctrine, suggesting that Congress cannot impose its interpretation of the law on the courts.[14]

As a consequence of this court decision, Seattle Audubon reinstituted its law suit, and as a result an injunction against the logging of old-growth in Pacific Northwest national forests was put into effect. On May 23, 1991, Judge William Dwyer granted a permanent injunction against timber sales in spotted owl habitat until the Forest Service complied with the National Forest Management Act and ruled that the Forest Service was to do so by March 5, 1992.[15] Under NFMA, "fish and wildlife shall be managed to maintain viable populations of existing native and desired non-native vertebrate species in the planning area."[16] This means that the Forest Service must manage its old growth in such a manner as to maintain viable populations of the spotted owl.

Judge Dwyer's decision includes a fascinating account of how the Forest Service and the Fish and Wildlife Service had systematically refused to comply with laws protecting wildlife. After admitting that its 1988 spotted owl environmental impact statement was inadequate, the Forest Service did not comply with a 1989 court order (*Seattle Audubon v. Robertson*) to produce spotted owl management guidelines in 30 days. Moreover, it did not comply with the requirements of the Hatfield-Adams bill (section 318, 1990 Interior Appropriations Bill) to develop a new plan for managing the spotted owl. The Fish and Wildlife Service at the same time was breaking the law by first refusing to list the spotted owl as a threatened species and then by failing to designate critical habitat as required under the Endangered Species Act.

In 1989, the Interagency Scientific Committee was established by the Forest Service, the Bureau of Land Management, the Fish and Wildlife Service, and the National Park Service to develop a "scientifically credible" conservation strategy for the northern spotted owl. The report of this committee was released on April 2, 1990, and could have served as the basis of a Forest Service spotted owl management plan. However, cabinet level decisions prevented the Forest Service from carrying out its congressional mandate under section 318. The administration wanted to work something out that had a less drastic impact on the timber industry than the approach taken by the Interagency Scientific Committee, but it never devised a feasible alternative.[17]

Judge Dwyer also considered the economic consequences of the injunction and concluded that during the period of the injunction, Forest Service timber sales would drop between 2.07 and 2.93 billion board feet in 1991 and 1992. This is a substantial amount, but the judge pointed to mitigating factors, including 4.764 billion board feet under contract and free of legal challenge, the likelihood of increased supplies from private lands as stumpage prices increase, and the probable diversion of some logs that would otherwise be exported to the domestic market. The judge also argued that a ban on log exports would divert logs to the domestic market, and he pointed out that many timber jobs have already been lost as a consequence of automation and that the Pacific Northwest economy is no longer driven by the timber industry. In his view, "job losses in the wood products industry will continue regardless of whether the northern spotted owl is protected." He also noted that in contrast to earlier episodes of economic disruption, programs for dislocated workers are currently available to facilitate adjustments.[18]

The Portland Audubon Society reinstituted its law suit in May of 1991 on slightly different grounds than it used in the original suit, grounds that were eventually accepted by the district court in Portland after a successful appeal. In February of 1992, Judge Helen Frye granted a preliminary injunction against logging in spotted owl habitat on BLM lands in Oregon.[19] The Portland Audubon Society claimed in its suit that the BLM had failed to file a supplemental environmental impact statement that would address new scientific information on the threat to the spotted owl from habitat loss and fragmentation due to logging. By this time, the Hatfield-Adams bill was no longer in force, and a key section of it had been declared unconstitutional as noted above. In its response, the BLM claimed that it was in the process of developing spotted owl management plans that would take into account the information provided in the Interagency Scientific Committee report on the spotted owl. However, the resource management plans and environmental impact statements containing the spotted owl management plans were not to be published by the BLM until the Spring of 1993, a delay that the court viewed as unacceptable.

As a consequence of court suits, timber harvests in old-growth forests were again tied up on national forest and BLM lands in Washington and Oregon pending the development of plans to preserve spotted owl habitat. The legal strategies employed by environmental and preservationist groups to protect old-growth forests in the 1980s and 1990s were unprecedented in terms of their success. On the other hand, the economic consequences for the timber industry have been equally unprecedented. Employment declines resulting from technological improvements and the restricted availability of old growth have been significantly accelerated as a consequence of spotted owl protection.[20]

In both court cases restricting old-growth timber harvesting, the key issue was the preservation of a species threatened with extinction, the spotted owl. Even though a threatened species was the central issue in both cases, the 1973 Endangered Species Act was not the key point of contention. One case relied primarily on provisions in the National Forest Management Act, while another relied on the National Environmental Policy Act. However, the listing of the spotted owl as a threatened species under the Endangered Species Act undoubtedly added weight to the plaintiffs' arguments in both cases.

Spotted Owls and the Value Foundation of the Endangered Species Act

While the listing of the spotted owl as a threatened species lurked in the background of key court cases halting old-growth timber harvesting, the Endangered Species Act was brought to the forefront of the spotted owl and old growth preservation controversy when Secretary of the Interior Manuel Lujan, Jr., convened the Endangered Species Committee in September of 1991 to consider whether the Fish and Wildlife Service could block forty-four timber sales involving 240 million board feet of timber on Oregon BLM lands because they would jeopardize the spotted owl. Under the Endangered Species Act, the BLM must consult with the Fish and Wildlife Service when its actions could threaten a listed species. However, the Endangered Species Act permits the convening of the

Endangered Species Committee to evaluate such decisions not only on the basis of scientific information, but on economic grounds as well. This committee (often referred to as the "god squad") once convened can, in theory, rule that a government agency's actions may be undertaken even though they jeopardize a listed species if there are compelling economic reasons for doing so.[21] In the absence of this committee, the Fish and Wildlife Service cannot take into account the economic and social costs of species preservation under the Endangered Species Act. Because the Endangered Species Committee is seldom used, the Endangered Species Act on the whole is a relatively powerful tool for protecting species and their habitats.

Given the potential of the Endangered Species Act as a means of preserving species and their habitats, even at the expense of economic activity, the reason for the existence of the act and the human values that underpin it become issues of considerable interest. The central goal in this chapter is to explore the value foundations of spotted owl and old-growth preservation, both of which are ultimately tied to the threatened species issue. For many preservationists and ecologists, the spotted owl is an indicator species, one whose health serves as an indicator of the health of the larger old-growth ecosystem it belongs to. The decline of the spotted owl would thus mean that the decline of the old-growth ecosystem is soon to follow. Consequently, to understand the values that underpin the old-growth/spotted owl issue, it is useful to first explore the rationale for the Endangered Species Act and the values upon which the act was founded. Then we will be in a better position to consider the values underlying support for spotted owl and old-growth preservation.

The key provision of the Endangered Species Act of interest in the spotted owl controversy is section 7, whose major requirement reads as follows:

All other Federal departments and agencies shall, in consultation with and with the assistance of the Secretary [Interior or Commerce], utilize their authorities in furtherance of the purposes of this Act by carrying out programs for the conservation of endangered species and threatened species listed pursuant to section 4 of this Act and by taking such action necessary to insure that actions authorized, funded, or carried out by them do not jeopardize the continued existence of such endangered species and threatened species or result in the destructions or modification of habitat of such species which is determined by the Secretary, after consultation as appropriate with the affected States, to be critical.[22]

In other words, federal agencies are precluded from doing anything that would harm endangered or threatened species or their habitat no matter what the resulting economic or social consequences. In 1978, Congress created the high-level Endangered Species Committee, which could grant exemptions under section 7. To do so, however, the committee had to demonstrate that there were no reasonable alternatives to the agency actions at issue, and that the benefits of the action clearly outweighed species preservation.[23] This provision was added in response to the halting of the Tellico Dam project as the result of listing of the snail darter, a small fish believed time to live only in habitat that was to be flooded by the dam. The Endangered Species Committee, however, refused to grant an exemption in the Tellico Dam case, although Congress did approve continuation of the project in a rider attached to an appropriations bill after snail darters were removed to nearby waters.[24] Prior to the spotted owl case, the Endangered Species Committee had never used its power to grant an exemption. Given the general tendency of Congress to give priority to economic interests, the passage of a measure that largely precludes consideration of economic criteria in government agency decisions affecting threatened or endangered species seems unusual. In the early 1970s, public concern with environmental issues was clearly on the rise, including concern for endangered species, and the 1966 and 1969 endangered species acts had been found to be ineffective in dealing with the problem. President Nixon himself pointed out the limitations of the existing law, and his administration proposed new legislation. Apparently sentiment for a stricter law was widespread.[25] Although Congress at the time of passage of the act may not have realized what the ultimate costs of endangered species preservation might be in terms of reduced economic opportunities, it is also true that Congress has been reluctant to substantially weaken the act since.[26]

Congressional testimony on the 1973 Endangered Species Act reveals little about the values underlying it. Much of the testimony dealt with technical issues, and only a few who testified provided philosophical justification for the act.[27] Those who did generally reflected the instrumental values of endangered species expressed in the act itself: "These species of fish, wildlife, and plants are of aesthetic, ecological, educational, historical, recreational, and scientific value to the Nation and its people."[28] One individual testifying in the hearings did refer to the intrinsic worth of plants, while another argued that species ought to be preserved for future generations.[29]

In earlier hearings on the 1969 Endangered Species Act, however, noninstrumental values were expressed as a justification for preserving species. Russell Train, then an under secretary in the Department of the Interior, suggested that animals have value in their own right: "Many governments have for centuries given protection to those wild animals used for sport and food. It is only recently that attention has been given to the preservation of animals for their own sake and for the appreciation of future generations".[30] David Scott of the Sierra Club argued that an endangered species bill would be a step in "developing a land ethic" and quoted Joseph Wood Krutch, a noted environmental writer:

> To live healthily and successfully on the land we must also live with it. We must be part not only of the human community, but of the whole community; we must acknowledge some sort of oneness not only with our neighbors, our countrymen, and our civilization but also some respect for the natural as well as the manmade community.[31]

Lee Talbot of the Smithsonian Institution noted that "our deep concern with the problem of threatened species has two not totally separated bases—the ethical and the scientific."[32] Richard Cowan of the National Museum of Natural History quoted Russell Train who argues that "Man in hastening the extinction of other species bears a troublesome and terrifying ethical burden."[33] And James Peters, also of the National Museum of Natural History, suggested that "the Texas blind salamander has just as long an evolutionary history behind it as I have. Therefore, it has an equal right to the opportunity to survive as I have."[34] At least some who supported protecting endangered species thus did so on the grounds that species have value in their own right.

Ethical Holism, the Spotted Owl, and Old Growth

Like these supporters of species protection, we saw in Chapter 7 that some advocates of Pacific Northwest wilderness preservation in the 1970s and 1980s justified their position on the grounds that ecosystems and organisms in wilderness areas have value independent of any instrumental value they deliver to human beings. Some of these individuals justified their support for this position by arguing that they along with members of all other species are a part of a larger evolutionary process and a larger biotic community. And some gave special priority to preserving ecosystems, species, and large-scale evolutionary processes as opposed to individual organisms. With this background, we are now in a position to consider specifically the extent to which advocates of spotted owl preservation support their position on the basis of instrumental or noninstrumental values, as well as the extent to which they accept a holistic view of ecological systems and evolutionary processes. Are the advocates of spotted owl preservation interested in preserving the spotted owl as an individual species, or is their real interest in preserving the old-growth ecosystem as a whole on which the spotted owl is dependent? Moreover, are they interested in preserving spotted owls and old growth because of instrumental benefits provided to human beings, or do they take the position that spotted owls and old-growth forests are valuable in their own right?

The vehicle for investigating these questions is a content analysis of public hearings held in Portland, Oregon, on February 12 and 13, 1992, before representatives of the Endangered Species Committee on the question of whether the BLM should be exempted from the provisions of section 7 of the Endangered Species Act and allowed to harvest timber from spotted owl habitat. The content analysis results are presented in Table 8-1.

The list of preservation arguments presented in Chapter 7 was used in the analysis underlying Table 8-1 with one addition (17). This was done even though some of the arguments refer to preserving natural areas as opposed to preserving members of a particular species. Because spotted owl preservation amounts to preserving large amounts of old-growth forest, species preservation is in this case equivalent to natural area preservation. Consequently, the same sort of arguments can be used in justifying preservation of the spotted owl as were used in justifying wilderness preservation.

The one argument not used previously in content analysis and thus added to Table 8-1 is number 17, measures to preserve employment. Spotted owl preservation would substantially reduce timber harvesting and therefore employment in the forest products industry. If measures could be undertaken to offset these employment losses, the case for preserving the spotted owl is obviously bolstered. Measures suggested by those testifying included a ban on log exports, employment training programs, employment in reclamation and reforestation of cutover areas, a shift from clearcutting to more labor intensive selective cutting of forests, more extensive precommercial thinning in second growth to increase productivity, and substitution of labor intensive brush control for pesticides. Just over half of those testifying made suggestions for diminishing the impact of lost employment. Some blamed the current plight of timber industry workers on large corporate timber owners who had overcut timberlands in the past.[35]

The most striking result of the content analysis (Table 8-1) is the large percentage of testifying preservationists mentioning the need to preserve old-growth forests (75.9 percent). This figure was even higher than the percentage of those mentioning the need to preserve endangered species (51.9 percent). The real issue for many in the hearings was, therefore, the

Table 8-1
Arguments Made by Advocates of Spotted Owl Preservation
in Hearings before the Endangered Species Committee

Argument	Percentage of advocates making argument
1. Natural beauty	7.4
2. Spiritual reflection	1.9
3. Solitude	0.0
4. Cultural resources	0.0
5. Outdoor recreation	5.6
6. Preserve ecosystems	44.4
7. Preserve wildlife, plantlife	9.2
8. Preserve endangered species	51.9
9. Preserve watersheds	5.5
10. Preserve ecosystem services	16.7
11. Preserve old-growth forests	75.9
12. Nature valued in its own right	31.5
13. Preserve for future generations	31.5
14. Worthless lands	7.4
15. Preserve for scientific purposes	3.7
16. Preserve for economic purposes	20.4
17. Measures to preserve employment	51.9
Total testifying	54.0

Source: Bureau of Land Management v. U.S. Fish and Wildlife Service, Transcript of Proceedings before the Endangered Species Committee, Portland, Ore., February 12-13, 1992.

preservation of old-growth forests; the spotted owl problem was seen as important, but it was generally viewed as an indicator of a much larger problem, the decline of the old-growth ecosystem. The depth of concern with ecosystem decline is indicated by the relatively large percentage (44.4) of advocates testifying that ecosystem preservation is an important goal of restrictions on timber harvests.

By comparison to the content analysis for wilderness area testimony in the previous chapter, the proportion of advocates for spotted owl preservation making purely instrumental arguments is unusually low (Table 8-1). For example, outdoor recreation is hardly mentioned as a justification for preserving the spotted owl (5.6 percent), and it hardly could be given the reclusive nature of the bird and the difficulty of observing it in the wild for the nonscientist. Old-growth is not mentioned very often either as a recreation resource. However, a fair proportion

(16.7 percent) of those testifying refer to the importance of preserving old-growth for the ecosystem services they provide, and a significant number (20.4 percent) recognize that preserved old-growth has economic value, for example as a stimulus to tourism and as commercial salmon spawning habitat.

A key result of the analysis in Table 8-1 is the relatively high proportion of those testifying (31.5 percent) making essentially noninstrumental arguments in their defense of the spotted owl and old-growth forests. Remember, in Chapter 7 only 5 to 6 percent of wilderness advocates used noninstrumental values to support their position. Specific comments of individuals making noninstrumental arguments in the spotted owl hearings can be found in Appendix 8A. An argument was considered to be noninstrumental for purposes of coding in Table 8-1 (i.e., it could be coded under number 12) if the individual testifying directly stated that either spotted owls or old-growth forests were valuable in their own right, had intrinsic or inherent value, or possessed a right to exist. In addition, noninstrumental value was inferred if the individual testifying argued that spotted owls and forests were sacred objects deserving of respect, were morally equated to human beings in some way, or were viewed as priceless (like human beings) and thus not subject to a purely instrumental or economic form of valuation. Finally, noninstrumental value was also inferred if individuals argued that neither the "god squad" nor any human individual or group of individuals had the right to determine the fate of a species. If the spotted owl were strictly an instrument, then it would be legitimately subject to human control. If it were not viewed as being legitimately subject to any kind of human control, then it must have some sort of noninstrumental value.

Not only did a relatively large number look upon either the spotted owl or old-growth as noninstrumentally valuable in testimony, but many justified preservation on the grounds that ecosystems ought to be preserved for their own sake or for the sake of continued human survival. Some who made noninstrumental valuations justified the preservation of old growth on the grounds that ecosystems in their entirety should be preserved.[36] Some also justified species and old-growth preservation on holistic grounds without implying that ecosystems or species are valuable in their own right, and some of those justified preservation on the grounds that human beings are part of a larger ecological whole and dependent upon that whole.[37]

To summarize, those who argued in favor of preserving the spotted owl before the Endangered Species Committee to a significant extent saw the natural world as having value in its own right and believed that the primary human concern should be with the preservation of ecosystems. Many of these same individuals also expressed deep concern with the economic disruptions resulting from the decline of the timber industry in the Pacific Northwest, but suggested possible ways of mitigating the effects of this decline. Many were loath to see the issue as pitting owls against timber workers.

Conclusion

The spotted owl issue has raised the stakes in the conflict over old-growth preservation to unprecedented heights. To date, the government plans to restrict logging on 5.4 million acres of ancient forests in the Pacific Northwest in order to protect the spotted owl.[38] The government has estimated that the number of jobs lost as a result will be 32,500.[39] The amount of economic disruption anticipated by the passage of the 1984 Washington and Oregon wilderness acts pales in comparison to the consequences of spotted owl preservation. The issue has gone beyond a simple accounting of costs and benefits to become a moral one involving a conflict between the basic material interests of an industry and its workers and the continued existence of a species and an ecosystem. The reluctance of a relatively conservative administration to come down strongly on one side or the other in this conflict is illustrated by the middle ground sought in the ruling of the Endangered Species Committee. Of the forty-four timber sales it was asked to rule on, it approved only thirteen of them.[40] At this point in time, the decision is moot because of court injunctions against logging.

All this brings us to the central question of this book. How should old-growth forests and ecosystems in general be valued? Should we rely on the methodology of cost-benefit analysis suggested by economists? Or should decisions on questions of ecosystem survival be looked at in ethical terms? If this is the case, what sacrifices should human societies be willing to make on the behalf of ecosystems, and more importantly who should bear those sacrifices? These are the questions we will now take up in Chapter 9 in the context of the old-growth preservation issue.

Appendix 8A
Noninstrumental Evaluations and
Environmental Holism: Comments from the
Endangered Species Hearings on the
Spotted Owl

The following are comments of spotted owl preservation advocates who expressed some type of noninstrumental evaluation of spotted owls or old-growth forests or else discussed the issue in terms of the larger ecological or environmental effects of not preserving old-growth forests and spotted owls. The comments are numbered sequentially as they appear in the hearings.

Noninstrumental Valuation

1. The ancient forests of the Pacific Northwest are living spiritual entities from the roots deep underground to the tips of the giant, lofty conifers which touch the face of the creator. The ferns, frog-eyed salmon, and spotted owls are all a very important part of that living spiritual force. . . . On behalf of the spotted owl and future endangered wildlife, do the right thing. . . . We can and must learn to live in harmony with creatures we share space with on this small, beautiful planet. And also do the right thing for our children's sake. It's their world tomorrow.[41]

2. This God Squad fraud is a disgrace. And we are all shamed by it. Not you, not I, not anyone here has the right to say whether or not a whole species or, worse yet, a whole ecosystem is expendable. I hope when you go back to the beltway and places like that and tell people what you have learned here in Oregon that you will be able to tell them first-hand what this old-growth forest dilemma is all about. I hope that you will have made the time to walk in the cathedral forests of the Northwest and listen to the sounds of God. If you had, you will know what you must do. If not, then listen to those of us who are speaking for the forests, which cannot be here today to speak for itself.[42]

3. I am going to read a poem that I wrote about two years ago, and this is called "The Forest Speaks."

> Trails of shadows of darkness with glistening light shining through mystical branches of beauty, the trees of mystery, the mountains of dreams. Beauty overlooking the destiny of life entwined of death. Trees perceive death in the faces of man. Why do they destroy such love, shared through the beauty of the earth? Do they not realize I am the soul of breath to which they live? As a being of love, I share many secrets, many mysteries through these branches of light.
> Would you not like to be in a trail of mystery as my family looks upon you? Our arms wide open, giving love, shade and coolness. The beauty of earth's bright blue sky above as I perceive your smiling awe-filled faces. I understand the freedom of your spirit. Know that we are one and can live in harmony. Know also that, even though my roots are firmly planted, my spirit is free, too. Many a human walks through these trails with hatred, destruction, and greed in mind.
> Do you not have a price for your life? Of course not. No amount of life and beauty of the soul has a price. Let me be free of these evils and

let there be freedom of love and warmth in your heart. Maybe some day, my generation can be free of destruction, and therefore my beauty put smiles upon the faces of another generation. Let us stop the destruction and let my family reach into your souls with our light, life, and love.[43]

4. I oppose exemptions to protection measures for the northern spotted owl, for I believe that we must preserve the remaining ancient forests, both for its own sake and also as a basis for the restoration of natural ecosystems in the Pacific Northwest. We don't hear too much anymore about the quality of life, but I believe, as a home-grown Oregonian, that we need the ancient forests so that future generations will have their chance at life, liberty and the pursuit of happiness.[44]

5. . . . my main point is, what you are deciding is the possible fate of a species, a life form. Can we take it in our hands to determine the fate of a life form just because we can? Do we have the right to do so? I would like to ask that question.[45]

6. The owl is simply a domino. If it goes belly up, then, the whole chain starts to go down. Marbled murrelet, tailed frog, goshawk, you name it—oh, not to mention a couple dozen species of wild salmon. It's time to start addressing real issues here and stop Mickey Mousing with them. The Endangered Species Act is here to save lives. Ultimately, it will save your own.

Any species that depends on the extinction of other species is in itself doomed to extinction.

Stop looking for a cheap way out of the problem and address the real issue. The owls, the trees, the salmon have as much a right to live as we do.[46]

7. So the larger question then is whether we will continue to treat the earth as a collection of resources to be exploited for human use and profit or shift our perspective to realize that all species have a right to exist for their own sake, that wilderness needs no human justification, and to realize that if we destroy the earth's life systems, we destroy our own life support.[47]

8. And when you take these messages home and make those decisions, your children are going to learn from those decisions you make. They will learn to be just as destructive as you.

None of the animals can be here to testify of their fear and pain of losing their shelter, watching their homes being destroyed every day, watching their waters being poisoned, the air being poisoned. You think about that.

The wildlife can't lobby in Washington, D.C. They can't do those things.

They don't have a voice. And it's your responsibility to be their voice, to protect their habitat, their environment. That belongs to them, not me. It doesn't belong to you either. The land belongs to the animals that live there. We are only guests when we walk onto the land.[48]

9. We will never get back the 90 to 95 percent we have given up, but we can surely exercise the common sense and decency to respect god's creation a little bit. . . .

If we have to change jobs, as I do, or retrain ourselves in order to not squander our creator's gifts to us, then I say, by God, let's do the right thing and make the sacrifices.

Let's ask ourselves how our actions will help us solve real survival issues like global warming, the ozone hole, the dwindling rain forests, and our endangered wild fellow travelers on our planet.

Finally, I might hope, or even expect my fellow human animals to share the pain of my job loss, but I cannot ask in good conscience human or nonhuman animals to die for the sake of my job security.[49]

10. The second thing I would like to say is, I think not only is this God Squad ridiculous but it is completely immoral. The idea of taking life, endangered species, old-growth forests, things of beauty and of substance and putting them on the balance scale with money and economic stability is disgusting to see which one weighs more.[50]

11. These BLM forests we are talking about are public forests, and they belong to the animals that live there, the trees that live there, and they also belong as much to me and the young kids and babies here in Oregon and in New York and in Florida and all over the country as much as they do to these timber companies.[51]

12. I want to be able to recognize that both them, spotted owls and freckled children, are endangered species that deserve our love, deserve our support and deserve our care.[52]

13. My question today is, who gave you the power to decide the survival of future generations of plant, animal, and human species alike? Surely it was not the God I know of. A sensible God would have chosen one who respected and honored His creations and allowed them to flourish, not one who is making this world unsafe for even his own survival.

Before you make any decisions, walk on the silent earth. Feel that you too are a part of it.[53]

14. Do you really believe that owls and trees and salmon have no bearing on our survival? Global warming is not just greenhouse gasses. It is also disappearing forests, and these forests aren't just disappearing in the tropics. I would be angry that I was even being asked to make a

decision that no human being has the right to make. To knowingly cause and allow the extinction of an entire living thing is not something for a human to decide. Only God can decide, not a God Squad.

The ancient Greeks had a word to describe the transgression or, more to the point, the crime of any human who would assume godly powers. It was called hubris.[54]

15. Our grandfathers with creation entrusted and mandated that we nurture, love, and protect our living mother, this earth.[55]

This is a wilderness, and it belongs to God and the animals that we are here to protect first, not the profiteers or not—not our creature comforts.

So please take into consideration the crying out that I do and that we all really feel, not just because we are looking to fill our pockets, but somewhere deep down in our soul we are looking for—to do something right instead of just continuing the status quo.[56]

16. The creator placed spotted owls in ancient forests. And when our owls die, we are all in trouble. Hard times have descended upon the Northwest. Our flagrant disregard for the health and well-being of our holy sacred mother, the earth, has ended the heyday of logging.[57]

The old-growth logger and the spotted owl are brothers, standing closer together on this sacred circle than most.

I would only hope that you remember this holy sacred circle and the fact that our loggers and our owls both occupy a place on that sacred circle. And I would like to ask you, please, to listen to the women that you hear giving testimony in your hearing and listen to the voice tones, not the words, because the voice tones of a mother of children who may be put out of work because of this controversy are the same voice tones of a mother spotted owl or a mother tree.[58]

17. I think that this issue is actually one of the most important since the issue . . . of slavery because the question really is, who and what deserves to live in freedom. And also, are we willing to make the changes in our society and in the way that we live?[59]

And I am not real comfortable doing that, but there is a verse in Genesis that says, . . . "God saw it all and it was very good." And God did not say that it's all very good except for the spotted owls.

God also . . . did not say it's all very good except for people, except for loggers.[60]

The preservation of us and of the spotted owl and of our ecosystem here in the Northwest and around the world is going to cost.

God never said it would be easy.[61]

Holism

1. . . . . you have to consider the big picture once in a while. And the big picture is that we have a serious global ecological crisis going on, and every small forty-four timber sales that we—we are marginalizing our own existence.[62]

2. I think that we should heed the words of the American Indian who was here earlier today and we should respect and take care of the land. We should honor future generations. I think our actions should begin with those values. I think we should realize that clean water and clean air and the forests that clean the water and air sustain us.[63]

3. How have we become so disconnected from the earth that we are actually allowing these six men to make a choice between short-term economic benefit and the lives of thousands of species?

We are all part of nature, not above it. Any harm that we do to our environment ultimately comes back to harm ourselves.[64]

4. So we need to save our Northwest ecosystems, contribute to stabilizing global climate, maintain biological diversity, and save our families and communities, too.[65]

I urge all of us to organize behind programs of reclamation and restoration so your grandchildren will also have jobs and a living earth.[66]

5. The near wipeout of the Indian population itself was an ecological disaster. We could have learned much from these people. The previous 10 or 20,000 years was a friendly interaction between all diverse creatures, including the human beings, and all the living beings on this continent.

By saving what is left of the old forest ecosystem and using it as a seed—understanding, as a seed to expand it, to promote diversity. How to regain the strength of expansion of all living creatures and planet and trees should be the present goal. That's what I am asking. Leave the old growth alone and use it as a seed and as an example to start growing new old growth.[67]

Notes

1. Victor M. Sher and Andy Stahl, "Spotted Owls, Ancient Forests, Courts and Congress: An Overview of Citizens' Efforts to Protect Old-Growth Forests and the Species That Live in Them," *Northwest Environmental Journal* 6 (1990): 362-63.

2. See Chapter 5 for a discussion of Franklin's and Forsman's research.

3. T. H. Watkins, "The Conundrum of the Forest," *Wilderness* 49 (Spring 1986): 13-49.

4. T. H. Watkins, "Blueprint for Ruin," *Wilderness* 52 (Fall 1988): 56-60; Wilderness Society, "End of the Ancient Forests: Special Report on National Forest Plans in the Pacific Northwest (Washington, D.C.: Wilderness Society, 1988).

5. Peter H. Morrison, "Old Growth in the Pacific Northwest."

6. Donald G. Balmer, "United States Federal Policy on Old-Growth Forests in Its Institutional Setting," *Northwest Environmental Journal* 6 (1990): 339-42.

7. Balmer, "United States Federal Policy," pp. 355-57; Sher and Stahl, "Spotted Owls," pp. 368-71.

8. Sher and Stahl, "Spotted Owls," pp. 372-75.

9. Ibid. pp. 365-67.

10. Ibid. pp. 373-74.

11. U.S. House of Representatives, *Forestry Issues in the Pacific Northwest*, Hearing before the Subcommittee on Forests, Family Farms, and Energy of the Committee on Agriculture, 101st Congress, 2d. Session, Olympia, Wash., August 31, 1990 (Washington, D.C.: U.S. Government Printing Office, 1990), pp. 40-44.

12. Balmer, "United States Federal Policy," pp. 348-50; Patricia Byrnes, "A Compromise More Pragmatic Than Pleasing: Ancient Forest Agreement," *Wilderness* 53 (Winter 1989): 3-4.

13. Byrnes, "Compromise," p. 4.

14. Sher and Stahl, "Spotted Owls," p. 382.

15. *Seattle Audubon v. Evans*, 771 F. Supp. 1081 (W.D.Wash. 1991).

16. Ibid., p. 1083.

17. Ibid., pp. 1085, 1089-90.

18. Ibid., pp. 1094-95.

19. *Portland Audubon v. Lujan*, 784 F. Supp. 786 (D.Or. 1992).

20. The extent of harvest reductions and employment declines resulting from spotted owl protection will be addressed more fully in Chapter 9.

21. "Land Bureau Seeks Timber Sales Despite Presence of Protected Owl," *New York Times*, September 12, 1991, p. A13.

22. PL 93-205, 81 Stat. 884 (Dec. 28, 1973).

23. Daniel J. Rohlf, *The Endangered Species Act: A Guide to Its Protections and Implementations* (Stanford, Calif.: Stanford Environmental Law Society, 1989), p. 29; 16 U.S.C. Section 1536(h).

24. Rohlf, *The Endangered Species Act*, pp. 3, 29.

25. Ibid. p. 23.; U.S. Senate, *Endangered Species Act of 1973*, Hearings before the Subcommittee on Environment of the Committee on Commerce, 93rd Congress, 1st Session, on S. 1592 and S. 1983, Washington, D.C., June 18, 21, 1973 (Washington, D.C.: U.S. Government Printing Office, 1973), pp. 51-75.

26. Rohlf, *The Endangered Species Act*, p. 25.

27. Ibid., pp. 23-24.

28. U.S.C. Section 1531(a).

29. U. S. Senate, *Endangered Species Conservation Act of 1972*, Hearings before the Subcommittee on the Environment, Committee on Commerce, 92nd

Congress, 2d. Session, on S. 249, S. 3199, and S. 3818, Washington, D.C., August 4, 10, 1972 (Washington, D.C.: U.S. Government Printing Office, 1972), p. 314; U.S. Senate, *Endangered Species Act of 1973*, p. 120.

30. U.S. House of Representatives, *Endangered Species*, Hearings before the Subcommittee on Fisheries and Wildlife Conservation of the Committee on Merchant Marine and Fisheries, 91st Congress, 1st Session, on H.R. 248, 992, 3790, 4812, 5252, 6634, Washington, D.C., Feb. 19, 20, 1969 (Washington, D.C.: U.S. Government Printing Office, 1969), p. 18.

31. Ibid., p. 73.

32. Ibid., p. 153.

33. U.S. Senate, *Endangered Species*, Hearings before the Subcommittee on Energy, Natural Resources, and the Environment of the Committee on Commerce, 91st Congress, 1st Session, on S. 335, S. 671, and S. 1280, Washington, D.C., May 14, 15, 1969 (Washington, D.C.: U.S. Government Printing Office, 1969), p. 80.

34. Ibid., p. 93.

35. For one example, see *Bureau of Land Management v. U.S. Fish and Wildlife Service*, Transcript of Proceedings before the Endangered Species Committee, Portland, Oregon, February 12 and 13, 1992 (Portland, Ore.: Bricker Nodland Studenmund Inc., 1992), pp. 319.

36. In Appendix 8A, under Noninstrumental Evaluation, see comments 6, 7, 9, and 14.

37. See the comments under the Holism section of Appendix 8A.

38. Keith Schneider, "Acting Grudgingly to Guard Owl, White House Backs New Logging," *New York Times*, May 15, 1992, p. 1.

39. Ibid.

40. "Panel Votes for Jobs, against Spotted Owl," *Milwaukee Journal*, May, 14, 1992, p. A.

41. *Bureau of Land Management v. U.S. Fish and Wildlife Service*, pp. 11-12.

42. Ibid., p. 18.

43. Ibid., p. 19.

44. Ibid., pp. 27-28.

45. Ibid., p. 29.

46. Ibid., pp. 31-32.

47. Ibid., p. 34.

48. Ibid., pp. 38-39.

49. Ibid., pp. 59-60.

50. Ibid., p. 71.

51. Ibid., p. 98.

52. Ibid., p. 102.

53. Ibid., pp. 126.

54. Ibid., pp. 164, 166-67.

55. Ibid., p. 307.

56. Ibid., pp. 309-310.

57. Ibid., p. 337.

58. Ibid., pp. 338-39.
59. Ibid., p. 340.
60. Ibid., p. 341.
61. Ibid., p. 343.
62. Ibid., pp. 47-48.
63. Ibid., p. 93.
64. Ibid., pp. 138-39.
65. Ibid., p. 181.
66. Ibid., p. 182.
67. Ibid., p. 356.

9

How Should Old-Growth Forests Be Valued?

Our discussion, to this point, has focused on providing insight into how old-growth forests have been valued in the past. To understand the various ways in which forests have been valued is a necessary first step in addressing the explicitly normative question of how forests should be valued.

The valuing of forests has historically gone through a cycle. Prior to European contact, Pacific Northwest Indians treated nature generally and forests specifically with deference and respect and exercised restraint in their exploitation of nature's resources (Chapter 3). European settlers, on the other hand, looked at Pacific Northwest forests in instrumental terms and were primarily interested in harvesting the wealth of timber the forests provided or in clearing them away for agriculture (Chapter 4). Timber harvesting since settlement has resulted in the elimination of old-growth forests containing very large trees, some of which were more than 600 years old, the replacement of old growth with young stands permitted to grow no older than 40 to 90 years prior to harvesting, and the disappearance of a biologically unique old-growth ecosystem type (Chapter 5). With the relative decline of the timber industry beginning as early as the 1930s, a strict adherence to an instrumental evaluation of forests solely for the wood fiber they contained was no longer an economic necessity. With declining timber dependency in the Pacific Northwest, alternative views of old-growth forests became possible, and a movement to preserve wilderness and old growth emerged (Chapter 6).

In the beginning years of this movement, wilderness and forests were seen to be instrumentally valuable as recreational resources; as places for the enjoyment of natural beauty, solitude, and spiritual reflection; and as watersheds and habitats needed for the preservation of valuable species, such as the salmon. Later on, wilderness and old-growth preservationists also began to see forests and the species they contain as valuable for noninstrumental reasons, and, in addition, they began to look upon forests as ecological wholes and to see that the preservation of whole ecosystems is necessary for the continued health of all living species including human beings (Chapters 7 and 8). Many old-growth preservationists by the early 1990s looked upon forests as valuable in their own right and valuable as a part of an ongoing evolutionary process from which all life has emerged. Like the presettlement Pacific Northwest Indians, preservationists now want to see nature treated with respect and restraint.

What does all this mean for the question of how old growth should be valued in the modern world? Should we use the cost-benefit approach suggested by economists in valuing old-growth forests and in deciding whether they should be cut or preserved? Or, should we use some sort of ethical principle in this decision, and if we do, how do we ethically compare old-growth forests and spotted owls with the livelihood of timber industry workers? The goal of the rest of this chapter is to address these questions, taking into account the historical material on valuing old-growth covered in the preceeding eight chapters. The first step will be to consider the cost-benefit approach as an evaluative procedure. The limitations of cost-benefit analysis will suggest the need for an ethical standard in valuing old-growth forests. The second step will be to describe and evaluate a holistic environmental ethic applicable to resource decisions, such as the issue of old-growth preservation. The final step will be to address the issue of the need to mitigate the human costs of old-growth preservation in order for it to be a valid ethical choice.

The Economic Approach to Valuing
Old Growth and Its Limitations

The economic justification for harvesting old growth is relatively simple. Old-growth forests are decadent in the sense that increments to woody biomass through growth are offset by death and decay of trees and tree branches. Also, old-growth timber is highly valued because it is contained in large trees that produce high-quality, defect-free wood. Old-growth forests thus have large volumes of valuable wood, but additions to wood volume are no longer occurring. Young forests, however, add wood at a comparatively high annual rate up to approximately 100 years of age. Consequently, to maximize the amount of woody material available for human use, old-growth forests should be harvested and converted to managed, even-aged forests that are harvested every 40 to 90 years. By harvesting old growth now, there will be an initial pulse of high-quality timber and then, after a 40-to-90-year gap, a steady flow of timber production in the future. By leaving old-growth forests standing, there will be no net production of new wood, the standing wood will go to waste, and future timber flows from managed second growth stands will be forgone.[1]

If attitudes toward forests are strictly instrumental and the only instrumental value in forests is wood, the above analysis would be sufficient. However, when other instrumental values are recognized in old-growth forests, the analysis needs to be expanded. Such values, as previously noted, could include hunting, observing, or photographing wildlife that find habitat in old growth; hiking, scenic observation, and scientific research; and the storing of genetic diversity and exotic compounds for society's future use. An example of the latter is the recent discovery that taxol found in Pacific yew bark and needles can be used for the treatment of cancer. These uses of old growth are not normally obtainable through market transactions and thus require public sector intervention to assure their supply.

To determine whether the economic value of these uses of old growth in a preserved state exceeds the value of timber harvesting requires a method of evaluation that mimics the assignment of value in normal market processes. Natural resource economists have devised an approach called the contingent valuation method involving the use of surveys to estimate the amount individuals would be willing to pay to preserve specified amounts of natural areas, such as old-growth forests. These surveys are constructed as carefully as possible so as to elicit reasonably accurate, unbiased responses. Additional old-growth forests ought to be to preserved under the contingent evaluation and cost-benefit methodology so long as the total of society's willingness to pay for preservation exceeds the present value of added land in timber production. To the extent that values, such as preserving old growth for future generations or preserving old growth for itself, motivate willingness to pay, the willingness-to-pay criterion could be said to have an ethical content. However, this approach, as we will see, is not equivalent to the application of an environmental ethic.[2]

As discovered in Chapters 7 and 8, some of those who favor the preservation of old growth do so on the grounds that it is valuable in its own right. To make this claim is equivalent to a moral commitment to preserve whatever it is that has this kind of value. Given such an attitude, the moral sphere encompasses not only human beings but the world of nature as well. To view old-growth forests as morally considerable is to be committed to their continued existence and well-being even if they will never be observed or never provide any kind of benefit flow. The idea of commitment goes beyond the notion of utility interdependence, implying an abstract commitment to a being of a particular kind, not just to an arbitrary individual that happens to generate a sympathetic emotional response.[3] Judging some being outside the self, such as spotted owls or old-growth forests, as morally considerable is the ultimate altruistic act, suggesting a willingness to defend that being's existence and make personal sacrifices in the process without expectation of reward. Given the logical possibility that natural entities are morally considerable, what are the consequences for the economic approach to valuing the natural world generally and old-growth forests specifically?

The standard goal of cost-benefit analysis is to discover those allocations of natural resources that will maximize net benefits. When net benefits are maximized, those who receive benefits in excess of costs will be able to compensate any losers (who experience costs in excess of benefits) and still be better off than if resources were not efficiently exploited. This is the central justification for seeking the net benefits maximizing solution. Once a morally considerable nature is admitted, however, compensation for losses is no longer possible where a particular resource allocation results in the destruction of something in nature that is held to be morally considerable, such as spotted owls or an old-growth forest. Neither the destroyed entity nor the moral agent who holds that entity to be worthy of moral consideration can be compensated. If one holds, say, the spotted owl as a species to be of moral concern, it is obvious that the species itself cannot be compensated for its destruction. If it could, the moral problem would disappear. If the moral agent could be compensated, the moral problem would also disappear, at least for the moral agent. However, a moral agent cannot be compensated in the form of instrumental values for such a loss, as we will now see.

A moral position is a commitment to some end that is not readily given up by the holder. A true moral position cannot be bought off in exchange for something of instrumental value.[4] Attaining a moral end is always preferred to not attaining it no matter what the level of income received for instrumental uses. In other words, no increase in income is sufficient to render the individual indifferent between the income gain and the loss of a moral end. Indifference between a moral end and an instrumental value is ruled out, and compensation for the loss of a moral end is not possible. A wedge is driven between personal well-being and moral choice.[5] If I view old-growth forests as morally considerable, then there is nothing of instrumental value you can give me to convince me to alter my position. Moral ends are commensurable, but moral ends and instrumental values are not, except to the extent that instrumental values can be a means of achieving moral ends.[6] If I control the fate of old-growth forests, then no amount of money would convince me to permit them to be destroyed, unless doing so allowed me to achieve some more highly ordered moral end. Even if the latter were the case, it would not really be a form of compensation because it would force me into a moral dilemma, to choose one moral end over another. Even though they are commensurable, moral ends are traded one for the other with great reluctance.

In using cost-benefit analysis to determine the disposition of a publicly owned, exploitable natural resource such as old-growth forests, the normal procedure would be to determine the sum total of the public's willingness to pay to have the resource preserved or willingness to be compensated for the exploitation of the resource, and then compare that with the market value of the exploited resource. Willingness-to-pay is the maximum payment the public is willing to make for preservation of the resource and assumes the public has no prior right to use the resource. Willingness-to-be-compensated is the minimum amount the public is willing to accept for giving up the resource in a preserved state and presumes a prior right of use. If the market value of the exploited resource is larger than willingness-to-pay and if no prior use right is judged to exist, then the resource should be exploited rather than preserved. If there is a prior use right for the preserved resource, then the market value of the exploited resource would have to be greater than the willingness to be compensated for cost-benefit analysis to support exploitation. If preservation is perceived as an instrumental value, then the maximum payment by each individual to preserve the resource in the willingness-to-pay case leaves the individual indifferent between preservation and the higher income level in the absence of the payment. In the willingness-to-be-compensated case, the minimum acceptable level of compensation leaves each individual indifferent between preservation and compensation for exploitation.

If preservation is instead a moral end, in the willingness-to-pay case the individual is willing to sacrifice income up to some maximum amount where other moral ends take precedence, such as the survival and well-being of one's self and one's family.[7] If preservation requires such a payment, then the individual will be rendered worse off by the resulting loss of income, being forced in effect to pay tribute in order to preserve something that ought not be valued in instrumental terms.[8] If exploitation prevails because payments offered for preservation are insufficient, those holding preservation to be a moral end will be rendered worse off and cannot be compensated for their loss. Remember, moral ends cannot be bought off by instrumental values. The question of a prior right of access is moot because access is irrelevant to the attachment of moral considerability to a natural entity. Thus, the normal procedure of cost-benefit analysis cannot yield a solution where some can be made better off without making others worse off; resource exploitation will always cause someone to be worse off where at least one person views the resource destroyed to be morally considerable. In the willingness-to-be-compensated case, if the natural entity in question is morally considerable, then there will be no acceptable level of compensation, and the costs of resource exploitation cannot be defined. Again, moral ends are not exchangeable for instrumental values.

To summarize, whenever anyone views old-growth forests or any other entity in nature as morally considerable, the premises of cost-benefit analysis are violated. Cost-benefit analysis cannot be legitimately applied. In Chapter 8 a significant proportion of those favoring the preservation of old growth were found to do so on noninstrumental and ethical grounds. Consequently, cost-benefit analysis is not the right approach to use in evaluating whether old-growth forests ought to be preserved or cut down. The cost-benefit approach presumes that everything in nature, including old-growth ecosystems, is an instrument capable of being valued through quasimarket processes. To place morally considerable entities in the flow of commerce or to value them through quasimarket processes is essentially to treat them as instruments or things. Much as those who hold human beings to be morally considerable object to the institution of slavery, those who hold the natural world to be morally considerable object to its being placed in the stream of commerce and treated strictly as an instrument. Cost-benefit analysis is designed for the allocation of instrumental values; ethical standards of conduct are needed for decisions involving anything deemed to be of moral concern, including old-growth forests.

The Ethics of Old-Growth Forests

Human ethics deals with the human individual. The focus of moral concern is the individual, not groups of individuals or society as a whole. Societies and cultures in the context of human ethics are evaluated on how well they treat human individuals. In his book *Respect for Nature*, Paul Taylor extends the idea of an individualistic human ethic to encompass the whole of the natural world. He does this by arguing that all biotic organisms, like human beings, have goods of their own and are teleological centers of life. Given an attitude of respect for nature, and given that all organisms in nature have goods of their own and as a consequence are intrinsically valuable, all such organisms are morally considerable and should be treated as ends in themselves. The good of a spotted owl or a Douglas fir can be discovered through observation of their life cycles, and human beings can thus learn how to act in ways that preserve and promote the good of those organisms.[9]

The central limitation of an individualistic ethic is that nature is not always very kind to individual organisms. The sick and the weak are culled from deer populations by predators; Douglas firs are often destroyed by fire or disease; rabbit overpopulation may be resolved by a hard winter and starvation; millions of salmon fry emerge each year, but very few make it to adulthood. These events, however, may function to preserve life in the longer term. Douglas fir snags and downed logs become the source of life for a variety of organisms; natural limits on deer and rabbit populations reduce habitat damage; reproductive strategies involving a large number of offspring are an adaption to harsh and constantly changing environmental conditions. Ecosystems function to protect their own integrity, not necessarily the well-being of a particular individual organism. Human societies, on the other hand, often function differently. Even where overpopulation may be a problem, the natural human inclination is to supply the starving with the food they need. In human society, the concern is generally with the well being of individuals. In the world of nature, priority is given to the preservation of the ecosystem and the species as opposed to the individual organism.

This suggests that a holistic ethic may be more appropriate in the case of natural systems than an individualistic ethic.[10] While preserving the full life cycle of all individual organisms is probably an impossible task, we can attempt to preserve the well-being of ecosystems and species.[11] As suggested in Chapters 7 and 8, wilderness and old-growth preservationists have justified their position, with increasing frequency over time, by arguing for whole ecosystem preservation. Because an old-growth Douglas fir forest is disturbance generated, a holistic ethic is more appropriate than an individualistic ethic. In order to perpetuate old-growth Douglas fir, patches of forest will have to be opened up to sunlight in order to allow shade-intolerant Douglas fir saplings to flourish. If fires are not allowed to play this role, some artificial form of disturbance will have to be employed that will destroy individual organisms.

A holistic environmental ethic, like any other, needs a philosophical underpinning. Preservationists themselves often refer to human membership in the larger biotic community, as did Aldo Leopold, or to our common origin with other species in the evolutionary process as the philosophical basis for their views. (See discussion in Chapters 7 and 8.)

They hint at the idea that we should as a consequence feel a sense of identity with whole ecosystems and the evolutionary processes that created them, and for this reason should project noninstrumental value onto them and treat them with moral concern.[12] This suggests that fact and value arise together in violation of the traditional philosophical standard that values must be formed prior to the determination of facts, but language, the only vehicle we have to describe nature and our relationship to it, is itself value laden.[13] We find that we have an "evolutionary kinship with all living things" and at the same time judge that the processes that create life are valuable for themselves.[14] If this is the path we follow in devising ethical principles, then the fact/value distinction is itself a questionable standard.

To claim that ecosystems are of moral concern does not in itself help much in resolving conflicts that arise in the political arena between ecosystem and human well-being. What is really needed is a principle of behavior that reconciles an individualistic human ethic with a holistic environmental ethic. This principle should be structured so as to indicate the circumstances under which human need takes priority over ecosystem survival or vice versa. One such principle that does this is as follows:

Natural ecosystems and species should be preserved unless doing so reduces the material well being of individuals below levels necessary for the leading of a decent human life.

Component parts of this principle are subject to interpretation, but this will be the case for any ethical principle. Clearly, there will be differences of opinion over what constitutes material well-being adequate to the leading of a decent human life. We do devise such standards in the political process, however; the U.S. government, for example, has an official income standard it uses in measuring the extent of poverty. Disagreement could also arise over the definition of an ecosystem. The old-growth ecosystem in the Pacific Northwest, for example, is made up of a number of forest types that could be interpreted as being separate ecosystems (see Chapter 2). Some suggest that ecosystem preservation should be approached at a landscape level. This might mean that certain habitats could be exploited or altered within a landscape area so long as certain other habitats were left alone or allowed to return to natural conditions in order to maintain a diversity of species and ecosystem types.[15] The point is, any political decision-making process will necessarily involve coming up with appropriate definitions of the terms in any ethical principle.

Why accept this principle for determining whether an ecosystem should be preserved or exploited? It does provide a standard for reconciling an individualist human ethic with a holistic environmental ethic. Deep ecologists might object to it on the grounds that it is anthropocentric, and indeed it is. It gives priority to human beings when their ability to lead a decent life is threatened. It does, however, recognize the moral status of ecosystems and species. Some might argue that it is tilted excessively in the favor of human individuals because it will always be the case in resource allocation decisions that someone's income will suffer excessively if ecosystems or species are preserved. On the other hand, some will argue that it is tilted excessively in the favor of ecosystems for precisely the opposite reason—it will seldom be the case that incomes are reduced to the point where leading a decent life is impossible. The best way to judge an ethical principle is through its application, a task to which we now turn.

An Environmental Ethic
and the Old-Growth Debate

In order to retain the northern spotted owl as a self-perpetuating species, the best scientific evidence available suggests that many of the remaining stands of old growth will have to be preserved. If the idea of the spotted owl as an indicator species is valid, then preserving the spotted owl is equivalent to preserving the old-growth ecosystem in Oregon and Washington. Given that these points are not at issue, the only question remaining to be resolved under the ethical standard of behavior described above is whether the decline of human material well-being that could result from old-growth preservation is acceptable. Will individual material well-being, as a result, be reduced to the point where people can no longer live decently? In answering this question, there are two possible approaches. One is to assume that no other measures will be taken to alleviate the economic suffering of those who would lose employment as the result of spotted owl protection. The other is to assume that measures will be undertaken to alleviate economic suffering.

Estimates of timber harvest and employment reductions resulting from preservation of the spotted owl vary widely depending upon assumptions made about the spotted owl conservation strategy chosen and other variables. The most credible strategy developed so far and the one that is likely to determine future public policy is contained in the Interagency Scientific Committee report entitled "A Conservation Strategy for the Northern Spotted Owl."[16] The committee was created by Congress for the express purpose of devising a strategy for preserving the northern spotted owl. The authors of the report found that forest habitats chosen by the owl exhibited moderate to high canopy closure; a multilayered multispecies canopy dominated by large overstory trees; a high incidence of large trees with large cavities, broken tops, and other indications of decadence; numerous large snags; heavy accumulations of logs and other woody debris on the forest floor; and considerable open space within and beneath the canopy.[17]

While the committee noted that young forests sometimes exhibit such characteristics, it suggested that they are most commonly found in old-growth forests. The committee also noted that habitats containing these characteristics had declined significantly in the past century, and that as a result of timber harvesting methods much of the existing habitat was being fragmented, reducing the ability of spotted owls to disperse and exposing them to competition from other species. As a key part of its strategy, the committee mapped networks of habitat conservation areas with each area containing a minimum of 20 pairs of owls and being located no further than 12 miles from another area. The committee indicated that logging should be prohibited in these areas and that forests around them should be managed such that 50 percent of the land base contains trees 11 inches or greater in diameter with at least a 40 percent canopy closure. The committee argued that if this strategy were carried out on public lands, it would conserve around 1,465 pairs of owls.[18]

Estimates of employment losses in the timber industry, assuming that this strategy is applied to public lands only, range in three different studies from a low of 12,383 to a high of 29,421, with a figure of 16,341 in the middle.[19] Authors of two of the studies also provide total employment loss estimates taking into account secondary employment losses outside the timber industry that roughly double the timber industry figures. Two of the studies also included employment losses assuming that the spotted owl strategy is applied to private as well as public lands. However, since there is no concrete reason to believe that this will be the case, this option is not considered here. The timber harvest reduction estimates underlying these figures range from 2.3 billion board feet to 3.0 billion board feet per year.[20] One study suggests that the social value of the old-growth timber harvest reduction would be $591 million in the first year and would have a present value of approximately $24 billion for 50 years of forgone harvests.[21] These are rough estimates of what society loses by not harvesting in terms of the value of the timber itself. The U.S. per capita value for the first year loss would be approximately $2.50, while the per capita present value for the full 50 years would be approximately $100. In practical terms, the loss will be reflected in lower government revenues from timber sales and higher timber prices. The latter will ultimately result in slightly higher housing costs. The final burden of the social cost from the forgone timber harvests should be relatively widespread, and given that the per capita cost is not very large, it is not likely to cause a reduction of living standards below levels needed to live decently.

The burden from unemployment is another matter. As noted above, anywhere from 12,000 to 29,000 jobs could be lost in the first year from spotted owl protection. However, many of the workers losing jobs will find employment elsewhere, particularly since the Oregon and Washington economies have experienced rapid employment growth outside of the forest products industry in recent years (see Chapter 6). In a period of large employment layoffs in Oregon sawmills from 1980 to 1982, 92 percent of those becoming unemployed held jobs one year later.[22] Nonetheless, workers suffering layoffs will lose wages during the period of unemployment, and, in all likelihood, new jobs will pay less than the old. Assuming that reemployment is at the average wage for the state, and that the typical worker has 20 years of potential employment remaining, the present value of the lost wages per worker for both the layoff period and the reemployment period is estimated to be approximately $71,000. The figure per worker for the first year alone would be approximately $14,000.[23] These are clearly substantial losses of income, particularly in the first year, and such losses could conceivably cause incomes for some to fall below levels necessary to live decently. Moreover, in the more remote timber dependent communities, some may have great difficulty finding new jobs, and they may have to move to other locations where jobs are more readily available, breaking their community ties and experiencing significant capital losses on homes that would have to be sold in a depressed housing market.

Economic dislocations of this sort are not uncommon in market economies and are often looked upon as a necessary price individuals in society must pay for economic progress. The consequences of such dislocations can be serious, however, taking the form of increased family violence, illness, and death rates among those affected.[24] Improvements in technology in the Pacific Northwest lumber industry has resulted in significant employment losses in recent years. Between 1970 and 1988, for example, total lumber and plywood production in western Washington and Oregon was constant at approximately 13 billion board feet, while total employment dropped by 13,000 jobs.[25] Beyond unemployment insurance and welfare, little has been offered to help people deal with such economic dislocations. One could argue that dislocations caused by spotted owl preservation are not fundamentally different from those caused by technological change or changing market conditions. If so, then nothing special needs to be done to alleviate any resulting economic suffering.

To accept this line of reasoning, however, would likely result in violation of the ethical premise that everyone should have the opportunity to gain a material standard of living that allows them to live a decent human life. Are there measures available that would significantly reduce the economic dislocation resulting from spotted owl preservation? If there are, then spotted owl preservation can be undertaken without violating the "decent human life" ethical standard. If not, then preserving the spotted owl is open to question on ethical grounds.

The single most effective measure for reducing the impact of old-growth preservation on the timber industry is the banning of log exports from public and private lands in the Pacific Northwest. The annual volume of log exports in recent years from Washington, Oregon, and California has been approximately 3.8 billion board feet. An export ban would divert much of this volume to domestic processing, although some portion of it would not be harvested because of lower stumpage prices (prices paid for uncut timber). Some of the additional lumber processed would be exported, some would enter the domestic market, and some would replace lumber imports from Canada. Taking into account the reduced imports from Canada, the international balance of payments deficit would increase by $1.2 billion a year, although this would be offset, to some extent, by increased lumber exports. However, as many as 15,000 new jobs could be created by additional processing, assuming the full volume of logs exported is eventually harvested each year. This would be the case if stumpage prices do not decline, and they most likely would not if stumpage is taken off the market because of spotted owl preservation.[26] This measure alone would replace the bulk of the jobs lost from spotted owl preservation. The increase in the balance of payments deficit would likely reduce the value of the dollar in foreign currency markets somewhat. This could make imported goods slightly more expensive for U.S. consumers, but it could also stimulate exports by making them cheaper to foreigners and, in turn, increase domestic employment.

While a log export ban has been the centerpiece of plans to offset employment declines and economic dislocation from spotted owl preservation, a number of other measures have been suggested as well. In a report that has not been given wide circulation or attention, the U.S. government suggests a variety of measures in addition to a log export ban that it could utilize in offsetting the affects of spotted owl preservation. These measures include the development of a task force to ensure the rapid delivery of available government programs for education and job training, unemployment benefits, and employment services to timber-dependent communities; the expansion of government loans and grant programs for local economic development; increased national forest tax equivalency payments to affected communities from 25 percent to 50 percent of net revenues received by national forests from timber sales; increased federal public works projects in affected areas; and improvements in land stewardship, including trail construction and the construction of tourist facilities, the reclamation of roads in spotted owl habitat conservation areas, and increased timber presale work in areas where timber sales are permitted.[27] Improved silviculture practices have been suggested not only to increase the productivity of second-growth forests but to create employment as well. One such measure is to increase the thinning and pruning of second growth in order to improve wood quality, and to then use the material removed in low-value wood products. This could lead to the creation of a new "thinning and pruning" industry and the creation of a high-quality, second-growth timber industry in the long run.[28] Others have suggested the creation of businesses that add significant value to harvested timber or use low-value abundant wood resources, such as alder or timber thinnings. One example is a furniture manufacturer that uses alder, and another is one that uses Douglas fir thinnings.[29]

These measures for mitigating the impact of timber harvest declines by no means exhaust the possibilities, but what has been presented here suggests that measures are available to potentially diminish employment and income losses. In all likelihood, spotted owls and old-growth forests can be preserved and incomes for timber industry workers can be prevented from falling below levels needed to lead a decent human life. If mitigation measures are undertaken, the "decent life" ethical standard can be met; if not, the ethical standard may well be violated. The point is a simple one. Decisions to preserve natural areas often impose harsh economic burdens on a few people, but those burdens can usually be spread through appropriate public action to the larger society, which can bear them more readily. Preservationists who believe that nature is morally considerable and also accept the notion that human beings ought to be able to live decently should press for public sector intervention to offset the harm done to individuals as a result of the preservation of nature. In other words, full employment at decent wages is an environmental issue. To avoid unnecessary ethical dilemmas that pit the basic economic interests of human individuals against those of ecosystems and species, assured employment at a decent income is needed and ought to be a goal of the environmental movement.

To apply an ethical standard of behavior such as the one just described is not unprecedented. In the court case *Seattle Audubon Society v. Evans*, Judge William Dwyer went through an ethical balancing act not unlike the one suggested by the "decent human life" principle. As noted in

Chapter 8, the Forest Service was enjoined in this case from harvesting old growth until it came up with a reasonable spotted owl management plan that would satisfy provisions of the National Forest Management Act. In granting injunctive relief in cases of this type, there must be an irreparable injury and the injury must be serious enough to outweigh any adverse effects from the issuance of the injunction.[30] Judge Dwyer noted that environmental injury can seldom be remedied by money damages and is often permanent and therefore irreparable.[31] In his written court opinion, the judge went on to argue that irreparable harm was likely in the absence of an injunction because the spotted owl was threatened with extinction.[32] While noting that the sales of timber from the national forests would be reduced more than 2 billion board feet during the period of the injunction, Judge Dwyer also indicated that programs and measures were available to mitigate the impact of sales reductions, including an export ban as well as programs for dislocated workers. He also noted that the industry is slated to lose upwards of 30,000 jobs in the next 20 years because of worker productivity increases, and that other industries in the area are now the major driving force in the economy.[33] In concluding his opinion, the judge made the following statement:

> To bypass the environmental laws, either briefly or permanently, would not fend off the changes transforming the timber industry. The argument that the mightiest economy on earth cannot afford to preserve old growth forests for a short time, while it reaches an overdue decision on how to manage them, is not convincing today. It would be even less so a year or a century from now.[34]

In sum, the harm to individuals employed in the timber industry was seen as not sufficient enough to outweigh the irreparable harm that would be done to the spotted owl. The reduction of living standards by those affected was indeed considered, but not viewed as substantial enough to preclude imposing the injunction and protecting spotted owls. While the spotted owl is not explicitly viewed in this decision as being a subject of moral concern, by virtue of seeing its extinction as an irreparable harm, it was implicitly treated as such.

Is a Noninstrumental Environmental Ethic Necessary?

The premise of the discussion so far is that a noninstrumental evaluation of species and ecosystems may be essential to the preservation of spotted owls and old-growth forests. But is this the case? Why go so far as to postulate that ecosystems and species are subjects of moral concern if an instrumental evaluation is adequate to justify the preservation of ecosystems?[35] In other words, why bother with a noninstrumental environmental ethic at all, particularly in a world where we realize that our own existence is intertwined with the health of natural ecosystems on a world scale? If the survival of the human species requires the preservation of ecosystems, isn't that enough?

There are several possible responses to this question. A simple one is that, in fact, human beings attach moral concern to nature, and we ought not to deny this in the realm of environmental policy making. This view has been the focal point of Chapters 7 and 8 in this book. At least some preservationists advocate saving spotted owls and old-growth forests on the grounds that they are valuable in their own right. Another response is that an environmental ethic may be necessary for a vigorous environmental movement. Moral values are more intensely held than instrumental values, for which there are usually ready substitutes, and such intensity is likely to bring forth a greater commitment to an environmental movement. The movement for old-growth preservation has certainly increased in fervor in recent years, a trend that has been paralleled by increasing expressions of moral concern for old growth by preservationists.

It is also possible that the premise of the question—that our own existence is intertwined with the health of natural ecosystems—may not be correct. Instrumental valuations of old-growth may well be insufficient to justify its preservation. Such valuations may not add up to the $24 billion or so needed to offset the value of the wood fiber given up. The harvesting of old growth may add somewhat to global warming through the release of carbon dioxide, but this could be offset with modest improvements in energy conservation. There may be loss of species diversity and the availability of cancer-fighting drugs, such as taxol from the old-growth-dependent Pacific yew tree, but perhaps genetic engineering can make up for this. There will be a loss of salmon habitat, but wild salmon populations may be doomed anyway because of dams, irrigation, and overfishing, and pen-raised salmon are becoming increasingly available in fish markets. Recreation opportunities will decline, but perhaps like the Europeans we will find that we can do perfectly well without wilderness. In sum, it may be possible to construct an anthropogenic world ecology that excludes wild ecosystems, and it may function just fine. We may find ourselves willing to substitute one instrumental value for another, and the one given up may be wild nature.

So, to preserve wild nature, an environmental ethic that views nature as valuable in its own right may be necessary. To preserve spotted owls and old-growth forests may well require a moral commitment.

Ecosystem Preservation
and Holistic Forestry

The movement to preserve wilderness and old-growth forests has been exactly that—a movement to preserve ecosystems from exploitation by human beings. As we have seen, when jobs are threatened by preservation, political polarization is the result. While efforts to mitigate the consequences of economic dislocation can diminish conflicts between preservation and exploitation, there may be another answer—the reintroduction of human economic activity into forests while at the same time maintaining natural forest ecosystem characteristics. The goals of such a holistic forestry would not only be the harvesting of wood fiber but the retention of whole ecosystem characteristics.[36] In the case of old-growth forests, timber could be harvested under holistic forestry, but only to the extent that old-growth characteristics, such as a certain number of large trees and snags per unit area, a certain amount of woody debris on the forest floor, a diversity of tree species and sizes, a multilayered canopy, and a patchy shrub layer on the forest floor, are maintained. Second growth forests could also be managed to ultimately create old-growth, with pruning and thinning providing harvestable wood fiber.

One approach to developing holistic forestry on public lands would be to sign long-term leases with groups of foresters or forestry cooperatives to manage forestlands according to holistic principles. Foresters would be paid not only for wood fiber extracted but also for maintenance of forest ecosystem characteristics and long-term forest growth.[37] This means that foresters would be concerned not only with timber harvesting but also with such things as maintenance of wildlife populations, prevention of erosion into streams, production of snags and downed wood, and retention of large old trees. The production and harvesting of wood fiber would continue to be a goal, but it would be constrained by the needs to preserve forest ecosystem characteristics.

Because Douglas firs require exposed mineral soils for germination and open sunlight for early growth, some form of disturbance will be needed for the long-term perpetuation of old-growth Douglas fir forests. Prior to European settlement, this role was fulfilled to a large extent by infrequent stand-replacing wildfires, particularly in the more northerly areas of the Pacific Northwest. Because of the danger of such fires to human beings, they are generally no longer allowed to burn. Without major forest fires, old-growth Douglas fir regeneration is threatened. One answer is to devote some second-growth Douglas fir stands to long rotations (200–400 years). Another answer may be the "new forestry" developed by Jerry Franklin and others. The basic idea is essentially the same as holistic forestry, to manage forests for both commodities and ecological values.[38] Franklin argues for the management of public forestlands for structural diversity as well as commodity production as a middle ground between tree farms and wilderness reserves. When harvesting, Franklin suggests that some large trees should be left standing and retained throughout the rotation to provide structural diversity. In addition, stream corridors and areas of unstable soil should be reserved from cutting, snags and downed logs should be retained in cutover areas, and the practice of patch cutting, which fragments the remaining forest into areas that are too small to provide habitat for some species, should be stopped.[39] The goal is to create landscape patterns in Pacific Northwest forests more like those caused prior by wildfires instead of those resulting from the standard practice of removing all trees, burning slash, and replanting. The result would be the creation of young forests that would preserve some of the structural diversity of older forests. For old growth to be created in the long term under the new forestry, harvest rotations would have to be lengthened from the current 40-90 years to at least 200 years. Such a forest management scheme could be accomplished under the holistic forestry arrangements described above.

Conclusion

The point of holistic forestry is a simple one: certain human uses of nature are compatible with ecosystem preservation. Human use of natural resources and moral concern for nature are not necessarily incompatible ideas. To see nature as valuable in its own right is not necessarily to place it above human needs. The economic task before us when we value nature for itself is to find forms of human activity that promote rather than threaten the health of ecosystems and species.

Notes

1. Barney Dowdle and Steven H. Hanke, "Public Timber Policy and the Wood Products Industry," in Deacon and Johnson, *Forestlands*, pp. 94-96.

2. The economic approach and the concept of contingent evaluation are summarized in Steven Edwards, "In Defense of Environmental Economics," *Environmental Ethics* 9 (1987): 73-85. A critique of the economic approach can be found in Mark Sagoff, "Some Problems with Environmental Economics," *Environmental Ethics* 10 (1988): 55-74. Sagoff correctly points out that the economic approach and many ethical approaches to environmental issues are not really equivalent or comparable. The incomparability of economic value and

inherent value is also suggested in Tom Regan, "The Nature and Possibility of an Environmental Ethic," *Environmental Ethics* 3 (1981): 32.

3. This idea of commitment is more fully developed in Amartya K. Sen, "Rational Fools: A Critique of the Behavioral Foundations of Economic Theory," *Philosophy and Public Affairs* 6 (1977): 317-44. For an elaboration of this notion of commitment, see Amitai Etzioni, "The Case for a Multiple-Utility Conception," *Economics and Philosophy* 2 (1986): 159-83.

4. Etzioni, "Case for a Multiple-Utility Conception," p. 168.

5. Drawing on Sen, "Rational Fools," other authors have made this point in their critiques of contingent evaluation methodology. See Steven F. Edwards, "Ethical Preferences and the Assessment of Existence Values: Does the Neoclassical Model Fit?," *Northeastern Journal of Agricultural and Resource Economics* (1986): 146-47, and David S. Brookshire, Larry S. Eubanks, and Cindy F. Sorg, "Existence Values and Normative Economics: Implications for Valuing Water Resources," *Water Resources Research* 22 (1986): 1509-18.

6. This presumes a dichotomy between moral and instrumental decision making. The ordering of moral preferences is independent of the ordering of preferences over instrumental values. This is exactly what is suggested in Etzioni, "The Case for a Multiple-Utility Conception," p. 166-70.

7. For a theoretical exposition of this point, see Edwards, "Ethical Preferences and the Assessment of Existence Values," pp. 147-149.

8. Steven Kelman, "Cost-Benefit Analysis: An Ethical Critique," *Regulation* 5 (January/February 1981): 33-40. Kelman argues that placing a price on something valued for itself degrades it, reducing it to the level of a mere instrument.

9. Taylor, *Respect for Nature*, pp. 60-80.

10. One of the strongest advocates of a holistic ethic is J. Baird Callicott. See his *In Defense of the Land Ethic: Essays in Environmental Philosophy* (Albany: State University of New York Press, 1989).

11. For a more extensive treatment of the issue of an individualist versus a holistic ethic for old-growth forests, see Douglas E. Booth, "The Economics and Ethics of Old-Growth Forests," *Environmental Ethics* 14 (1992): 43-62. Portions of this article are reprinted here with the permission of the editor.

12. This position is not too far from J. Baird Callicott's. See "Intrinsic Value, Quantum Theory, and Environmental Ethics," pp. 257-73.

13. This point is put most succinctly in Elizabeth M. Harlow, "The Human Face of Nature: Environmental Values and the Limits of Nonanthropocentrism," *Environmental Ethics* 14 (1992): 27-42.

14. Ibid., p. 41.

15. For a readable overview of this approach, see Norton, *Toward Unity Among Environmentalists*, pp. 148-51, 155-83.

16. Jack Ward Thomas, Eric. D. Forsman, Joseph B. Lint, E. Charles Meslow, Barry R. Noon, and Jared Verner, "A Conservation Strategy for the Northern Spotted Owl" (Portland, Ore.: Interagency Scientific Committee to Address the Conservation of the Northern Spotted Owl, May 1990).

17. Ibid.

18. Ibid.

19. Walter J. Mead, Dennis D. Muraoka, Mark Schniepp, and Richard B. Watson, "The Economic Consequences of Preserving Old Growth Timber for Spotted Owls in Oregon and Washington" (Santa Barbara: Community and Organization Research Institute, University of California, Santa Barbara, October, 1990), p. iii; Bruce R. Lippke, "Three State Impact of Spotted Owl Conservation and Other Timber Harvest Reductions: A Cooperative Evaluation of Economic and Social Impacts, A Report to the United States House of Representatives, Agriculture Committee, Subcommittee on Forests, Farms and Energy" (Seattle: College of Forest Resources, University of Washington, August 31, 1990), p. 8; John H. Beuter, "Social and Economic Impacts in Washington, Oregon and California Associated with Implementing the Conservation Strategy for the Northern Spotted Owl: An Overview" (Portland, Ore.: Mason, Bruce & Girard, Inc., July 9, 1990), p. 23.

20. Mead et al., "The Economic Consequences of Preserving Old Growth Timber," p. iii; Beuter, "Social and Economic Impacts," p. 19.

21. Mead et al., "The Economic Consequences of Preserving Old Growth Timber," p. v.

22. Ibid., p. 128.

23. These figures are derived from Mead et al., pp. iv-v.

24. Barry Bluestone and Bennett Harrison, *The Deindustrialization of America: Plant Closings, Community Abandonment, and the Dismantling of Basic Industry* (New York: Basic Books, 1982), pp. 49-81.

25. Mead et al., "The Economic Consequences of Preserving Old Growth Timber," p. 124.

26. USDA Forest Service and USDI Bureau of Land Management, "Actions the Administration May Wish to Consider in Implementing a Conservation Strategy for the Spotted Owl," May 1, 1990, pp. 15-16.

27. Ibid., pp. 3-5.

28. U.S. House, *Forestry Issues in the Pacific Northwest*, p. 239.

29. Ibid., p. 222.

30. *Seattle Audubon Society v. Evans*, 771 F. Supp. 1081 (W.D.Wash. 1991), p. 1086-87.

31. Ibid., p. 1087.

32. Ibid., pp. 1091-94.

33. Ibid., pp. 1094-95.

34. Ibid., p. 1096.

35. Some have looked upon a noninstrumental evaluation of species and ecosystems with skepticism. For example, see Norton's *Toward Unity Among Environmentalists*, pp. 220-43 and *Why Preserve Natural Variety?* (Princeton: Princeton University Press, 1987), pp. 151-82.

36. For a discussion of holistic forestry, see Ray Raphael, *Tree Talk: The People and Politics of Timber* (Covelo, Calif: Island Press, 1981).

37. For a detailed discussion of this approach, see Raphael, pp. 211-55.

38. U.S. House of Representatives, *Management of Old-Growth Forests of the Pacific Northwest,* Joint Hearings before the Subcommittee on Forests, Family Farms, and Energy, Committee on Agriculture and the Subcommittee on National Parks and Public Lands of the Committee on Interior and Insular Affairs, 101st Congress, 1st Session, Washington, D.C., June 20 and 22, 1989 (Washington, D.C.: U.S. Government Printing Office, 1989), p. 138.

39. Ibid., p. 139.

Bibliography

Abbott, Helen Betsy, ed. "Life on the Lower Columbia, 1853-1866." *Oregon Historical Quarterly* 83 (1982): 248-57.

Aikens, C. Melvin. "Archaeological Studies in the Willamette Valley, Oregon," *University of Oregon Anthropological Papers* no. 8 (1975): 3-13.

Allin, Craig W. *The Politics of Wilderness Preservation.* Westport, Conn.: Greenwood Press, 1982.

Andersen, Dennis A. "Clark Kinsey: Logging Photography." *Pacific Northwest Quarterly* 74 (1983): 19-24.

Andrews, H. J., and R. W. Cowlin. *Forest Resources of the Douglas-Fir Region.* USDA Forest Service, Pacific Northwest Forest and Range Experiment Station, Washington, D.C.: U.S. Government Printing Office, 1940.

———. *Forest Resources of the Douglas-Fir Region: A Summary of the Forest Inventory of Western Oregon and Western Washington.* Portland, Ore.: USDA Forest Service Pacific Northwest Range and Experiment Station, Research Note 13, 1934.

Baker, Abner. "Economic Growth in Portland in the 1880s." *Oregon Historical Quarterly* 67 (1966): 105-23.

Balmer, Donald G. "United States Federal Policy on Old-Growth Forests in Its Institutional Setting." *Northwest Environmental Journal* 6 (1990): 339-42.

Beuter, John H. "Social and Economic Impacts in Washington, Oregon and California Associated with Implementing the Conservation Strategy for the Northern Spotted Owl: An Overview." Portland, Ore.: Mason, Bruce & Girard, Inc., July 9, 1990.

Bluestone, Barry, and Bennett Harrison. *The Deindustrialization of America: Plant Closings, Community Abandonment, and the Dismantling of Basic Industry.* New York: Basic Books, 1982.

Booth, Douglas E. "The Economics and Ethics of Old-Growth Forests." *Environmental Ethics* 14 (1992): 43-62.

————. "Estimating Prelogging Old-Growth in the Pacific Northwest." *Journal of Forestry* 89 (1991): 25-29.

————. "Timber Dependency and Wilderness Selection: The U.S. Forest Service, Congress, and the RARE II Decisions." *Natural Resources* 31 (1991): 715-39.

Boyd, Robert T. "The Introduction of Infectious Diseases among the Indians of the Pacific Northwest, 1774-1874," Ph.D. diss., University of Washington, 1985.

Bradley, Charles C. "Wilderness and Man." *Sierra Club Bulletin,* 37 (December 1952): 5-9, 67.

Brady, Eugene A. "The Role of Land Policy in Shaping the Development of the Lumber Industry in the State of Washington." MA thesis, University of Washington, 1954.

Brennan, Andrew. *Thinking about Nature.* London: Routledge, 1988.

Brookshire, David S., Larry S. Eubanks, and Cindy F. Sorg. "Existence Values and Normative Economics: Implications for Valuing Water Resources." *Water Resources Research* 22 (1986): 1509-18.

Brower, David R. "Definitions for Inner Space." *Sierra Club Bulletin* 47 (December 1962): 37-41.

————. "The Irreplaceables, Foundations, and Conventional Heresy." *Sierra Club Bulletin* 49 (December 1964): 9-12.

————. "Scenic Resources for the Future." *Sierra Club Bulletin* 41 (December 1956): 1-10.

————. "Toward an Earth International Park." *Sierra Club Bulletin* 52 (October 1967): 20.

————. "Wilderness Conflict and Conscience." *Sierra Club Bulletin* 42 (June 1957): 1-12.

Brown, David. "Oregon Wilderness Handbook." BA thesis, Honors College, University of Oregon, 1977.

Brown, E. Reade, ed. *Management of Wildlife and Fish Habitats in Forests of Western Oregon and Washington.* Portland, Ore.: USDA Forest Service, Pacific Northwest Region, 1985.

Buchanan, Iva L. "Lumbering and Logging in the Puget Sound Region in Territorial Days." *Pacific Northwest Quarterly* 27 (1936): 34-53.

Bureau of Corporations. *The Lumber Industry, Part I.* Washington, D.C.: U.S. Government Printing Office, 1913-1914.

Bureau of Land Management v. U.S. Fish and Wildlife Service. Transcript of Proceedings before the Endangered Species Committee. Portland, Ore.: Briker Nodland Studenmund, February 12 and 13, 1992.

Byrnes, Patricia. "A Compromise More Pragmatic Than Pleasing: Ancient Forest Agreement." *Wilderness* 53 (Winter 1989): 3-4.

Callicott, J. Baird. *In Defense of the Land Ethic: Essays in Environmental Philosophy.* Albany: State University of New York Press, 1989.

―――. "Intrinsic Value, Quantum Theory, and Environmental Ethics." *Environmental Ethics* 7 (1985): 257-73.

―――. "Traditional American Indian and Western European Attitudes Toward Nature: An Overview." *Environmental Ethics* 4 (1982): 293-318.

Carey, Andrew B. "Wildlife Associated with Old-Growth Forests in the Pacific Northwest." *Natural Areas Journal* 9 (1989): 151-62.

Carter, Harry R., and Spencer G. Sealy. "Inland Records of Downy Young and Fledgling Marbled Murrelets in North American." *Murrelet* 68 (1987): 58-63.

Clawson, Marion. "Forests in the Long Sweep of American History." *Science* 204 (June 1989): 1168-74.

Cohn, Edwin J., Jr. *Industry in the Pacific Northwest and the Location Theory.* New York: Columbia University Press, 1954.

Collins, June McCormick. "The Mythological Basis for Attitudes toward Animals among Salish-Speaking Indians." *Journal of American Folklore* 65 (1952): 353-60.

————. *Valley of the Spirits: The Upper Skagit Indians of Western Washington.* Seattle: University of Washington Press, 1980.

Collins, Lloyd R. "The Cultural Position of the Kalapuya in the Pacific Northwest." MS thesis, University of Oregon, 1951.

Coman, Edwin T., Jr., and Helen M. Gibbs. *Time, Tide and Timber: A Century of Pope and Talbot.* New York: Greenwood Press, 1968.

Corn, Paul Stephen, and Bruce R. Bury. "Habitat Use and Terrestrial Activity by Red Tree Voles (*Arborimus longicaudus*) in Oregon." *Journal of Mammalogy* 67 (1986): 404-6.

————. "Logging in Western Oregon: Responses of Headwater Habitats and Stream Amphibians." *Forest Ecology and Management* 29 (1989): 39-57.

Cox, Thomas R. *Mills and Markets: A History of the Pacific Coast Lumber Industry to 1900.* Seattle: University of Washington Press, 1974.

Craig, Joseph A., and Robert L. Hacker. "The History and Development of the Fisheries of the Columbia River." *Bulletin of the Bureau of Fisheries* 49 (1940): 133-215.

Crutchfield, J. A., and G. Potecorvo. *The Pacific Salmon Fisheries: A Study of Irrational Conservation.* Washington D.C.: Resources for the Future, 1969.

Dana, Samuel T., and Sally K. Fairfax. *Forest and Range Policy: Its Development in the United States.* 2d ed. New York: McGraw-Hill, 1980.

DeVoto, Bernard. "Shall We Let Them Ruin Our National Parks." *Saturday Evening Post*, 223 (1950): 44.

Dobyns, Henry F. "Estimating Aboriginal American Population: An Appraisal of Techniques With A New Hemispherical Estimate." *Current Anthropology* 7 (1966): 395-416.

Dowdle, Barney, and Steven H. Hanke. "Public Timber Policy and the Wood Products Industry." In Robert T. Deacon and M. Bruce Johnson, eds., *Forestlands: Public and Private*, San Francisco: Pacific Institute, 1985.

Drucker, Philip. *Cultures of the North Pacific Coast.* New York: Harper and Row, 1965.

Edwards, Steven F. "Ethical Preferences and the Assessment of Existence Values: Does the Neoclassical Model Fit?" *Northeastern Journal of Agricultural and Resource Economics* (1986): 145-50.

———. "In Defense of Environmental Economics." *Environmental Ethics*, 9 (1987): 73-85.

Ellerman, David P. "On the Labor Theory of Property." *Philosophical Forum* 16 (1985): 293-326.

Emergency Conservation Committee. "Protect the Roosevelt Elk." Publication no. 69. New York: Emergency Conservation Committee, March, 1938.

Endangered Species Act Amendments of 1978, 16 U.S.C. Section 1536(h).

Endangered Species Act of 1973, PL 93-205, 81 Stat. 884 (Dec. 28, 1973).

Engstrom, Emil. *The Vanishing Logger.* New York: Vantage Press, 1956.

Etzioni, Amitai. "The Case for a Multiple-Utility Conception." *Economics and Philosophy* 2 (1986): 159-83.

Fahnestock, George R., and James K. Agee. "Biomass Consumption and Smoke Production by Prehistoric and Modern Forest Fires in Western Washington." *Journal of Forestry* 81 (1983): 653-57.

Ficken, Robert E. *The Forested Land: A History of Lumbering in Western Washington.* Seattle: University of Washington Press, 1987.

———. *Lumber and Politics: The Career of Mark E. Reed.* Seattle: University of Washington Press, 1979.

Fiddler, Richard. "The Alpine Lakes . . . Seattle's Backyard Wilderness." *Sierra Club Bulletin* 61 (February 1976): 4-7.

Fogel, Robert. "Mycorrhizae and Nutrient Cycling in Natural Forest Ecosystems." *New Phytologist* 86 (1980): 199-212.

Forbes, Reginald D. *Forestry Handbook.* New York: Ronald Press, 1955.

Forsman, Eric D., Charles E. Meslow, and Howard M. Wight. "Distribution and Biology of the Spotted Owl in Oregon." *Wildlife Monographs* 87 (1984): 1-64.

Fox, Stephen. *The American Conservation Movement: John Muir and His Legacy.* Madison: University of Wisconsin Press, 1985.

Fox, Warwick. *Toward a Transpersonal Ecology: Developing New Foundations for Environmentalism.* Boston and London: Shambhala Publications, 1990.

Franklin, J. F., K. Cromack, Jr., W. Denison, A. McKee, C. Maser, J. Sedell, F. Swanson, and G. Juday. *Ecological Characteristics of Old-Growth Douglas-Fir Forests.* Portland, Ore.: USDA Forest Service, GTR, PNW-118, 1981.

Franklin, Jerry F., and C. T. Dyrness. *Natural Vegetation of Oregon and Washington.* Portland, Ore.: USDA Forest Service, GTR, PNW-8, 1973.

Franklin, Jerry F., H. H. Shugart, and Mark E. Harmon. "Tree Death as an Ecological Process: The Causes, Consequences, and Variability of Tree Mortality." *BioScience* 37 (1987): 550-56.

Franklin, Jerry F., and Thomas A. Spies. "Characteristics of Old-Growth Douglas-Fir Forests." In *New Forests for a Changing World,* pp. 328-34. Bethesda, Md.: Society of American Foresters, 1984.

Gates, Paul W. *History of Public Land Law Development.* Washington D.C.: U.S. Government Printing Office, 1968.

Goodpaster, Kenneth E. "On Being Morally Considerable." *Journal of Philosophy* 75 (1975): 168-76.

Gunther, Erna. "An Analysis of the First Salmon Ceremony." *American Anthropologist* n.s. 28 (1926): 605-17.

―――. *Ethnobotany of Western Washington: The Knowledge and Use of Indigenous Plants by Native Americans.* Seattle: University of Washington Press, 1973.

―――. "A Further Analysis of the First Salmon Ceremony." *University of Washington Publications in Anthropology* 2 (1928): 133-73.

―――. "Klalam Ethnography." *University of Washington Publications in Anthropology* 1 (1927): 186-90.

Gunther, Erna, and Hermann Haeberlin. "The Indians of Puget Sound." *University of Washington Publications in Anthropology* 4 (1930): 1-84.

Gutierrez, R. J. "An Overview of Recent Research on the Spotted Owl." In Ralph J. Gutierrez and Andrew B. Carey, eds., *Ecology and Management of the Spotted Owl in the Pacific Northwest.* Portland, Ore.: USDA Forest Service, GTR, PNW-185, 1985.

Habeck, James R. "The Original Vegetation of the Mid-Willamette Valley, Oregon." *Northwest Science* 35 (1961): 65-77.

Halpern, Charles B. "Early Successional Pathways and the Resistance and Resilience of Forest Communities." *Ecology* 69 (1988): 1703-15.

Hansen, Henry P. "Postglacial Forest Succession, Climate, and Chronology in the Pacific Northwest." *Transactions of the American Philosophical Society, New Series* 37, part 1 (1947): 1-130.

Hargrove, Eugene C. "Anglo-American Land Use Attitudes." *Environmental Ethics* 2 (1980): 121-48.

Harlow, Elizabeth M. "The Human Face of Nature: Environmental Values and the Limits of Nonanthropocentrism." *Environmental Ethics* 14 (1992): 27-42.

Harmon, Mark E., and Jerry F. Franklin. "Tree Seedlings on Logs in *Picea-Tsuga* Forests of Oregon and Washington." *Ecology* 70 (1989): 45-59.

Harris, Larry D. *The Fragmented Forest: Island Biogeography Theory and the Preservation of Biotic Diversity.* Chicago: University of Chicago Press, 1984.

Hayes, Samuel. *Conservation and the Gospel of Efficiency.* Cambridge: Harvard University Press, 1959.

Haynes, Richard W. *Inventory and Value of Old-Growth in the Douglas-Fir Region.* Portland, Ore.: USDA Forest Service, GTR, PNW-118, 1986.

Hemstrom, Miles A. "A Recent Disturbance History of Forest Ecosystems at Mount Rainier National Park." Ph.D. diss., Oregon State University, 1979.

Hewes, Gordon Winant. "Aboriginal Use of Fishery Resources in Northwestern North America." Ph.D. diss., University of California, Berkeley, 1947.

Hidy, Ralph W., Frank E. Hill, and Allan Nevins. *Timber and Men: The Weyerhaeuser Story.* New York: Macmillan, 1963.

Holtby, L. Blair. "Effects of Logging on Stream Temperatures in Carnation Creek, British Columbia, and Associated Impacts on the Coho Salmon (*Oncorhynchus kisutch*)." *Canadian Journal of Fisheries and Aquatic Science* 45 (1988): 502-15.

Hughes, J. Donald. *American Indian Ecology.* El Paso: Texas Western Press, 1983.

Hughson, Oliver Greeley. "When We Logged the Columbia." *Oregon Historical Quarterly* 60 (1959): 173-209.

Hutchinson, Bruce. *The Fraser*. New York: Rinehart and Co., 1950.

Hyde, William F. *Timber Supply, Land Allocation, and Economic Efficiency*. Washington, D.C.: Resources for the Future, 1980.

Ise, John. *The United States Forest Policy*. New Haven: Yale University Press, 1920.

Jensen, Vernon H. *Lumber and Labor*. New York: Arno Press, 1971.

Johannessen, Carl L., William A. Davenport, Artimus Millet, and Stephen McWilliams. "The Vegetation of the Willamette Valley." *Annals of the Association of American Geographers* 61 (1971): 286-302.

Johnson, Ronald N. "U.S. Forest Service Policy and its Budget." In Robert T. Deacon and M. Bruce Johnson, eds., *Forestlands: Public and Private*. San Francisco: Pacific Institute, 1985.

Kelman, Steven. "Cost-Benefit Analysis: An Ethical Critique." *Regulation* 5 (January/February 1981): 33-40.

Kozloff, Eugene N. *Plants and Animals of the Pacific Northwest*. Seattle: University of Washington Press, 1976.

Krech, Shepard, III, ed. *Indians, Animals, and the Fur Trade: A Critique of Keepers of the Game*. Athens: University of Georgia Press, 1981.

"Land Bureau Seeks Timber Sales Despite Presence of Protected Owl." *New York Times*, September 12, 1991, p. A13.

Lane, Barbara Savadkin. "A Comparative and Analytic Study of Some Aspects of Northwest Coast Religion." Ph. D. diss., University of Washington, 1953.

Lang, Frank Alexander. "A Study of Vegetation Change on the Gravelly Prairies of Pierce and Thurston Counties, Western Washington." MS thesis, University of Washington, 1961.

Leibhardt, Barbara. "Interpretation and Causal Analysis: Theories in Environmental History." *Environmental Review* 12 (Spring 1988): 23-36.

Leopold, Aldo. *A Sand County Almanac: With Essays From Round River*. New York: Ballantine Books, 1966.

Leopold, A. Starker. "Wilderness and Culture." *Sierra Club Bulletin* 42 (June 1957): 33-37.

Lien, Carsten. *Olympic Battleground: The Power Politics of Timber Preservation.* San Francisco: Sierra Club Books, 1991.

Lippke, Bruce R. "Three State Impact of Spotted Owl Conservation and Other Timber Harvest Reductions: A Cooperative Evaluation of Economic and Social Impacts." A Report to the United States House of Representatives, Agriculture Committee, Subcommittee on Forests, Farms and Energy, August 31, 1990. Seattle: University of Washington, College of Forest Resources, 1990.

Locke, John. *Two Treatises of Government*, Thomas I. Cook, ed. New York and London: Hafner Press, 1947.

Lotspeich, Frederick B., Jack B. Secor, Rose Okazaki, and Henry K. Smith. "Vegetation and a Soil-forming Factor on the Quillayute Physiographic Unit in Western Clallam County, Washington." *Ecology* 42 (1961): 53-68.

Mannan, R. William, Charles E. Meslow, and Howard M. Wight. "Use of Snags by Birds in Douglas-Fir Forests, Western Oregon." *Journal of Wildlife Management* 44 (1980): 787-97.

Manuwal, David A., and Mark H. Huff. "Spring and Winter Bird Populations in a Douglas-Fir Forest Sere." *Journal of Wildlife Management* 51 (1987): 586-95.

Martin, Calvin. *Keepers of the Game: Indian-Animal Relationships and the Fur Trade.* Berkeley: University of California Press, 1978.

Martinson, Arthur D. "Mountain in the Sky: A History of Mount Rainier National Park." Ph. D. diss., Washington State University, 1966.

———. *Wilderness Above the Sound: The Story of Mount Rainier National Park.* Flagstaff, Ariz.: Northland Press, 1986.

Maser, Chris, and James M. Trappe, eds. *The Seen and Unseen World of the Fallen Tree.* Portland, Ore.: USDA Forest Service, GTR, PNW-164, 1984.

Maser, Chris, James M. Trappe, and Ronald A. Nussbaum. "Fungal-Small Mammal Interrelationships with Emphasis On Oregon Coniferous Forests." *Ecology* 59 (1978): 799-809.

Maser, Chris, Zane Maser, Joseph W. Witt, and Gary Hunt. "The Northern Flying Squirrel: A Mycophagist in Southwestern Oregon." *Canadian Journal of Zoology* 64 (1986): 2086-89.

McCloskey, Michael. "Wilderness Movement at the Crossroads." *Pacific Historical Review* 41 (1972): 346-61.

McDonald, Alexander N. "Seattle's Economic Development, 1880-1910." Ph.D. diss., University of Washington, 1959.

Mead, Walter J., Dennis D. Muraoka, Mark Schniepp, and Richard B. Watson. "The Economic Consequences of Preserving Old Growth Timber for Spotted Owls in Oregon and Washington." Santa Barbara: Community and Organization Research Institute, University of California, Santa Barbara, October, 1990.

Meany, Edmond S. "The History of the Lumber Industry in the Pacific Northwest to 1917," Ph. D. diss., Harvard University, 1935.

Meeker, Ezra. *Pioneer Reminiscences of Puget Sound*. Seattle: Lowman and Hanford, 1905.

Milbrath, Lester W. *Environmentalists: Vanguard for a New Society*. Albany: State University of New York Press, 1984.

Mooney, James. "The Aboriginal Population of America North of Mexico." *Smithsonian Miscellaneous Collections* 80 (1928): 1-40.

Moravets, F. L. "Production of Lumber in Oregon and Washington: 1869-1948." Portland, Ore.: Pacific Northwest Forest and Range and Experiment Station, Forest Survey Report No. 100, December, 1949.

Morris, William G. "Forest Fires in Western Oregon and Western Washington." *Oregon Historical Quarterly* 35 (1934): 313-39.

Morrison, P. H., and F. J. Swanson. "Fire History and Pattern in a Cascade Range Landscape." Portland, Ore.: USDA Forest Service, GTR, PNW-254, 1990.

Morrison, Peter H. "Old Growth in the Pacific Northwest: A Status Report." Washington, D.C.: Wilderness Society, 1988.

Munger, Thornton T. "Timber Growing and Logging Practice in the Douglas Fir Region." Washington, D.C.: U.S. Government Printing Office, USDA Department Bulletin No. 1493, June 1927.

Murphy, Michael L., and James D. Hall. "Varied Effects of Clear-cut Logging on Predators and Their Habitat in Small Streams of the

Cascade Mountains, Oregon." *Canadian Journal of Fisheries and Aquatic Science* 38 (1981): 137-45.

Nash, Roderick. *The Rights of Nature: A History of Environmental Ethics.* Madison: University of Wisconsin Press, 1989.

———. *Wilderness and the American Mind.* 3d ed. New Haven: Yale University Press, 1982.

Nelson, Robert H. "Mythology Instead of Analysis: The Story of Public Forest Management." In Robert T. Deacon and M. Bruce Johnson, eds., *Forestlands: Public and Private.* San Francisco: Pacific Institute, 1985.

Netboy, Anthony. *The Columbia River Salmon and Steelhead Trout: Their Fight for Survival.* Seattle: University of Washington Press, 1980.

Norse, Elliott A. *Ancient Forests of the Pacific Northwest.* Washington, D.C.: The Wilderness Society and Island Press, 1990.

North Cascades Conservation Council. "Prospectus for a North Cascades." Seattle, October 1963.

North Cascades Study Team. *The North Cascades: A Report to the Secretary of the Interior and the Secretary of Agriculture.* Washington, D.C.: U.S. Government Printing Office, 1965.

Northwest Power Planning Council. *Appendix D of the 1987 Columbia River Basin Fish and Wildlife Program, Compilation of Information on Salmon Steelhead Losses in the Columbia River Basin.* Portland, Ore.: Northwest Power Planning Council, March, 1986.

Norton, Bryan G. "Intergenerational Equity and Environmental Decisions: A Model Using Rawls' Veil of Ignorance." *Ecological Economics* 1 (1989): 137-59.

———. *Toward Unity among Environmentalists.* New York: Oxford University Press, 1991.

———. *Why Preserve Natural Variety?* Princeton: Princeton University Press, 1987.

Nourse, Hugh O. *Regional Economics.* New York: McGraw-Hill, 1968.

Oberg, Kalervo. *The Social Economy of the Tlingit Indians.* Seattle: University of Washington Press, 1973.

Obsidians, Inc., Chemeketans, The Mountaineers Conservation Division, Oregon Cascades Conservation Council, Pacific Northwest Chapter of the Sierra Club, and Oregon Wildlife Federation. "A Proposal for a Mt. Jefferson Wilderness Area." Eugene Oregon, December 22, 1961.

O'Callaghan, Jerry. *The Disposition of the Public Domain in Oregon.* Washington, D.C.: U.S. Government Printing Office, 1960.

Oelschlaeger, Max. *The Idea of Wilderness: From Prehistory to the Age of Ecology.* New Haven: Yale University Press, 1991.

Olson, Ronald L. "The Quinault Indians." *University of Washington Publications in Anthropology* 6 (1936): 1-190.

Osgood, Charles E., George J. Suci, and Percy H. Tannenbaum. *The Measurement of Meaning.* Urbana: University of Illinois Press, 1957.

O'Toole, Randal. *Reforming the Forest Service.* Covelo, Calif.: Island Press, 1988.

"Panel Votes for Jobs, Against Spotted Owl." *Milwaukee Journal*, May, 14, 1992, p. A9.

Perkins, J. Mark, and Stephen P. Cross. "Differential Use of Some Coniferous Forest Habitats by Hoary and Silver-Haired Bats in Oregon." *Murrelet* 69 (1988): 21-24.

Pettitt, George A. "The Quileute of La Push: 1775-1945." *Anthropological Records* 14 (1950): 1-105.

Pike, Lawrence H., Robert A. Rydell, and William C. Denison. "A 400-Year-Old Douglas Fir Tree and Its Epiphytes: Biomass, Surface Area, and Their Distributions." *Canadian Journal of Forest Research* 7 (1977): 680-99.

Polanyi, Karl. *The Great Transformation.* Boston: Beacon Press, 1957.

Portland Audubon Society v. Lujan, 784 F. Supp. 786 (D.Or. 1992).

Powell, John Wesley. *Report on the Lands of the Arid Region of the United States.* Wallace Stegner, ed. Cambridge: Belknap Press, 1962.

Pyne, Stephen J. *Fire in America: A Cultural History of Wildland and Rural Fire.* Princeton: Princeton University Press, 1982.

Rakestraw, Lawrence W. "A History of Forest Conservation in the Pacific Northwest." Ph. D. diss., University of Washington, 1955.

Raphael, Ray. *Tree Talk: The People and Politics of Timber.* Washington, D.C.: Island Press, 1981.

Regan, Tom. "The Nature and Possibility of an Environmental Ethic." *Environmental Ethics* 3 (1981): 19-34.

Richardson, Elmo. "Olympic National Park: 20 Years of Controversy." *Journal of Forest History* 12 (1968): 6-15.

Robbins, Roy. *Our Landed Heritage, 1776-1936.* Lincoln: University of Nebraska Press, 1976.

Robbins, William G. *Hard Times in Paradise: Coos Bay, Oregon, 1850-1986.* Seattle: University of Washington Press, 1988.

Rohlf, Daniel J. *The Endangered Species Act: A guide to Its Protections and Implementations.* Stanford, Calif.: Stanford Environmental Law Society, 1989.

Rolston, Holmes, III. *Environmental Ethics: Duties to and Values in the Natural World.* Philadelphia: Temple University Press, 1988.

―――. "Values in Nature." *Environmental Ethics* 3 (1981): 113-28.

―――. "Valuing Wildlands." *Environmental Ethics* 7 (1985): 23-48.

Rosenberg, Kenneth V., and Martin G. Raphael. "Effects of Forest Fragmentation on Vertebrates in Douglas-fir Forests." In Jared Verner, Michael L. Morrison, and John C. Ralph, eds., *Wildlife 2000: Modeling Habitat Relationships of Terrestrial Vertebrates,* pp. 263-72. Madison: University of Wisconsin Press, 1986.

Roth, Dennis M. *The Wilderness Movement and the National Forests: 1964-1980.* Washington, D.C.: USDA Forest Service, 1984.

Rounsefell, George A., and George B. Kelez. "The Salmon Fisheries of Swiftsure Bank, Puget Sound, and the Fraser River." *Bulletin of the Bureau of Fisheries* 48 (1938): 693-823.

Runte, Alfred *National Parks: The American Experience.* 2d ed. Lincoln: University of Nebraska Press, 1987.

Sagoff, Mark. "Some Problems with Environmental Economics." *Environmental Ethics* 10 (1988): 55-74.

Sahlins, Marshall. *Stone Age Economics.* Chicago: Aldine-Atherton, 1972.

Sauter, John, and Bruce Johnson. *Tillamook Indians of the Oregon Coast.* Portland: Binfords and Mort, n.d.

Schneider, Keith. "Acting Grudgingly to Guard Owl, White House Backs New Logging." *New York Times*, May 15, 1992, p. 1.

Schrepfer, Susan R. *The Fight to Save the Redwoods: A History of Environmental Reform: 1917-1978.* Madison: University of Wisconsin Press, 1983.

Scrivener, J. C., and M. J. Brownlee. "Effects of Forest Harvesting on Spawning Gravel and Incubation Survival of Chum (*Oncorhynchus keta*) and Coho Salmon (*O. kisutch*) in Carnation Creek, British Columbia." *Journal of Fisheries and Aquatic Science* 46 (1989): 681-96.

Seattle Audubon v. Evans, 771 F. Supp. 1081 (W.D.Wash. 1991).

Sen, Amartya K. "Rational Fools: A Critique of the Behavioral Foundations of Economic Theory." *Philosophy and Public Affairs* 6 (1977): 317-44.

Shankland, Robert. *Steve Mather of the National Parks*. 3d ed. New York: Knopf, 1970.

Sher, Victor M., and Andy Stahl. "Spotted Owls, Ancient Forests, Courts and Congress: An Overview of Citizens' Efforts to Protect Old-Growth Forests and the Species That Live in Them." *Northwest Environmental Journal* 6 (1990): 362-63.

Sierra Club v. Butz, 349 F. Supp. 934 (N.D. Cal. 1972).

Sierra Club v. Morton et al., 405 U.S. 727 (1972).

Smith, Marian W. *The Puyallup-Nisqually*. New York: Columbia University Press, 1940.

Smith, Robert Leo. *Ecology and Field Biology*. 3d ed. New York: Harper and Row, 1980.

Solins, P., C. C. Grier, F. M. McCorison, K. Cromack, Jr., and R. Fogel. "The Internal Element Cycles of an Old-Growth Douglas-Fir Ecosystem in Western Oregon." *Ecological Monographs* 50 (1980): 261-85.

Sommarstrom, Alan R. "Wild Land Preservation Crisis: The North Cascades Controversy," Ph.D. diss., University of Washington, 1970.

Spies, Thomas A., and Jerry F. Franklin. "Course Woody Debris in Douglas-Fir Forests of Western Oregon and Washington." *Ecology* 69 (1988): 1689-702.

———. "Old Growth and Forest Dynamics in the Douglas-Fir Region of Western Oregon and Washington." *Natural Areas Journal* 8 (1988): 190-201.

Steen, Harold K. *The U.S. Forest Service: A History*. Seattle: University of Washington Press, 1976.

Suttles, Wayne. *Coast Salish Essays*. Vancouver: Talon Books, 1987.

Swan, James B. *The Northwest Coast; or, Three Years' Residence in Washington Territory*. New York: Harper and Brothers, 1857. Reprinted, Seattle: University of Washington Press, 1972.

Tattersall, James N. "The Economic Development of the Pacific Northwest to 1920," Ph. D. Diss., University of Washington, 1960.

Tautges, Alan. "The Oregon Omnibus Wilderness Act of 1978 as a Component of the Endangered American Wilderness Act of 1978, Public Law 95-237." *Environmental Review* 13 (1989): 43-62.

Taylor, Herbert C., Jr. "Aboriginal Populations of the Lower Northwest Coast." *Pacific Northwest Quarterly* 54 (1963): 158-65.

Taylor, Paul W. *Respect for Nature: A Theory of Environmental Ethics*. Princeton: Princeton University Press, 1986.

Thedinga, John F., Michael L. Murphy, Jonathan Heifietz, K. V. Koski, and Scott W. Johnson. "Effects of Logging on Size and Age Composition of Juvenile Coho Salmon (*Oncorhynchus kisutch*) and Density of Presmolts in Southeast Alaska Streams." *Canadian Journal of Fisheries and Aquatic Science* 46 (1989): 1383-91.

Thomas, Donald W. "The Distribution of Bats in Different Ages of Douglas-Fir Forests." *Journal of Wildlife Management* 52 (1988): 619-26.

Thomas, Jack W., Leonard F. Ruggiero, William R. Mannan, John W. Schoen, and Richard A. Lancia. "Management and Conservation of Old-Growth Forests in the United States." *Wildlife Society Bulletin* 16 (1988): 252-62.

Thomas, Jack Ward, Eric D. Forsman, Joseph B. Lint, E. Charles Meslow, Barry R. Noon, and Jared Verner. "A Conservation Strategy for the Northern Spotted Owl." Portland, Ore.: Interagency Scientific Committee to Address the Conservation of the Northern Spotted Owl, May, 1990.

Towle, Jerry C. "Changing Geography of Willamette Valley Woodlands." *Oregon Historical Quarterly* 83 (1982): 67-87.

————. "Woodland in the Willamette Valley: An Historical Geography," Ph.D. diss., University of Oregon, 1974.

Twight, Ben W. *Organizational Values and Political Power: The Forest Service Versus the Olympic National Park.* University Park: Pennsylvania State University Press, 1983.

U.S. Bureau of the Census, *County Business Patterns, 1951, 1959, 1970, 1980, 1986.* Washinton, D.C.: U.S. Government Printing Office, 1953, 1961, 1972, 1982, and 1988.

————. *1980 Census of Population, Vol. 1, Chapter A,* Parts 39 and 49. Washington, D.C.: U.S. Government Printing Office, 1983.

————. *Tenth-Sixteenth Census of the United States, Manufactures, Vol. III.* Washington, D.C.: U.S. Government Printing Office, 1883, 1893, 1903, 1913, 1923, 1933, 1943.

————. *Twelfth-Fourteenth Census of the United States, Population, Vol. III.* Washington, D.C.: U.S. Government Printing Office, 1903, 1913, 1923.

U.S. House of Representatives, Committee on Interior and Insular Affairs, Subcommittee on National Parks and Recreation. *Alpine Lakes Area Management Act: Hearings on H.R. 3977, H.R. 3978, H.R. 7792,* 94th Congress, 2d Session, June 17, 1975. Washington, D.C.: U.S. Government Printing Office, 1975.

————. *The North Cascades, Part I: Hearings on H.R. 8970 and Related Bills,* 90th Congress, 2d Session, Seattle, Wash., April 19-20, 1968. Washington, D.C.: U.S. Government Printing Office, 1968.

————. *The North Cascades, Part II: Hearings on H.R. 8970 and Related Bills,* 90th Congress, 2d Session, Wenatchee, Washington, July 13, 1968. Washington, D.C.: U.S. Government Printing Office, 1968.

U.S. House of Representatives, Committee on the Public Lands. *Mount Olympus National Park: Hearings on H.R. 7086,* 74th Congress, 2d Session, April 23-25, 27-30, May 1 and 5, 1936. Washington, D.C.: U.S. Government Printing Office, 1936.

U.S. House of Representatives, Subcommittee on Fisheries and Wildlife Conservation, Committee on Merchant Marine and Fisheries. *Endangered Species: Hearings on H.R. 248, 992, 3790, 4812, 5252,*

6634, 91st Congress, 1st Session, February 19-20, 1969. Washington, D.C.: U.S. Government Printing Office, 1969.

U.S. House of Representatives, Subcommittee on Forests, Family Farms, and Energy of the Committee on Agriculture. *Forestry Issues in the Pacific Northwest: Hearing*, 101st Congress, 2d Session, Olympia, WA, August 31, 1990. Washington, D.C.: U.S. Government Printing Office, 1990.

U.S. House of Representatives, Subcommittee on Forests, Family Farms, and Energy, Committee on Agriculture and the Subcommittee on National Parks and Public Lands, Committee on Interior and Insular Affairs. *Management of Old-Growth Forests of the Pacific Northwest: Joint Hearings*, 101st Congress, 1st Session, June 20 and 22, 1989. Washington, D.C.: U.S. Government Printing Office, 1989.

U.S. House of Representatives, Subcommittee on Indian Affairs and Public Lands, Committee on Interior and Insular Affairs. *Endangered American Wilderness Act: Hearings on H.R. 3454*, 95th Congress, 1st Session, February 28, March 1, May 2 and 6, 1977. Washington, D.C.: U.S. Government Printing Office, 1977.

U.S. House of Representatives, Subcommittee on Irrigation and Reclamation, Committee on Interior and Insular Affairs. *Colorado River Storage Project: Hearing on H.R. 4449, H.R. 4443, and H.R. 4463*, 83rd Congress, 2d Session, January 18-23, 25-28, 1954. Washington, D.C.: U.S. Government Printing Office, 1954.

U.S. House of Representatives, Subcommittee on National Parks and Recreation, Committee on Interior and Insular Affairs. *Alpine Lakes Area Management Act: Hearing on H.R. 3977, 3978, 7792*, 94th Congress, 1st Session, Wenatchee, Wash., July 19, 1975. Washington, D.C.: U.S. Government Printing Office, 1975.

————. *Alpine Lakes Area Management Act: Hearing on H.R. 3977, 3978, 7792*, 94th Congress, 1st Session, Seattle, Wash., June 28, 1975. Washington, D.C.: U.S. Government Printing Office, 1975.

U.S. House of Representatives, Subcommittee on Public Lands and National Parks, Committee on Interior and Insular Affairs. *Additions to the National Wilderness Preservation System: Hearings on H.R. 7340*, 97th Congress, 2d Session, December 2 and 6, 1982. Washington, D.C.: U.S. Government Printing Office, 1982.

————. *Additions to the National Wilderness Preservation System:*

Hearings on H.R. 1149, 98th Congress, 1st Session, February 14, 1983. Washington, D.C.: U.S. Government Printing Office, 1983.

U.S. House of Representatives, Subcommittee on Public Lands and National Parks of the Committee on Interior and Insular Affairs. *Additions to the National Wilderness Preservation System: Hearings on S. 837*, 98th Congress, 2d Session, June 7, 1984. Washington, D.C.: U.S. Government Printing Office, 1984.

U.S. Senate, Committee on Interior and Insular Affairs. *Alpine Lakes Management Act of 1976: Hearing on H.R. 7792*, 94th Congress, 2d Session, June 22, 1976. Washington, D.C.: U.S. Government Printing Office, 1976.

———. *National Wilderness Preservation Act: Hearings on S. 4028*, 85th Congress, 2d Session, Bend, Oregon, November 7, 1958. Washington, D.C.: U.S. Government Printing Office, 1958.

———. *National Wilderness Preservation Act—1959: Hearings on S. 1123*, 86th Congress, 1st Session, Seattle, Wash., March 30-31, 1959. U.S. Government Printing Office, 1959.

U.S. Senate, Committee on Interior and Insular Affairs, Subcommittee on Public Lands. *San Gabriel, Washakie, and Mount Jefferson Wilderness Areas: Hearings on S. 2531, S. 2630, and S. 2751*, 90th Congress, 2d Session, February 19, 20, 1968. Washington, D.C.: U.S. Government Printing Office, 1968.

U.S. Senate, Subcommittee on Energy, Natural Resources, and the Environment, Committee on Commerce. *Endangered Species: Hearings on S. 335, S. 671, S. 1280*, 91st Congress, 1st Session, May 14, 15, 1969. Washington, D.C.: U.S. Government Printing Office, 1969.

U.S. Senate, Subcommittee on Environment, Committee on Commerce. *Endangered Species Act of 1973: Hearings on S. 1592 and S. 1983*, 93rd Congress, 1st Session, June 18, 21, 1973. Washington, D.C.: U.S. Government Printing Office, 1973.

———. *Endangered Species Conservation Act of 1972: Hearings on S. 249, S.3199, S. 3818*, 92nd Congress, 2d Session, August 4, 10, 1972. Washington, D.C.: U.S. Government Printing Office, 1972.

U.S. Senate, Subcommittee on Irrigation and Reclamation, Committee on Interior and Insular Affairs. *Colorado River Storage Project: Hearing on S. 1555*, 83rd Congress, 2d Session, Washington, D.C.,

June 28-30, July 1-3, 1954. Washington, D.C.: U.S. Government Printing Office, 1954.

————. *Colorado River Storage Project: Hearing on S. 500*, 84th Congress, 1st Session, Washington, D.C., February 28, March 1-5, 1955. Washington, D.C.: U.S. Government Printing Office, 1955.

U.S. Senate, Subcommittee on Parks and Recreation, Committee on Energy and Natural Resources. *Endangered American Wilderness Act of 1977: Hearings on S. 1180*, 95th Congress, 1st Session, September 19-20, 1977. Washington, D.C.: U.S. Government Printing Office, 1977.

————. *Oregon Omnibus Wilderness Act: Hearings on S. 658*, 95th Congress, 1st Session, April 21, 1977. Washington, D.C.: U.S. Government Printing Office, 1977.

U.S. Senate, Subcommittee on Parks and Recreation, Committee on Interior and Insular Affairs. *The North Cascades: Hearings on S. 1321*, 90th Congress, 1st Session, Washington, D.C., Seattle Wash., Mt. Vernon, Wash., and Wenatchee, Wash., April 24-25, May 25, 27, and 29, 1967. Washington, D.C.: U.S. Government Printing Office, 1967.

U.S. Senate, Subcommittee on Public Lands and Reserved Water of the Committee on Energy and Natural Resources. *Oregon Wilderness Act of 1983: Hearings on H.R. 1149*, 98th Congress, 1st Session, Bend, Ore., July 21, 1983, Salem, Ore., August 25, 1983. Washington, D.C.: U.S. Government Printing Office, 1983.

————. *Oregon Wilderness Act of 1983: Hearing on H.R. 1149*, 98th Congress, 1st Session, October 20, 1983. Washington, D.C.: U.S. Government Printing Office, 1983.

————. *Washington State Wilderness Act of 1983: Hearings on S. 837*, 98th Congress, 1st Session, Spokane, Wash., June 2, 1983, Seattle, Wash., June 3, 1983, Washington, D.C., September 30, 1983. Washington, D.C.: U.S. Government Printing Office, 1983.

U.S. Senate, Subcommittee on the Environment and Land Resources of the Committee on Interior and Insular Affairs. *Oregon Omnibus Wilderness Act: Hearings on S. 1384*, 94th Congress, 2d Session, Grants Pass, Ore., October 25, 1976. Washington, D.C.: U.S. Government Printing Office, 1976.

USDA Forest Service. "Draft Environmental Statement on a Recommended Land Use Plan for the Alpine Lakes Area in the State of Washington." Portland, Ore.: USDA Forest Service, Pacific Northwest Region, 1973.

———. *Production, Prices, Employment, and Trade in Northwest Industries, First Quarter 1976.* Portland, Ore.: USDA Forest Service, Resource Bulletin, PNW-130, 1976.

———. *Production, Prices, Employment and Trade in Northwest Forest Industries, Fourth Quarter 1985.* Portland, Ore.: USDA Forest Service, Resource Bulletin, PNW-130, 1986.

———. *Mt. Jefferson Wilderness: A Proposal.* Portland, Ore.: USDA Forest Service, Pacific Northwest Region, 1967.

———. *RARE II Final Environmental Statement.* Washington, D.C.: U.S. Government Printing Office, 1979.

———. "Report on the Proposed Alpine Lakes Wilderness." Portland, Ore.: USDA Forest Service, Pacific Northwest Region, 1975.

———. "Timber Resource Statistics for Non-Federal Forest Land in Northwest Oregon." Portland, Ore.: USDA Forest Service, Resource Bulletin, PNW-140, 1986.

———. "Timber Resource Statistics for Non-Federal Forest Land in Southwest Oregon." Portland, Ore.: USDA Forest Service, Resource Bulletin, PNW-138, 1986.

———. "Timber Resource Statistics for Non-Federal Forest Land in West-Central Oregon." Portland, Ore.: USDA Forest Service Resource Bulletin, PNW-143, 1987.

———. *Wildlife and Vegetation of Unmanaged Douglas Fir Forests.* Portland, Ore.: USDA Forest Service GTR, PNW-285, 1991.

USDA Forest Service and USDI Bureau of Land Management. "Actions the Administration May Wish to Consider in Implementing a Conservation Strategy for the Spotted Owl." May 1, 1990.

Van Wagner, C. E. "Age-Class Distribution and the Forest Fire Cycle." *Canadian Journal of Forest Research* 8 (1978): 220-27.

Vecsey, Christopher. "American Indian Environmental Religions." In Christopher Vecsey and Robert W. Venables, *American Indian Environments: Ecological Issues in Native American History,* pp. 19-37. Syracuse: Syracuse University Press, 1980.

Walcott, Francis, et al. "Report of the Wilderness Classification Study Committee." *Sierra Club Bulletin* 55 (Nov.-Dec. 1970): 17-19.

Wall, Brian R. *Log Production in Washington and Oregon: An Historical Perspective.* Portland, Ore.: USDA Forest Service, Resource Bulletin, PNW-42, 1972.

Waring, R. H., and J. F. Franklin. "Evergreen Coniferous Forests of the Pacific Northwest." *Science* 204 (1979): 1380-85.

Washington Department of Natural Resources, "Timber Harvest Reports," 1970-1980. Olympia, Wash.: Department of Natural Resources, 1970-1980.

Waterman, T. T., and Ruth Greiner. "Indian Houses of Puget Sound." *Indian Notes and Monographs* (1921): 1-61.

Watkins, Alfred J. *The Practice of Urban Economics.* Beverley Hills: Sage, 1980.

Watkins, T. H. "Blueprint for Ruin." *Wilderness* 52 (Fall 1988): 56-60.

———. "The Conundrum of the Forest." *Wilderness* 49 (Spring 1986): 13-49.

Wazeka, Robert T. "Organizing for Wilderness: The Oregon Example." *Sierra Club Bulletin* (October 1976): 48-52.

White, Richard. *Land Use, Environment, and Social Change: The Shaping of Island County, Washington.* Seattle: University of Washington Press, 1980.

Wilderness Act of 1964, *U.S. Code*, Public Law 88-577.

Wilderness Society. "End of the Ancient Forests: Special Report on National Forest Plans in the Pacific Northwest." Washington, D.C.: Wilderness Society, 1988.

Worster, Donald. *Nature's Economy: A History of Ecological Ideas.* Cambridge: Cambridge University Press, 1984.

Yonce, Frederick J. "Lumbering and the Public Timberlands in Washington: The Era of Disposal." *Journal of Forest History* 21 (1978): 4-17.

Zahniser, Howard. "The Need for Wilderness Areas." *National Parks Magazine* 29 (1955): 161-66, 187-88.

Zarnowitz, Jill E., and David A. Manuwal. "The Effects of Forest Management on Cavity-Nesting Birds in Northwestern Washington." *Journal of Wildlife Management* 49 (1985): 255-63.

Index

About the Author

Douglas E. Booth lives in Milwaukee, Wisconsin, with his wife, Carol Brill, and their two sons, Edward and Jeremy. He teaches environmental and natural resource economics and other courses at Marquette University, where he is the coordinator of an interdisciplinary program on urban and environmental affairs. His research is primarily concerned with the relationship between the economy and the natural environment. He is an avid backpacker and sea kayaker and enjoys exploring natural areas in the Pacific Northwest, the desert southwest, the Rockies, and the upper Great Lakes.